IMPROVING PUBLIC SECTOR PRODUCTIVITY

To Milton

IMPROVING PUBLIC SECTOR PRODUCTIVITY

CONCEPTS AND PRACTICE

Ellen Doree Rosen

SAGE Publications
International Educational and Professional Publisher
Newbury Park   London   New Delhi

For reprinted material we give grateful acknowledgment to the following: © 1982/88 by The New York Times Company. Reprinted by permission; Fortune, © 1985 Time Inc. All rights reserved; © 1987, 1991, AARP Bulletin. Reprinted with permission; From Newsweek, © 1992, Newsweek, Inc. All rights reserved. Reprinted by permission; Reprinted with permission from *The Guide to Management Improvement Projects in Local Government*, published by the International City/County Management Association; Reprinted with permission from *Law Enforcement News*, John Jay College of Criminal Justice, New York; October 1992 *Corrections Today*, Vol. 54, No. 7. Reprinted with permission of the American Correctional Association; Reprinted with permission from PA Times © by the American Society for Public Administration; Reprinted with permission from the Court Technology Bulletin published by the National Center for State Courts.

Copyright © 1993 Ellen Doree Rosen

For information address:

SAGE Publications, Inc.
2455 Teller Road
Newbury Park, California 91320

SAGE Publications Ltd.
6 Bonhill Street
London EC2A 4PU
United Kingdom

SAGE Publications India Pvt. Ltd.
M-32 Market
Greater Kailash I
New Delhi 110 048 India

Printed in the United States of America

Library of Congress Cataloging-in-Publication Data

Rosen, Ellen Doree, 1924-
  Improving public sector productivity : concepts and practice / Ellen Doree Rosen.
        p.   cm.
  Includes bibliographical references and index.
  ISBN 0-8039-4572-8.   — ISBN 0-8039-4573-6 (pbk.)
  1. Government productivity. I. Title.
JF1525.P67R67   1993
350.1'47—dc20   93-13276
                                                              CIP
93 94 95 96   10 9   8 7 6 5 4 3 2 1

Sage Production Editor: Megan M. McCue

Contents

Preface

Although they would probably be surprised to hear me say so, it is my students who have inspired and shaped this book. In many years of teaching public productivity to practitioners—in formal Masters of Public Administration programs, in workshops, and in training sessions—I have been struck by the transformation that occurs, typically, somewhere in the second half of a course. The defensive, guarded, skeptical attitude with which in-service students arrive gives way to excitement and creative thinking at the point where they begin to feel confident that they understand enough about the field to assess realistically the possibilities, the instrumentalities, and the pitfalls. I have learned from my students that many of the lies we tell are true: There is, even in the most jaded public servants, tremendous potential energy and a desire to believe; practical ideas, which are obvious to those who do the work, can make significant improvements in efficiency and the quality of services.

Public agencies *can* be made more productive, serviceable, and humane if those who control the reward system appreciate their role in productivity improvement and those who would design and implement changes know what they are doing. This book is intended to provide a basic understanding of the public productivity field to policy makers and practitioners, whether reading independently or enrolled in formal courses on organizational performance.

For instructors using this as a textbook, I suggest that the formal sequence of chapters, arranged to provide a logical progression of ideas to a reader, need not be followed in the classroom. In my experience, students find the material on improvement techniques (Chapters 6-10) exciting, while the material on concepts and measurement (Chapters 3-5) takes time to absorb and needs reinforcement. I tend therefore to present the measurement material piecemeal, over a period of several weeks, by devoting only the first half-hour of class to some aspect of measurement and then moving on to the major topic for the day.

My usual term assignment is to have each student assume the role of productivity consultant to his or her own organization or subunit. The student is asked to identify real productivity problems, brainstorm a set of potential improvement undertakings, select one for scrutiny as to feasibility, and, finally, make a "go" or "no-go" recommendation on the project. Students participate in panels, organized as much as possible around substantive fields, presenting their work in progress for constructive suggestion from the class, thereby also providing the opportunity for everyone vicariously to experience productivity improvement in a number of settings. Every semester, one or two students report back that the productivity improvement suggestion they developed for their term paper has been adopted and is being implemented in their workplace: A new schedule has eliminated a redundant patrol unit, a simplified form has cut paperwork, route mapping has shortened travel time, or a new satellite "hazardous materials" center provides faster response to spills.

Acknowledgments

In the genesis of this book, I am indebted to many people. This is an opportunity to acknowledge the influence of Martin Landau, who first taught me to think about organizations and systems, and Marc Holzer, who introduced me to the subject of public productivity. The conceptualization of the book was strengthened by suggestions from Walter Balk, Beverly Cigler, and Seymour Mann, and I give them my thanks. I am particularly grateful to my colleagues Patrick O'Hara and Lotte Feinberg for reviewing a portion of the manuscript. Any failure to use all of this advice is, of course, my own.

My thanks to Marilyn Harris, Marc Holzer, Frank Conroy, and Harold Sullivan for helpful information and clarifications. The John Jay College of Criminal Justice Library has been a rich and hospitable resource. Harry M. Briggs and Nancy S. Hale of Sage Publications have guided me along the way. Finally, without my family this book would not have happened. My husband, children, and grandchildren have given me support, guidance, solitude, and encouragement; they know how much I owe them.

ELLEN DOREE ROSEN
Great Neck, New York

1

Introduction

Public Productivity

This book deals with public productivity: what it is, how it can be measured, and, most important, how it can be improved. The productivity of our public agencies has never been more important than now. Taxpayers, elected officials, clients, and public servants have a stake in making public agencies more efficient, effective, and respected. Taxpayers have drawn the line on what they are willing to pay for governmental programs and are increasingly worried about public debt. Elected officials are casting about for ways to meet a high level of citizen demand for services in the face of fiscal limitations. Clients are increasingly distrustful of government and critical of the quality of the public services they receive. Public administrators are demoralized, "much like abuse victims, demeaned yet dependent" (Holzer, 1989, p. 343).

The field of public productivity addresses these problems. Its central concern is making better use of the taxpayer's dollar by making agencies more efficient. Productivity measurement provides the kind of solid information that elected officials need in order to make rational and defensible decisions about the allocation of resources. Concern for service quality and client satisfaction occupy center stage in the productivity field today. Finally, the public productivity improvement field stresses attention to workers' perceptions and their potential for contributing to the generation and implementation of improvements.

Productivity addresses the bottom line; it expresses "what you get for what you give" (Fosler, 1980, p. 281). That matters today:

> If government provides such critical services as education, public safety, housing, provision of water and disposal of wastes, transportation, land-use management, and health, and if it expends an equivalent of one-third of the Gross National Product to do it, then how well it performs those functions and how efficiently it uses those resources is a matter of prime concern (Fosler, 1980, p. 283).

Impulses to Improvement

The improvement of public sector productivity is possible right now, on a much larger scale than heretofore, for two basic reasons: There is new motivation for change, and the technical and strategic know-how has been developed.

The climate is right. In 1991, one of every four U.S. cities had a revenue shortfall of more than 5% (Lemov, 1991, p. 28). Fiscal crises beset every level of government. Resources are in short supply; that creates a counterforce to complacency.

> "There's a little bit of good in austerity in that it makes it possible to do hard things that you can't do in good times," says Richard Nathan, provost at the Rockefeller College of Public Affairs in Albany, New York. "This is a good time to attack management issues, politics being what they are" (Walters, 1992, p. 38).

It is widely perceived that business as usual will not serve, and the search is on for better ways. Public sector managers, workers, and unions have begun to see themselves as interdependent, with interests in common, ready to cooperate and accept change. The competition presented by privatization is a major factor.

Intensified productivity improvement activity is possible now because—thanks to decades of work by innovative practitioners, academicians, and research groups—many productivity improvement models have been developed and now stand ready to borrow. Real productivity measurement has been done in a wide range of substantive public sector fields and at every level of government. Real public productivity improvement projects have taken place in many fields and jurisdictions, using a wide variety of techniques and strategies. These projects have yielded useful lessons as well as fertile models. We know a great deal now about the politics, psychology, and mechanics of improving the productivity of public organizations. In the early 1970s, when the first rush of enthusiasm for productivity improvement was felt, this body of experience with measurement and innovation was not yet available.

Impediments to Improvement

This optimistic assessment of what is possible provides the faith and drive that fuel action, but success depends on scouting out the terrain before advancing. Barriers do exist, arising from human nature, the nature of the American political system, and the status of the public productivity field. They are summarized here. Each will be treated more fully elsewhere in the book.

1. Resistance to any change is natural. Improving productivity means changing things. But it is a principle in biology, an axiom in organization theory, and observable in practice, that individuals and organizations tend to resist change (Katz & Kahn, 1966, pp. 24, 28). This means that productivity improvement is an uphill fight, and persuasion and motivation to overcome resistance must be part of the process.

2. The American political system inhibits change. Power is fragmented among federal, state, and local jurisdictions and executive, legislative, and judicial authorities. Actors change frequently as the electoral system rotates incumbents and their appointees. The annual budget provides a short time frame and discourages long-range thinking (Mann, 1980, p. 357). Productivity improvement strategies must conform to the reality that it is not easy to build support and invest in the future.

3. Public productivity is a relatively young field, applied and interdisciplinary in nature. Because it is applied and interdisciplinary, the knowledge

gained has come from experience in scattered places and been expressed in the vocabularies and mind-sets of many fields, among them politics, engineering, psychology, business, law, economics, and sociology. The title of Robert Quinn's article summed up the situation some years ago (1978): "Productivity and the Process of Organizational Improvement: Why We Cannot Talk to Each Other."

Because the field is relatively young, it is still plagued by ambiguities, myths, uncertainties, and distractions. There remain ambiguities about how public productivity is defined, myths about what productivity improvement implies, uncertainties about what really works, and, too often, a climate of exaggerated faith or cynicism. A great deal more is known than has been codified. Happily, these problems are waning. Through public productivity conferences, books, and journals there is increasing dialogue across jurisdictions and fields of practice. We can talk to each other, though we still have to be careful to define what we mean.

In sum, the field of public productivity improvement covers a lot of ground, some of it rough and uncharted. Let us start with some preliminary definitions and a brief survey.

Defining Public Productivity

What are we talking about when we talk about public productivity? In general terms, "productivity" is an efficiency measure: It tells how well resources have been used. The more produced with a given set of resources, the higher the productivity. We say someone is a productive worker if he or she turns out a lot of good work per day, week, or year. A productive organization, similarly, is one that turns out a high level of good quality product with its resources. Public productivity focuses on the efficiency of governmental (that is, publicly authorized and funded) administrative agencies and their subunits. Public productivity as a field is different from the private sector productivity field. Public agencies operate under significantly different conditions. They are more tightly constrained: Missions are legislatively fixed; operations are open to public scrutiny and reaction; volumes of rules and detailed procedures define options; civil service and budget systems limit freedom to redeploy labor and monetary resources. The major difference is in measurement: Goods and services produced in the private sector can be measured in terms of their dollar value because they are sold in the market. Public agencies produce services that are not for sale. This makes measurement quite different, and more difficult (but not impossible—valid and useful information is obtainable on the productivity of public sector organizations). To the extent that they resemble public agencies, "third sector," not-for-profit organizations also benefit from the techniques and principles developed for the public sector.

In specific terms, productivity expresses the ratio of outputs to the inputs consumed in producing them:

$$\text{Productivity} = \text{Outputs} \div \text{Inputs}$$
$$P = O \div I$$

Public sector outputs are the public services produced and delivered by agencies to their "clients." The quality, as well as the quantity, of output is significant. Inputs express the amount of labor, equipment, or other resources used in producing the services. The productivity level is determined by measuring outputs, measuring inputs, and calculating the ratio. It is the same idea as expressing the efficiency of a car in terms of miles per gallon of gasoline. Productivity is improved when the ratio is larger (more miles per gallon).

Public productivity measurement and improvement is applicable to any kind of work: purchasing, fire fighting, investigation, placing foster children, processing insurance claims, issuing motor licenses. It applies to work units of any size, from department of transportation to road crew. It applies to agencies at every level of government and every kind of jurisdiction.

The Dimensions of Productivity Improvement

Productivity is improved when more or better services or both are produced with the same (or fewer) resources. This may be the result of changing one factor:

- The quantity of output is increased (the same staff processes more workers' compensation claims each month);
- the quality of output is increased (the same staff handles the same number of claims but processes them more promptly); or
- the level of resources is decreased (the same number of claims are processed just as promptly but with less labor).

An increase in productivity may be the result of varying more than one factor at a time:

- More and better outputs are produced with the same resources (more claims, faster processing, same staff);
- more outputs of the same quality are produced with fewer resources;
- the same amount of output is produced with better quality and using fewer resources; or
- a large gain in quantity or quality of outputs or both is achieved through a smaller increase in resources (the payoff is larger than the investment).

The optimal in productivity improvement, of course, is realized where all three variables are improved:

- More and better is done with less.

Sometimes elements vary, but not in the same direction: for example, fewer claims processed, but more promptly and accurately. When there have been trade-offs among factors it becomes difficult to assess with any confidence whether productivity has been improved. The chapters on measurement will suggest a way.

We have discussed the dimensions of productivity improvement. The next question is, what means are available for making improvements?

Avenues to Productivity Improvement

The universe of established techniques for improving productivity is large and varied: quality circles, job redesign, contracting out, alternative work schedules, demand analysis—the list is almost endless. Fortunately, they fall naturally into three groups: (1) changes in the work process, (2) changes in the worker, and (3) changes in management options. These constitute three distinct approaches to productivity improvement based on different assumptions, emerging at different points in the history of the field, and tending to focus on different elements in the productivity formula.

The first avenue to productivity improvement concerns attention to operations, to how the work is structured and processed. In general, it reflects the engineer's perspective and stresses recording, analyzing, and streamlining to minimize waste and improve efficiency. The objective is, in general, to improve the quantity of output achieved with a set of resources. Some examples of the techniques reflecting this approach: work charting, reorganization, demand analysis, and technological innovation.

The second avenue to productivity improvement concerns attention to improving the contribution of the worker. It reflects the psychologist's perspective in assessing worker needs and improving motivation. The objective is, in general, to energize the major public sector input—labor. This avenue focuses on training, incentive systems, and worker participation in decision making. The techniques include monetary rewards, career development, quality circles, and joint labor-management committees.

The latest avenue to productivity improvement focuses on exploring new managerial options for meeting client needs in an environment of constraint, uncertainty, and change. In general, it reflects the open systems perspective in attention to the organization's environment, in welcoming feedback, and in pursuing alternative means. Efficiency remains an objective, but this approach stresses improved quality of outputs, and, as the title of the Second Annual Conference on Federal Quality and Productivity Improvement suggests, "Making Customers Count" (Achieving the Quality Difference, 1989). This approach encompasses such techniques as user surveys, alternative funding sources, alternative labor sources, intergovernmental cooperation, contracting out, and total quality management.

It is vital to recognize that, in undertaking any productivity improvement effort, success will depend on two factors. One is choosing the right technique. The innovation (for example, instituting a training program) must constitute a valid solution to a real problem. If work has to be redone (waste of labor) because workers lack the skill or knowledge they need, then a training program is appropriate. But if the problem lies elsewhere or if the training goes to the wrong people, has the wrong content, or is pitched at the wrong level, then it will not succeed.

There is a second vital condition, a "political" or behavioral factor. It must be feasible to obtain the necessary cooperation to effect the change. There are stakeholders both within and without the agency whose cooperation or opposition is relevant. If, for example, top administration will not support the action; or the legislature will not amend the rules; or if the union, workers, clientele, or any other significant actor withholds cooperation, then change will not be feasible.

Success depends on choosing a technique that will work and that will be allowed to work. The technical and the "political" must go hand in hand.

Orientation to the Book

This book is intended as a framework for understanding and a guide to action for the serious student of and practitioner in public administration. It is meant to serve as a textbook for formal courses and workshops. It is also meant as an introduction and resource for the practitioner or policy maker who wants to gain some command of the subject of public productivity by reading independently.

The Approach

Improving public productivity is not a simple matter. It involves organizational change within a highly political setting. It calls on a wide array of improvement techniques from mathematical to motivational. It requires a capacity for careful collection and analysis of data, together with a capacity for imagination and risk taking. It demands objectivity and empathy at the same time.

The productivity field is life at the administrative edge, challenging and exciting. Success depends on understanding the terrain, the actors, and the resources. The objective of arming the reader with that understanding has influenced the underlying model, depth of discussion, and range of subjects covered in this book.

Open Systems Model

It is possible to study an administrative organization by limiting attention only to what goes on inside the walls. Classical managerial principles and theories of human relations in organizations were derived using that approach. However, such a "closed system" model leaves out the relationships of an organization to environmental influences and provides no explanation for how and why organizations adapt and change.

The "open system" model conceptualizes an organization as receiving resources and information ("inputs") from outside sources and supplying goods or services ("outputs") for outside consumers. Filling some niche, providing some societal necessity, is what "earns" the organization continued resources. The organization maintains itself in a state of moving equilibrium, interacting with the environment but preserving its identity. In an environment that is not completely predictable and may contain surprises, the organization copes by monitoring, by taking in "feedback" about the results of its activities. If it is not meeting with success, the organization may modify its output, and even adapt its structure, in the effort to cope.

In today's world of rapid and unpredictable change, the environment cannot be disregarded. The past decade has brought an AIDS epidemic, the computer age, the demise of communism, and full dump sites. Both public and private sector organizations have been presented with new problems, new instrumentalities, and new priorities. Monitoring performance and making adaptive change are at the heart of gauging and improving productivity. It is not surprising that the language of productivity is open systems language: inputs, outputs, and, increasingly, feedback. This book rests on that model and employs that language.

Presentation

This is meant to be a practical book, presenting a range of possible productivity improvement undertakings in an organized way. Lively quotes from the field have been chosen to permit the reader to hear about ideas and innovations in the words of those who have experienced them firsthand. But informed application depends on basic understanding of underlying dynamics, elements, and limitations. For that reason, topics are placed within their theoretical frameworks. Finally, knowing that quantification is a necessary condition for, but psychological barrier to, systematic improvement, we have devoted liberal, user-friendly coverage to defining what productivity is (and what it is not) and presenting a "how-to" procedure for measuring it.

Plan of the Book

Orientation

Chapter 1 provides an introduction and orientation to the subject of public productivity and its improvement, a sort of preliminary look around and look back. The importance and scope of the field is set out. Some basic vocabulary is introduced. The chapter concludes with a brief historical perspective on public productivity.

The Politics of Productivity

The improvement of public sector productivity involves many interested parties, or stakeholders, and takes place in a complex political environment. Chapter 2 discusses the implications of the American political system as it sets the scene and defines the ground rules and pathways along which public productivity improvement can proceed. It then turns to another kind of politics, the power relationships and interactions among the many "actors," the people, groups, and institutions that have something to lose or gain from a change or innovation that improves productivity. Major stakeholders are identified, with special attention to their interests, motivations, and misgivings.

Productivity Concepts and Measurement

Clear thinking about productivity improvement starts with basic definitions: what productivity is; what distinguishes a focus on productivity from other perspectives on performance; and how output quantity, output quality, and inputs relate to the ideas of efficiency and effectiveness. Chapter 3 offers some fundamental definitions and distinctions. The information collected for the purpose of measuring productivity can also be used for other applications, to serve other management needs. Chapter 3 also reviews some of the ways that productivity data can be integrated into a management information system.

Chapter 4 prepares the background for measuring public productivity. It covers the theory, politics, and strategy of measurement, discussing the need for measurement, the nature of measurement, sources of data, the characteristics that make a measure good, and possible misuses to guard against. It deals with the politics of measuring productivity in the public sector and with the difference between the often-confused "measures" and "standards."

Chapter 5 offers a generic "recipe" for measuring the productivity of any public organization or subunit. It describes in step-by-step fashion how to measure public agency inputs, output quantity, and output quality, and then how to calculate productivity, efficiency, and effectiveness.

Improvement Techniques

The field of productivity is rich in practical, field-tested instrumentalities for identifying and dealing with problems that keep public agencies from their full potential. These practical ways of improving productivity form the heart of the book. For purposes of discussion, they are grouped under three rubrics: (1) focusing on the work process, (2) focusing on the worker, and (3) focusing on management options.

Chapter 6 is devoted to improving the work process, to "working smarter, not harder." It describes techniques for analyzing operations and improving the way the work is organized and structured. It also discusses productivity improvement through technological innovation.

Two chapters focus on the worker: Chapter 7 forms an introduction to the importance of worker skill and motivation. It provides some background to the subject, looking at how traditional ideas of organization management undervalued the full potential of workers and gave them little scope for contributing ideas or influencing decision making. It then explores how rewards can be built into the system so that workers develop a sense of ownership in the process of producing services, resulting in a more satisfying workplace that is also more efficient and provides a higher quality of service. Chapter 8 presents modes of providing for worker participation in making decisions about production. Such participation provides the worker with the highest form of motivation and brings to the organization and the public the insights, ideas, and energies of a knowledgeable, "liberated" work force.

Two chapters are devoted to the increased importance of organizational openness to new ideas, options, emphases, and possibilities, particularly as they provide instrumentalities for improved productivity. Chapter 9 focuses on new modes for obtaining monetary, labor, and other resources. Chapter 10 covers new alternatives for producing and delivering public services, as well as the new emphasis on managing for quality.

Strategy

The secret of successful productivity improvement is tackling the right problem with the right solution, including the necessary support and cooperation. Productivity improvement is an exercise in organizational change and needs to be understood in that light. Chapter 11 concludes the book with a discussion of the strategy and tactics of productivity improvement. It includes guidelines on selecting the right problem, technique, scale, and timing, and it concludes with suggestions for designing and administering a productivity improvement project.

History

The public productivity movement as we know it is the product of a history. Its shape, content, and emphases today can be best understood in the light of its evolution. History is a story of broad, powerful, flowing ideas and the unique persons and institutions that act upon them and give them form. What ideas have shaped public productivity? A few appear clear:

1. The emergence of public productivity as a concept and an issue has been impelled by three related thrusts: (a) a growing scarcity of resources in the face of undiminished demand for public services, (b) a public perception of governmental agencies as bloated and wasteful, and (c) the existence of the business organization as a model.

2. The behavioral revolution in the social sciences, with its emphasis on replacing journalistic impressions with observation and measurement, provided a foundation for the legitimacy and feasibility of measuring the productivity of public agencies, as it did for the sister field of program evaluation.

3. The field of organization theory has influenced the search for productivity improvement techniques. Organization theory has used a succession of explanatory models, each drawing attention to some special aspect of organizational structure and function. The machine model stressed the formal structure and conduct of the work operation; the human relations model that succeeded it stressed worker motivation and social relations; the open systems model stressed goals and adaptability in dealing with the environment. The development of productivity improvement techniques has followed that sequence, with attention first to work improvement methods, then to worker motivation vehicles, and, most recently, to results-oriented innovations, stressing alternative options and the use of feedback.

The history of the public productivity field has been divided into four periods by Geert Bouckaert (1990), and we will conform to his useful categories.

Government by the Efficient: 1900-1940

More than 100 years ago, Woodrow Wilson made the argument that the administrative side of government can, and should, be distinguished from politics. Administration could be studied as a proper field, with improvement the goal.

> The field of administration is a field of business. . . . It is a part of political life only as . . . machinery is part of the manufactured product. . . .
> [T]he hanging of a criminal, the transportation and delivery of the mails, the equipment and recruiting of the army . . . are all obviously acts of administration; but the general laws which direct these things to be done are as obviously outside of and above administration. The broad plans of

governmental action are not administrative; the detailed execution of such plans is administrative. . . (1987, pp. 18-19).

Wilson went on to defend the idea of seeking better methods wherever they are to be found:

> If I see a murderous fellow sharpening his knife cleverly, I can borrow his way of sharpening the knife without borrowing his probable intention to commit murder with it; and so, if I see a monarchist dyed in the wool managing a public bureau well, I can learn his business methods without changing one of my republican spots (1987, p. 24).

Wilson had laid the intellectual groundwork. The author of the first textbook in public administration, Frank Goodnow, saw the elimination of political patronage as the opportunity to improve administrative efficiency (Bouckaert, 1990, p. 54). The Bureau of Municipal Research, established in New York in 1906, became a model for other independent agencies conducting analyses of government operations (Bouckaert, 1990, p. 56). Models of efficiency were drawn from the world of business, from people such as Frederick Taylor, advocating a scientific approach to finding the "one best way" to produce. The dominant themes of this period were established: keep politics out of administration and conduct research. "The two components of the dichotomy reinforced each other, since political neutrality guaranteed efficiency, and efficiency legitimized political neutrality" (Bouckaert, 1990, p. 55).

Luther Gulick (who would live to become a centenarian) and Lyndall Urwick built on the work of Henri Fayol, who had identified universal principles of good management (Fayol, 1949). Their 1937 *Papers on the Science of Administration*, a report to the Brownlow Committee, which had been appointed by President Franklin D. Roosevelt "to correct perceived deficiencies in the federal bureaucracy," urged the application of such principles (Barton & Chappell, 1985, pp. 247-248).

Before the end of the 1930s, Clarence Ridley and Herbert Simon were pioneering the measurement of public agency performance (1943).

Government by Administrators: 1940-1970

From the productivity standpoint, this period was marked chiefly by an emphasis on controlling expenditures (Bouckaert, 1990, p. 58). Attention turned to budgeting systems that would better inform political decision makers about where the money went and what programs it served. This was the era of the planning program budgeting system and zero-based budgets.

The "principles" had been discredited in practice and, at the hands of Herbert Simon, by a devastating theoretical critique (1946). The pursuit of organizational improvement continued, but the search shifted. "Advocates of the neobureaucratic model . . . have continued the classical search for improved public administration through the use of positivist (scientific) methods" (Barton & Chappell, 1985, p. 249), but attention turned to behavioral phenomena, especially the process of decision making.

Although this period saw little attention to efficiency and productivity concepts as such, the ferment of activity in other areas was laying the groundwork for new advances in the productivity improvement effort. Attention to the worker was one focus. Another was an awakening to the organizational environment: concern for the client, for the relationship between organizational structure and how it functions, and for the importance of culture to administration. A light sketch will be sufficient for our purposes here.

Attention to the psychology of the worker and the influence of the work group on individual behavior had been growing since the Hawthorne studies in the 1930s. The 1940s were marked by a spate of research on motivation. The results were to find application in the "worker" approach to productivity improvement.

The structural-functional school established the idea that an organization "copes" with its environment. All through this period, open systems theory was becoming developed, from its genesis in the field of biology in the 1930s to its application to organizations in the 1950s.

After World War II, the breakup of colonial empires created newly independent countries seeking to adopt modern administrative methods. In the effort to transplant western institutions to different societies, the influence of the cultural setting became evident. That became one practical lesson that the environment was not irrelevant to administration.

By the 1960s concern for management yielded in the minds of many to concern for the potential of public administration in confronting the problems of society. The "new public administration" movement, as it came to be defined through the Minnowbrook Conference of 1968, emphasized relevance and responsiveness. Considerations of equity for the client and potential client became important, laying a foundation for goal-oriented management.

These themes were as yet prologue. Productivity as such lay dormant as an issue.

Government by the Managers: 1970-1980

Not for long. Developing problems in the U.S. economy led President Richard Nixon to establish a National Commission on Productivity in 1970 (reformulated in 1975 as the National Center for Productivity and Quality of Working Life). The commission divided itself into four working groups, one of which took as it focus the improvement of government productivity. Then-Secretary of Commerce Peterson explained the situation:

> Improving productivity in the public sector of the U.S. economy is fundamental to the success of the current federal effort to create . . . an environment that will spur a higher rate of productivity growth . . . in the economy as a whole.
>
> It is fundamental, first, because the public sector is such a large and rapidly growing part of the whole. But it is crucial, also, because no government program to encourage higher rates of productivity growth in the private sector will succeed if government itself sets a bad example (or . . . is widely thought of as a bad example) (1972, p. 740).

At the state and local level, urgent concern for productivity in the 1970s came as a legacy of the 1960s, as Governor Lucey of Wisconsin explained (1972):

> During the 1960's, AFDC [Aid to Families with Dependent Children] caseloads in Wisconsin doubled, public college enrollments tripled, and vocational rehabilitation cases went up 800 per cent. . . . Fields such as pollution control meant expenditures . . . in program areas which had not previously existed.
>
> Changes of this magnitude could not be funded without a corresponding escalation in state tax levels. Personal income tax rates were raised on four separate occasions. . . . A sales tax was instituted . . . as were state gas taxes and . . . cigarette taxes. [Local] property taxes . . . nearly matched the level of state tax growth. . . .
>
> One legacy of that growth is the nationwide "taxpayers' revolt" of the 1970's, which has already toppled a number of mayors and governors. Citizens . . . are demanding relief (p. 795).

The situation at the state level was paralleled at the local level. Struggling to maintain service and improve quality in the face of a two-year shrinkage in work force, New York City took a lead role at the local level by initiating the New York City Productivity Program (Hamilton, 1972, p. 784).

The national "Wingspread" Conference on Productivity in the Public Sector in 1972 gave rise to a special issue of the *Public Administration Review* (Vol. 32, No. 6), titled "Symposium on Productivity in Government"; another symposium issue (1978) provided a progress report and a forum for discussion of significant issues (Balk, 1978). The academic-based Center for Productive Public Management (later the National Center for Public Productivity) was established in 1975 by Marc Holzer, who founded the *Public Productivity Review* (later, *Public Productivity & Management Review*) the same year. Public sector productivity had become a conscious, defined, and focused field.

The 1970s was a decade of vibrant, fertile activity. Research projects were undertaken. The U.S. Civil Service Commission, General Accounting Office, and Office of Management and Budget joined forces in a project to explore ways of measuring the productivity of federal agencies (1972). The task force concluded that measurement of productivity is practicable for large segments of the federal sector and that work on measuring and enhancing productivity should continue (Kull, 1978, p. 5). An Urban Institute group, under the leadership of Harry Hatry, studied general measurement practices and productivity improvement techniques at the local level (Hatry & Fisk, 1971; Hatry, Blair, Fisk, Greiner, Hall, & Schaenmar, 1977; Hatry, 1979) and pioneered in assessing measurement problems and techniques in specific fields (see, for example, Blair & Schwartz, 1972; Hatry & Dunn, 1971; Winnie & Hatry, 1972; Webb & Hatry, 1973).

Experimentation was supported. The National Commission on Productivity encouraged experimentation with productivity bargaining in the public sector (Newland, 1972, p. 808). The Department of Housing and Urban Development was "extensively involved in efforts to improve productivity and strengthen management in local government" (Report to the National Productivity Council, 1980, p. 172). It funded state and local initiatives, like Washington state's productivity program to create a state technology office, do a measurement pilot study, and prepare a case study as a model for other governments (Ryan, 1978, p. 13). The Intergovernmental Personnel Act (IPA) grant program administered by the Office of

Personnel Management supported some 600 projects per year (Report to the National Productivity Council, 1980, p. 172). It made federal funds and mechanisms available to state and local jurisdictions for training, personnel management, and for projects such as the "team-building" experiments in Virginia (Giegold & Dunsing, 1978). The National Science Foundation supported programs to help state and local governments integrate science and technology research results into management support activities (Report to the National Productivity Council, 1980, p. 173).

The Office of Personnel Management issued a publication, *Performance*, that actively promoted productivity. An IPA grant supported the publication of *Productivity Probe* by the State Government Productivity Research Center, which was established by the Council of State Governments. IPA funding supported a clearinghouse, under the aegis of the Center for Productive Public Management, to serve as a reference and dissemination center (Holzer, 1980, p. 138).

These were important years.

> The search for productivity was now motivated not by better government, as it had been in the first stage, or by expense control, as it had been in the second stage, but by the desire to get more yield out of the taxpayer's money, more bang for the public buck (Bouckaert, 1990, p. 59).

Walter Balk's opening sentence as symposium editor of the 1978 special issue of the *Public Administration Review* was prophetic: "Productivity improvement in the public sector is alive and well. . . . Or is it?" (p. 1). The National Center for Productivity and the Quality of Working Life was eliminated in 1978. The demise of the IPA program was a blow to state and local efforts; for example, *Productivity Probe* had only a one-year life, as did the clearinghouse. Highly regarded productivity centers in Maryland and Georgia, active in the 1970s, no longer exist (Partners in Productivity, 1989, p. 2).

The 1970s fizzled out. One factor was the turnover in administrations, especially at the state level (certainly in Washington, Wisconsin, and, a few years later, in North Carolina). More important, too little impact of all this effort had become visible. That was a fault of the strategy: expectations had been raised high, too much was expected too soon, and, according to Balk, "the major problem was that there was a crash attempt to transfer incomplete and incompatible business productivity management action orientations to government" (1984, p. 152).

Government by Private Sector: 1980-

The early 1980s saw renewed activity around the subject of productivity. It was a period of reviewing and sharing what had been accomplished. In 1980, a large and still valuable handbook on productivity improvement for state and local government appeared (Washnis, 1980). There were two conferences in 1983: a White House Conference on Productivity and a conference sponsored by the National Center for Public Productivity, featuring reports on successful innovations from the field (Rosen, 1984, 1985).

The National Center for Public Productivity, the only center devoted exclusively to productivity in the public sector, has remained an active nucleus through its journal, *The Public Productivity & Management Review*, as well as conferences, workshops, and the International Productivity Network, which was begun in 1988. The International City/County Management Association's (ICMA) *Guide to Management Improvement Projects in Local Government* continues to serve as a catalyst for the dissemination of information about specific improvements in efficiency and service quality; examples will appear throughout this book. The Coalition to Improve State and Local Government Management unites such organizations as ICMA, the National League of Cities, and the National Governors' Association in a joint undertaking to facilitate information exchange and to provide guidance and training.

The last decade has seen two parallel trends. One has been a philosophy of downsizing government ("rightsizing" to its advocates) through privatization in its two senses (divesting whole governmental activities to the private sector and contracting out selected functions to the private sector). The other has been a reemphasis on improving agency performance, but, since the President's Private Sector Survey on Cost Control report, the emphasis has shifted from cost control (deficits and budget cuts have achieved much of that) and toward the improvement of service quality. The total quality management system first used in Japan has become a model, supported by the Office of Management and Budget. These recent trends will be discussed more fully in Chapter 10.

References

Achieving the quality difference: Making customers count. (1989). *Proceedings of the Second Annual Conference on Quality and Productivity Improvement.* Washington, DC: President's Council on Management Improvement and the Office of Management and Budget.

Balk, W. L. (1978). Productivity in government: Introduction. *Public Administration Review*, *38*, 1.

Balk, W. L. (1984). Productivity in government: A legislative focus. *Public Productivity Review*, *8*, 148-161.

Barton, R., & Chappell, W. L., Jr. (1985). *Public administration: The work of government*. Glenview, IL: Scott, Foresman.

Blair, L. H., & Schwartz, A. I. (1972). *How clean is our city? Measuring the effectiveness of solid waste collection operations*. Washington, DC: Urban Institute.

Bouckaert, G. (1990). The history of the productivity movement. *Public Productivity & Management Review*, *14*, 53-89.

Fayol, H. (1949). *General and industrial management*. London: Pitman.

Fosler, R. S. (1980). Local government productivity: Political and administrative potential. In C. Levine & I. Rubin (Eds.), *Fiscal stress and public policy* (pp. 281-301). Beverly Hills, CA: Sage.

Giegold, W. C., & Dunsing, R. J. (1978). Team-building in the local jurisdiction: Two case studies. *Public Administration Review*, *38*, 59-63.

Hamilton, E. K. (1972). Productivity: The New York City approach. *Public Administration Review*, *32*, 784-795.

Hatry, H. P. (1979). *Efficiency measurement for local government services*. Washington, DC: Urban Institute.

Hatry, H. P., Blair, L. H., Fisk, D. M., Greiner, J. H., Hall, J. R., Jr., & Schaenmar, P. S. (1977). *How effective are your community services? Procedures for monitoring the effectiveness of municipal services*. Washington, DC: Urban Institute.

Hatry, H. P., & Dunn, D. R. (1971). *Measuring the effectiveness of local government services: Recreation*. Washington, DC: Urban Institute.

Hatry, H. P., & Fisk, D. M. (1971). *Improving productivity and productivity measurement in local governments*. Washington, DC: Urban Institute.

Holzer, M. (1980). Sharing productivity information. *Public Productivity Review*, *4*, 138-145.

Holzer, M. (1989). Widening the dialogue. *Public Productivity Review*, *12*, 343-344.

Katz, D., & Kahn, R. L. (1966). *The social psychology of organizations*. New York: John Wiley.

Kull, D. C. (1978). Productivity programs in the federal government. *Public Administration Review*, *38*, 5-9.

Lemov, P. (1991, August). The axe and its victims. *Governing*, pp. 26-30.

Lucey, P. J. (1972). Wisconsin's productivity policy. *Public Administration Review*, *32*, 795-799.

Mann, S. Z. (1980). The politics of productivity: State and local focus. *Public Productivity Review*, *4*, 352-367.

Newland, C. A. (1972). Personnel concerns in government productivity improvement. *Public Administration Review*, *32*, 807-815.

Partners in Productivity. (1989, August). *Progress report: Research on performance and productivity measurement programs and management improvement efforts in other states and the federal government*. Tallahassee, FL: Author.

Peterson, P. G. (1972). Productivity in government and the American economy. *Public Administration Review*, *32*, 740-747.

Quinn, R. E. (1978). Productivity and the process of organizational improvement: Why we cannot talk to each other. *Public Administration Review*, *38*, 41-45.

Report to the National Productivity Council, November 1979. (1980). *Public Productivity Review*, *4*, 167-189.

Ridley, C. E., & Simon, H. A. (1943). *Measuring municipal activities: A survey of suggested criteria for appraising administrations*. Chicago: International City Management Association.

Rosen, E. D. (Ed). (1984, 1985). Proceedings of the Second National Public Sector Productivity Conference: Putting Productivity to Work. *Public Productivity Review, 8*, 7-84, 127-147; *9*, 83-107, 373-392.

Ryan, R. (1978). The impact of three years of experience and a new governor on the State of Washington's productivity program. *Public Administration Review, 38*, 12-15.

Simon, H. (1946). The proverbs of administration. *Public Administration Review, 6*, 53-67.

U.S. Civil Service Commission, General Accounting Office, and Office of Management and Budget. (1972). *Measuring and enhancing productivity in the federal sector*. Washington, DC: Joint Financial Management Improvement Program.

Walters, J. (1992, March). The shrink-proof bureaucracy. *Governing*, pp. 32-38.

Washnis, G. (1980). *Productivity improvement handbook for state and local government*. New York: John Wiley.

Webb, K., & Hatry, H. P. (1973). *Obtaining citizen feedback: The application of citizen surveys to local government*. Washington, DC: Urban Institute.

Wilson, W. (1987). The study of administration. In J. M. Shafritz & A. C. Hyde (Eds.), *Classics of public administration* (2nd ed.) (pp. 10-25). Homewood, IL: Dorsey.

Winnie, R. E., & Hatry, H. P. (1972). *Measuring the effectiveness of local government services: Local transportation*. Washington, DC: Urban Institute.

2

The Politics of Productivity

Productivity and politics are like oil and water: They are naturally incompatible but can be brought together with the right emulsifier and some deliberate shaking up. Productivity is based on facts, while politics is based on values and interests. Productivity utilizes measurement, analysis, and experimentation; politics utilizes persuasion, bargaining, and compromise. The rational thing to do may not be politically feasible; the politic decision may not make sense in terms of efficiency. Public productivity improvement represents an effort to bridge this gap and do the rational thing in a political environment.

This chapter discusses the politics of productivity improvement in two senses. One is **Politics**, with a capital **P**: how the American governmental structure, traditions, and culture define the playing field—the institutions and rules within which action is possible. The other, **politics** with a small **p**, resembles "office politics" in that it focuses on the importance of knowing all the actors—their interests, strengths, and connections. Let us start by looking at how the effort to measure and improve public productivity is affected by the structure of the American political system, the political culture, and contemporary political issues.

The Political System

The Structure of the Political System

Fragmentation of Power

The most noteworthy characteristic of the American political system is the degree to which power is fragmented. Two basic principles made this so: federalism and the separation of powers.

Federalism. Federalism was a practical solution to a real dilemma: how a new union of preexisting political entities, each jealous of its power, could produce the central authority necessary to action as a nation. The conclusion was to share powers between the central government and the states. In addition, power is also shared within states: The capitol makes policy in some matters, and local governments decide others. The result is confounding:

> Local government in Illinois defies description. First, there is so much of it—6,627 units in Illinois. . . . In addition to state government, there are cities, villages, towns, counties, townships, school districts and special taxing districts. . . .
> Second, these units are significantly different from each other in size, scope, structure, function, budgets, personnel practices, professional expertise and political influence ("Chicago Just One," 1992).

What does this mean for the productivity effort? It undercuts rational management. "The fragmentation of local government has long been cited as an impediment to coordination, accountability, equitable funding, and economies of scale" (Ammons, 1985, p. 296). The many layers of government make innovation slow, complicated, and risky:

> Federal wage and hour laws, equal employment opportunity (EEO) requirements, and intergovernmental grant provisions have limited local managerial

flexibility in areas such as working-hour variations, modified performance-appraisal techniques, shared-savings plans, and other employee incentive programs (Ammons, 1985, p. 299).

Some mandates are questionable or clearly inappropriate, according to the U.S. Advisory Commission on Intergovernmental Relations (Ammons, 1985, p. 298).

> A county hospital in Maryland is required by state law to keep its hot water temperature no less than 110 degrees. That same hospital is mandated by federal law to keep that very same water no more than 110 degrees. . . .
>   "It's called 'mandate madness' " (Cottman, 1980).

Wise or questionable, statesmanlike or nitpicking, mandates from numerous sources dot the field like land mines and the innovator must defuse them or dance around them. Obtaining waivers, rule changes, or special allocations involves the politics of persuading the relevant authorities.

Even intergovernmental assistance creates barriers. "Regulations governing grant-supported programs tend to be written with an eye toward controlling the behavior of the least responsible local governments, often resulting in tightly prescribed and cumbersome operating procedures that lead to red tape and delays, while eliminating flexibility in the development of improved methods" (Ammons, 1985, p. 297).

Fragmentation has its uses, however. So many governmental entities provides room for what Alice Rivlin has called "random innovation" (1971, p. 88): a quality circle here, privatization there, robotics somewhere else. From the successes and the failures come models and lessons. Also, governments can provide one another with impetus for action: The state may insist that the city improve its financial accounting system; two townships may invite a third to join a consortium to establish a new facility or service.

Separation of Powers. If the Founders shared one passion, it was the fear of tyranny. They wrought to forestall the accumulation of total power by establishing separate legislative, executive, and judiciary branches on the assumption that each would act to control the excesses of the others. This vertical division of power further compounded the horizontal fragmentation created by federalism.

What does the separation of powers imply for productivity improvement? As Norton Long pointed out in a seminal article:

> The lifeblood of administration is power. . . . Yet power is not concentrated by the structure of government or politics into the hands of a leadership with a capacity to budget it among a diverse set of administrative activities. . . . The agencies to which tasks are assigned must devote themselves to the creation of an adequate consensus to permit administration (1987, pp. 203-205, passim).

Because American agencies need to worry about finding and keeping support, they need to cultivate relationships with many outsiders. They tend to avoid any action that might arouse antagonism. This creates a bias against innovating or taking proactive risks to forestall future problems. The separation of powers politicizes administrative decisions:

> Since it must be responsive to multiple external and internal interests, government decision making resembles a bargaining process. In making decisions, a federal manager must try to avoid alienating the President, the Congress, various constituency groups, the public at large, and finally the agency's own staff—all of whose interests may clash (Usilaner, 1981, p. 238).

To this must be added the chilling effect created by anticipation that an innovative action might be challenged in the courts. If a state agency wants to prioritize the allocation of a scarce resource, such as medical care, will those denied benefits initiate a lawsuit? Will the attempt to improve personnel utilization by reclassifying jobs impel a suit on the grounds that the new system favors one group or another? The innovator may have second thoughts: better, perhaps, not to rock the boat, stir up a hornet's nest, or open a Pandora's box.

On the positive side, fragmented power opens avenues and leaves room for maneuvering. The budget allocation denied by the executive may be restored by the legislature. The agency view can be supported by a friendly reporter, a client group.

Equality

Because everyone's opinion counts, mandates often have to be worded ambiguously in order to receive enough political support. Rational assessment is therefore difficult: "The goals of a government agency are multiple, complex, vague, and subject to much debate. . . . Consequently, a public administrator is rarely able to determine unambiguously when an agency or one of its programs, policies, or projects is a success" (Behn, 1980,

p. 257). Furthermore, because "the views of all constituent groups are to be considered legitimate, . . . the managers of a government agency . . . make decisions less than they negotiate compromises—not only with outside constituencies, but also with subordinates who may have cultivated outside supporters" (Behn, 1980, p. 261). This points up the importance of both political and technical skills for productivity improvement efforts.

Short Time Frames

The U.S. political system inhibits long-range thinking. Terms of elective office are fixed and often short. Most governmental budgets are drawn for only one-year periods. "There may be no greater obstacle to the efficiency of government operations than the one-year budget horizon that encourages delaying management challenges for the future" (Lewis & Logalbo, 1980, p. 185). Seymour Mann (1980) has put the matter succinctly:

> Most productivity improvement efforts take considerable time to reach fruition and to yield visible benefits. Even the introduction of dramatic new technology, such as the computer, requires time-consuming groundwork with budget providers, line and staff workers, managers, and users, as well as time for easing the system in and awaiting results. Other productivity measures take even longer; many take years and years. Compared to such time frames, the political term appears short. Elected officials who sponsor such efforts, or the appointed bureaucrats who lead them, are likely to find that tension has been generated but that relief is not provided in time to serve the reelection or reappointment candidacy. There is no reward.
>
> The acquisition of monetary and other resources is subject to the same difficulties. Legislators are understandably disinclined to be held accountable for expenditures when the benefits of the spending will accrue to their successors (pp. 359-360).

Fixed terms have consequences not only for proposed improvements but also for productivity programs already under way. New incumbents may choose tactically, if not philosophically, to disassociate themselves from the preceding administration's project. The loss of top support has crippled more than one undertaking: "In late spring of 1976, Governor Evans announced he would not seek another term and would return to private life in January 1977. There was an immediate and perceptible loss of momentum in agency response to Productivity Program staff contacts" (Ryan, 1978, p. 14).

Accountability

Protection of individual rights, openness to scrutiny, due process of operations, and concern for financial propriety are jewels in the crown of American government, but they impede action. To the extent that productivity improvement is about creative new options and organizational change, these constraints upon public managers create circumstances in the public productivity field that are different from the circumstances in the private sector.

Protection of Constitutional Rights. Protection of the constitutional rights of employees, clients, and other individuals binds government agencies, but not private companies. "Rights secured by the U.S. Constitution are in every instance (except the prohibition against slavery) protected from only government infringement" (Sullivan, 1987, p. 461). Public officials can be sued personally.

Open Operations. Public agencies are subject to legislative oversight, investigations, and hearings. The Freedom of Information Act entitles members of the public to obtain copies of agency documents (with certain exceptions). Sunshine laws in many jurisdictions mandate that deliberations be open to the public. Legislators, and, in some jurisdictions, official ombudsmen, are free to probe administrative actions on behalf of complaining citizens.

Administrative Due Process. The Administrative Procedures Act sets requirements to prevent arbitrary action by agencies. The need to give advance notice and to provide opportunity for a hearing slows down the change process.

The Civil Service. Most jurisdictions select and manage most of their personnel under a merit system. This is intended to ensure open access to public positions and the rational placement of personnel. But the rules that guard this process also make it difficult to introduce alternative schedules or redesign jobs:

> New York State has 7,300 different job categories for its 285,000 state employees. Iowa has 1,254 different job titles for 44,000 employees; of those job titles, 364 apply to positions held by one individual. Under Florida's current civil service system, there are 23 categories of adminis-

trative assistant, none interchangeable. Civil service rules discourage moving people and jobs, because of the strict constraints of classification (Walters, 1992, p. 36).

The Budget. Budgets afford necessary control over the use of public resources. But the budget has been called "one of the most significant structural barriers to federal productivity improvement" (Usilaner, 1981, p. 238). Like narrow job descriptions, line-item budget categories prohibit shifting resources to meet changing problems and opportunities. The usual one-year budget cycle discourages long-range thinking, and the requirement that unspent funds be returned to the coffer provides no incentive for thrift.

The Political Culture

Alongside written laws and other formal provisions, custom and practice have shaped a set of shared public assumptions about what is right, a set of mutual expectations about how things should be done. Although never formally voted or written, these assumptions and expectations take on the force of rules that guide action in the public sphere. In general, productivity initiatives that fit into and flow with the cultural pathways have a better chance of success.

To take just one example, it is an important norm that no public servant gets fired just for the sake of efficiency. It is, however, acceptable to make fiscally required reductions in force and downsize staff through attrition, even though cuts based on seniority may eliminate productive workers while retaining solid goldbricks and attrition may leave some units untouched but others seriously understaffed. Worse, across-the-board cuts actually penalize past and current efficiencies (Lewis & Logalbo, 1980, p. 186).

Innovators can effect some judicious reshaping of norms by taking what is customary and then nudging it toward what is rational. For example, it is possible to introduce a system of points for performance, along with seniority, when making necessary reductions in force. Likewise, reduction through attrition may be supplemented by a program to retrain and transfer some individuals to understaffed units. That action will be facilitated if it follows the culturally acceptable pathway of offering "the right person" a "career development opportunity." This is not suggested cynically as nothing more than "packaging": The point is that, with some sensitivity to the culture and with some creativity, a rational action can also become a rewarding and thus welcomed action.

Although culture varies from place to place and from one level of govern-ment to another, there are some common elements, including a disincli-nation to eliminate existing programs and an expectation that everyone is entitled to service—even when people know that it is really impossible to investigate every burglary or inspect every facility. An attempt to ration-alize the allocation of resources or prioritize services is more likely to succeed if prevailing expectations are taken into account. The final chap-ter of this book will deal with some strategies for selecting and conducting productivity improvement undertakings.

Political Issues and Policies

Contemporary political issues and currently favored policies create a political climate that has implications for productivity improvement ef-forts. As successful veteran public managers know, these currents can be ridden like waves, smoothing and accelerating progress. The wise conduct of productivity improvement efforts includes a sense of which way the wind is blowing and how it shifts.

Today's political climate keeps productivity improvement an important issue. The public demand for services has been growing continuously since the Great Depression. It has never been higher, and it shows no sign of diminishing. On the other hand, the public taxpayer is unwilling to pay more. For two decades now, governments at all levels have been strug-gling to deal with the problem of how to meet the high demand for public services in the face of severe fiscal constraints. It is no coincidence that the productivity movement blossomed as fiscal crises emerged.

It has been called the irony of the productivity effort that the fiscal con-straints that make productivity improvement important also act to make productivity improvement difficult: The dime is not available to invest in the program that could save a dollar. Also, these constraints "aggravate the very conditions for which investment was needed in the first place. . . . [Infrastructures] deteriorate as maintenance is deferred, facilities and equipment cannot be repaired . . . and [work force] strains mount" (Mann, 1980, p. 353).

Other changes in the political climate are changing the nature of the productivity effort. Public dissatisfaction with politicians and bureaucrats is high. Therefore, it must be assumed that proposed service changes affecting clients (closing or moving a facility, for example) will not be accepted on trust. Also, client opinion and participation are becoming more important as vehicles for reestablishing credibility and ensuring the relevance of services. The probusiness, antigovernment philosophy of recent years offers favorable ground for private sector participation in administration (through volunteerism and citizen coproduction, for example) or turning public functions over to the private sector (through contracting out or voucher systems, for example). Thus, public-private partnerships and privatization have become acceptable options in the 1990s; they might not have been in another era.

The current openness to new options and the serious search for solutions to America's economic and social problems favor the removal of some of the impediments to change:

> The situation is not likely to improve any time soon. . . . So where do we go from here? . . .
>
> Perhaps this new low point will serve to encourage examination of alternative ways to meet public sector obligations. Every week I [an assistant county controller] read of initiatives aimed at continuing public service in new and creative ways (Carroll, 1992).

Given the continuing thrust of fiscal crises, the willingness to seek change, and the impressive reservoir of theoretical and practical know-how that has been amassed since public productivity first emerged as a concept, the scene may well be set for accomplishing productivity improvement now as never before.

The Actors

The "actors" in the productivity improvement story are the stakeholders, those who have vested interests and potential roles to play. They can be classified for convenience into two broad categories: those external to the agency and those within it. The external actors are the public (as taxpayers, clients, voters), elected officials (legislators, executives), the media, and the public sector unions. The internal actors are the top managers (political appointees and permanent civil servants), middle managers (including supervisors), and workers.

The roles and relationships of these actors can best be seen through a systems diagram developed from the original conceptualization of David Easton (1965) (see Figure 2.1). The central organ is the government, which is divided into legislative, executive, and judicial branches. The public provides inputs in the form of resources (taxes) and information (political

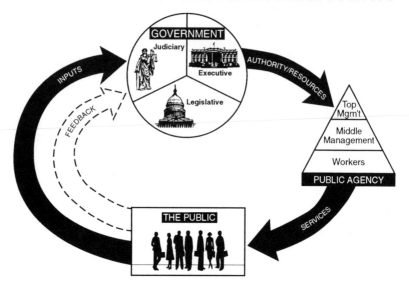

Figure 2.1. Systems Diagram of the Political System

demands). Based on these inputs, the government makes authoritative decisions about policies and programs. These decisions are turned into reality by administrative agencies (located on the output side of government), to which authorization and funding have been given.

The agency is drawn in the diagram as a three-tiered triangle. This is based on James D. Thompson's conceptualization of three significant suborganizational levels (institutional, managerial, and technical), each with a distinct level of responsibility and control (1967, pp. 10-12). Different interests and possibilities for action drive the top managers, the middle managers, and the workers.

Let us look at what concerns and motivates each group of stakeholders, starting with the external actors.

External Actors

The Public

As the diagram illustrates, the public is the supplier of resources and the recipient of services. Each member of the public feels the different roles:

Taxpayer. The taxpayer is that part of the personality of each of us which resists higher payments to government and yearns for reductions in government costs that will ease our tax burden. . . .

Consumer. There is another side of our nature. . . . As consumers, we may easily argue for more police officers, a new library, newer schools . . . and a host of other public services. . . . Just as the taxpayer side of us typically underestimates the importance of the services provided by government, the consumer side of us typically ignores the cost of what it is that we demand.

Voter. It is in the voting booth that the taxpayer and consumer sides of our nature must come to grips with each other. Elections also provide a test of political strength between those who see themselves principally as taxpayers and those who see themselves principally as consumers of government services (Fosler, 1980, pp. 284-285).

The public as taxpayer has asserted, consistently and strongly, its opposition to higher taxes:

Ballot Measure 5, which Oregon voters adopted in 1990, places restrictions on the dollar amount of taxes that local governments can impose on property owners, (h)arking back to California's Proposition 13 and Massachusetts' Proposition 2 ½, approved in 1978 and 1980, respectively (Petersen, 1992).

Public dissatisfaction with government services needs no documentation: Criminal justice, education, health, social service, tax collection, immigration, and postal agencies have been criticized as inefficient, ineffective, or both. Political candidates run against "the government," and the idea of privatization has become increasingly popular.

As the public becomes increasingly discontented with both taxes and services, it loses faith in government. We see that phenomenon today. Despite the quip that we are lucky that we do not get all the government that we are paying for, the public *does* want to get its money's worth. The productivity field can provide the means for improvement and a restoration of confidence, but, given the current level of mistrust, the public will respond only to carefully crafted changes, visible improvements, and impeccable claims.

Elected Officials

Elected legislators and executives achieve and hold their offices because they can obtain and hold the support of contributors and voters. Therefore, most politicians cannot afford to be seen as too far afield of the electorate when it comes to taxes or services. This does not absolve them from taking leadership, defining issues, and setting priorities, but it imposes limitations on how far and how fast they can go. Executives and legislators are most likely to interest themselves in public productivity when the public is concerned about costs and to favor those productivity improvement efforts that will produce visible benefits in time for the next election.

Elected officials, in disarray in the face of rising costs against a falling tax base and caught between the forces of tax revolt and demand for public services, have an important stake in productivity improvement. It can provide both the fact and the image of doing more and better with less. It can help restore public confidence in government.

Political leaders are the source of empowerment and motivation for agencies. Their actions ensure the rules, authority, and funding to permit improvements.

> Along with the executive office, [state legislatures] are the prime movers in making productivity improvement a major policy focus. Once this is accomplished, they have the power of the purse to encourage management action. . . .
>
> No roles are more important to productivity improvement policy than those of the counterparts of state governors and state legislatures in Federal and local government. . . .
>
> While they can deal with improvement techniques, make change in management style and take action inside their organizations, agency administrators can make little progress without the direct support, encouragement, and even prodding by executive and legislative leadership (Balk, 1984, pp. 157-158).

Executive and legislative actions also shape the reward system within which public managers operate. If savings bring only budget cuts, and if initiatives bring high risk of criticism from which no politician will defend them, then

> . . . agency managers keep a low profile. They put their energies into subtle efforts to get more resources and control, rather than engaging in the less certain, risk-laden outcomes involving productivity improvement.
>
> In order to bring about a change in agency management attitudes and directions, a good part of the answer seems to lie in giving productivity improvement a higher *political* priority and making it more of a satisfying activity for agency managers (Balk, 1984, p. 155).

Balk suggests that legislatures undertake to encourage the generation of measurement data by not misusing it, ensure that appointive agency heads have the necessary professional background, make long-term investments in training and facilities, reward competent administrators, and buffer agencies from strident media (Balk, 1984, pp. 159-160).

Outside Organizations

Every public sector agency is subject to the influence of outside organizations that are specifically concerned with its efficiency or the quality of its work. They provoke quantitative analyses, define quality standards, and serve as sources of information, inspiration, and guidance. These organizations are essentially of three types: (1) budgeting and auditing offices, (2) professional associations, and (3) productivity researchers and centers.

Budgeting and Auditing Offices. Budget offices at every level of government require a periodic effort by operating agencies to translate qualitative agendas into quantitative terms and to defend requests, often in programmatic categories. The need to project future resource requirements in terms of workload pushes agencies towards the output-to-resource ratio as a frame of reference. The accounting systems needed for budgeting and auditing purposes provide much of the data upon which agency productivity measurement rests. Not surprisingly, the agency's budget office is a common source of expertise and the site for productivity programs or projects.

Auditing agencies, from the federal General Accounting Office on down through state and city comptrollers, check not only for the correctness and legality of spending, but also for efficiency, management, and the quality of services. For cities in crisis, emergency control boards may be added to the list. Any and all of these agencies may be the spur to productivity measurement and to improvement initiatives.

Professional Associations. Organizations such as the Council of State Governments and the International City/County Management Association (ICMA) (formerly, the International City Management Association) provide forums and resources for the dissemination and exchange of productivity improvement experience; the ICMA annual *Guide* is one important example.

Professional societies in such fields as public administration, accounting, personnel, engineering, and the law serve as reference groups to which the public sector practitioner looks for the newest methods and for procedural and behavioral standards. They are a source of innovative ideas, as well as an objective source of quality criteria or standards.

Productivity Research Groups and Centers. Some of the most creative pioneering work in productivity measurement and improvement has come from research organizations such as the Urban Institute. Several productivity centers (National Center for Public Productivity, 1982) disseminate information. The National Center for Public Productivity has advanced academic-practitioner exchange through national conferences and its journal, the *Public Productivity & Management Review.* These organizations inspire and inform the process of productivity improvement.

The Media

The media may not be stakeholders in the productivity effort, but they play a role as shapers of public opinion. They bring issues to public attention, affect how the issues are framed, and give voice to selected opinion holders. Ideological bias can insinuate itself at every step, but there is a consistent skew toward undermining work force morale and public confidence: Failures, abuses, and other negatives make news; day-to-day performance and systematic improvement do not.

On the positive side, in their search for news and in the use that whistle-blowers and others can make of them, the media are effective in locating and publicizing problems to be addressed. There is nothing more dramatic and irrefutable than video footage documenting malingering by park crews, census workers, or other public employees. Action reporters publicize individual problems with public agencies. Agencies can and should use that information as feedback on performance and as a spur to action.

An invidious effect comes, however, from the pattern of bombarding the public with overwhelmingly negative information. This creates public cynicism and demoralizes the public work force. Conscious of their social responsibility and influence, the media can, and should, offset this bias by publicizing accomplishments and improvements.

The Unions

The most recent wave in the unionization of the American work force has been the organization of public sector workers. "While union membership overall in this country has been dropping over the past several years, unionization in the public sector has grown from about 900,000 in the late 1950s to over 6 million in 1987" (Naff, 1991, p. 23).

Since unionization, public sector workers have achieved pay levels and, more particularly, benefits programs (Methe & Perry, 1980, p. 366) that rival or outpace the private sector. Persistent fiscal crises now threaten unions' gains through personnel retrenchments, management requests for "give-backs," and contracting work out to the private sector. This situation is particularly acute because the most highly unionized jurisdictions are also those hardest hit by fiscal problems: the older, larger cities of the East.

The Impact of Change. The prime interest of unions has always been to maximize membership, protect jobs, increase compensation, and champion the rights of labor in general and members in particular. Other things being equal, unions would be expected to resist productivity efforts that reduce the work force or create differential rewards based on performance (Balk, 1975, p. 14; McGowan, 1984, p. 174). But other things have not been equal. The fiscal crises in many places made it clear that wages could go up only if productivity improved. Privatization emerged as a real source of competition and a threat to jobs. In addition, it is clear that changes will continue to take place in the profile of the public work force (better educated, more females, new ethnic groups) and in technology; it has become impractical to ignore change. "Employees and their unions have learned that without their input, they can become casualties in the plans for change" (Cohen-Rosenthal & Burton, 1987, pp. 10-13).

Productivity bargaining offers some contractual accommodation between management's desire to make productivity-enhancing changes and labor's desire to be rewarded for its contribution. During the collective bargaining process, management and labor thresh out new agreements in which concessions on such matters as work rules are accompanied by increases for the workers (Newland, 1972, p. 808; Balk, 1975, p. 8). But productivity bargaining has been criticized as representing a continuation of the traditional adversarial win-lose mode of bargaining between labor and management, with "limited prospects for long-term successes in governments and high potential for counterproductive, even dismal, consequences" (Newland, 1980, p. 526).

Labor has begun putting onto the bargaining table policy issues, such as changes in emergency room staffing and procedures. That represents the beginning of a new, win-win approach: "a bargaining process that identifie[s] problems in need of solution with the contract specifying the means by which such problems will be resolved through a continuing cooperative process engaged in by the designated representatives of the concerned parties" (Mann, 1989, p. 231).

Contract negotiations are confrontational in nature; in Chapter 8 we will see how a system of labor-management committees provides union and management with a collaborative vehicle for improving both productivity and the quality of working life.

Both sides stand to gain from cooperation. For unions, cooperation with management is a way to gain autonomy, use their expertise, enhance members' upward mobility through the opportunities for training and decision making, and recoup the reputation of the public work force. Cooperation also requires that managers become more knowledgeable and prepared to share information and decision making: Labor has long maintained that management is the barrier to effective production (Gotbaum & Handman, 1978, p. 19).

There are advantages for management. Union distrust breeds resistance to even reasonable concessions. A cooperative relationship gives management access to the union communication network. The union is a repository of experience and information and a source of stability despite turnover at the top of the agency (Mann, 1980, pp. 361-362). Finally, the current emphasis on managing for quality (see Chapter 10) depends on the awareness and sensitivity of the workers, who are the "boundary spanners" between the organization and the client.

Unions and management share common ground and critical interests. Both have an interest in worker health and safety and in training both workers and supervisors (Hodes, 1991, p. 164). Both want to restore public faith in and respect for public agencies; neither wants agency functions removed to the private sector. To a large extent, labor-management accommodation depends on mutual trust:

> [Uniformed Sanitationmen's Association leader] DeLury's membership trusted him and respected him; no other city union leader could have secured member acceptance of a 25 percent increase in work performed just by passing the word that it was ok. . . . DeLury's willingness to stick his neck out related in turn to his growing trust in [Commissioner] Elish and confidence in his managerial ability (Hayes, 1977, pp. 229-230).

Unions and Productivity Improvement. Surprisingly, it is still unclear to what extent, on balance, unions have helped or hindered the productivity effort (Methe & Perry, 1980, p. 367). Union-management relations may "evoke images of dueling gunfighters of the Old West," but, say Cohen-Rosenthal and Burton, that is a distorted view created by the media (1987, p. 5). In fact:

> Unions have not been actively involved in efforts to improve productivity in most governments. However, where informed management initiative has been exercised, employees and unions generally have accepted improvement programs, so long as their security and other interests have not been threatened or ignored (Newland, 1980, p. 504).

In his classic study of productivity programs in eight local governments, Frederick O'R. Hayes (1977) concluded his chapter on the unions as follows:

> There are few reported situations where the unions constitute the critical factor in productivity improvement. . . . [But in] the most difficult union situations, it may well be that the real issues are sociological and psychological rather than economic. To the rank and file in a large organization, aggressive union behavior has been an antidote to the feeling of powerlessness, to grievances against an insensitive management, to public criticism and complaints, and to just being pushed around. Such a situation probably symptomizes the need for new styles of management rather than new approaches to union-management relations (p. 241).

Internal Actors

Figure 2.1 showed the administrative unit as a three-tiered triangle. At the top sit those managers who are responsible for the agency in its dealings with the outside world. They interpret the mission, set programs, negotiate for opportunities and resources, and watch for events and trends with which the agency may have to deal. At the middle level are those people who manage routine operations. They plan, oversee, and control, making the necessary adjustments to prevent or offset potential disruptions (absences, a computer virus, a paper shortage). At the foundation are the workers, the group sometimes called the "technical" or "operating core." It is this group that actually performs the operations and carries out the activities that produce the mandated services.

Location and function give each group its own viewpoint, interests, and role to play with regard to productivity improvement.

Top Managers

In most agencies, top management comprises political appointees and high-level permanent civil servants. The political appointees represent the administration in power; the civil servants embody the history and identity of the organization. Ideally, this admixture works to ensure that agency priorities and policies move with the changing political preferences of the electorate. In practice, it is often a source of friction: "All too often, professional managers are used by appointees as 'fall guys' for program problems and failures. Hence, a 'working relationship' evolves that is built on political versus professional manager fingerpointing" (Usilaner, 1981, pp. 242-243). The political appointees are more likely to seek innovation (sometimes genuine, sometimes as window dressing) to demonstrate that the administration is making its mark. However, they generally lack administrative experience and familiarity with the agency; they tend to serve for short periods (Usilaner, 1981, pp. 243-244). The professionals, who tend to value the established ways, are aware that they can wait out each political wave.

Top administration as a whole can play, essentially, one of three roles in productivity improvement: do nothing, initiate, or support.

Do Nothing. The political reward system up to now has encouraged doing nothing. Why? For one thing, change is risky:

> The heads of most government agencies have learned over time that there is relatively little reward, aside from personal satisfaction, in doing things exceedingly well or showing imagination or initiative to improve programs. A city manager, a mayor, or a host of council members will always be ready to claim credit for successes. . . . On the other hand, if something goes wrong . . . there will be innumerable members of the public, an aggressive press, and a variety of elected officials who will be quick to point out the "failure" and to hold the agency head responsible for it. In short, there is little incentive for improvement, but a great price to be paid for failure (Fosler, 1980, pp. 286-287).

Initiate. A White House Conference on Productivity in 1983 called for both public and private sector managers to take the initiative in productivity improvement: "Government needs to be better managed. . . . A manager's job is productivity" (Aronson & Skancke, 1983, pp. 321, 323). However, as long as "substantial rewards often depend upon emotional political influence, rather than organizational-rational management influence," managers will prefer "surface acceptance" to substantive action (Balk, 1977, p. 47). They will seek the name, not the game.

Under what circumstances does action become more attractive? To begin with, the sanctions for failed efforts need to be lifted. Governmental agencies cope with uncertainty and change, which means that methods have to be discovered through trial and error. Lack of success does not necessarily mean incompetence; it may simply mean "back to the drawing board."

Next, performance and economy should be rewarded. The present reward system is perverse:

> The local government department head who finds ways to minimize the resources necessary to continue operating effectively can expect, instead of accolades and a substantial pay increase, the reassignment of current funds to cover the overruns of a less efficient department and a reduction in the upcoming budget (Ammons, 1985, pp. 302-303).

Finally, history suggests that top-down initiatives are most likely to occur in an agency that is clearly malfunctioning. If the old ways stand in disrepute, opposition to change is vitiated and radical action is not only accepted but also invited. Two famous successes share the characteristic that they overhauled agencies that were patently failing:

> In 1979, a new top administration came to PennDOT [Pennsylvania Department of Transportation] committed to revitalizing a department which was notorious for waste, poor management, and corruption. The highway system was described as follows: "Pennsylvania's highway system . . . once one of the finest in the world is on the verge of becoming a shambles" (Poister, 1983, p. 325).

> Streets became noticeably dirtier. . . . [C]ollections per week were reduced by over 27 percent. . . . Vehicle maintenance was a disaster, with . . . a fleet which was up to 50 percent incapacitated at any given time. . . . Ignored and overworked, maintenance personnel produced more and more shoddy work (Steisel, 1984, pp. 104-105, 110).

Support. Initiatives for improvement may spring from lower levels or smaller subunits within an agency. Top management can create a climate of encouragement by rewarding performance and risk taking. It can facilitate specific undertakings by welcoming proposals, allocating the necessary resources wherever possible, and helping to overcome resistance by consistent authoritative support for the fact that change will take place.

Middle Managers

In the organizational triangle, middle managers, including first-line supervisors, form the middle layer. They serve two crucial functions: operations management and vertical communication. As we will see, their roles predispose them to regard proposed change with suspicion.

The Functions of Middle Management. It is the job of middle management to guarantee the work process: to plan and monitor operations; make sure that personnel, equipment, space, transport, supplies, and other necessities are available; and to analyze reports and order adjustments.

Good management of operations also involves keeping the infrastructure in good condition. That translates into maintaining not only the physical plant and equipment, but also the morale and good will of the work force. Driving machinery into the ground or exploiting the workers may achieve short-term gains, but it does so at the cost of future capacity. Epstein and Fass (1989) urge doing the opposite: investing in capacity building for public sector agencies, so that their potential grows.

> Industry has traditionally depended on major investments for productivity growth . . . but it simply is not in our culture to think of investment as a necessary ingredient for sustained productivity growth of *public* organizations. . . .
>
> Traditional investments in new capital equipment and facilities are important . . . but they are only a small part of the answer. Government is a service industry. Services are delivered *by people* . . . to people. Investments to improve services should be seen as *investments in people.* . . . This does not mean simply adding more . . . staff. . . . It means investing in better training . . . and in anything else that *helps people do their jobs better in serving people* (p. 112).

The second major function of middle management is to serve the communications process as both conduit and gatekeeper. It is essential that the workers in the lower layer are clear about the purposes, programs, and policies that direct and guide operations from above. Conversely, it is important that top management gets realistic information on the internal condition and potential of the organization. This includes more than reports of operations: It includes feedback from the workers about their own perceptions and what they hear from the clients.

Interests and Perceptions. Most middle managers, and certainly most supervisors, have risen from the ranks. They know the operation: the skills, technology, work flow. That is their stock in trade. All too often, they have had little or no training in management skills, such as delegation, and are unsophisticated about organizational dynamics. Productivity improvement constitutes a threat, because it devalues the old ways and stresses the managerial art.

> Some studies have shown department heads and supervisors potentially to be among the most formidable barriers to productivity improvement— more formidable than employee unions. Supervisors, ideally situated to thwart the successful implementation of productivity-inspired changes, may . . . resent the intrusion of outside analysts; they may fear that ideas from others will suggest . . . that they are weak innovators themselves; they may fear that productivity analysis will result in loss of subordinate employees or other resources; they may be concerned that new procedures will expose their own technical weaknesses . . . or they may worry that organizational change will bring loss of status (Ammons, 1985, p. 309).

Motivating Change. It is clear that middle managers, as a class, are an unlikely source of impetus for productivity improvement. There are exceptions, including a newer generation of people, college-educated and often trained in management; but young managers need time to establish command of substantive operations before they are ready to lead change efforts.

It is not vital that innovation comes from middle managers; others can initiate change. It is vital, however, to overcome middle management's opposition. How? Chapter 11 will explore strategies in detail, but some points can be made here. First, managers have to be made to believe that stonewalling will not work, that change is inevitable; top management pressure is important for this. Second, fears have to be allayed. Supervisors and managers need reassurance that change will be done through and not around them, and that credit will be shared, not grabbed by top management. Familiarity with new techniques can be built through orientations, workshops, and more formal training. Proud managers can be offered training under the face-saving guise that it is a matter of bringing them up-to-date on what their staff is being taught.

In general, it must be recognized that middle management probably perceives itself as having much to lose and little to gain from change, and that fact must be taken into account and dealt with if innovation is to succeed.

The Workers

At the foundation of the organizational triangle are the workers who actually produce and deliver public services.

> Increased productivity ultimately comes from the perspiration and inspiration of workers. . . . They are the teachers in public schools, professors at institutions of higher education, highway patrol troopers, soldiers, social workers, prison guards, engineers, tax collectors, and wildlife officers. Virtually all want to do a good job (Kee & Black, 1985, p. 31).

But all too many public sector workers settle for less: for just following the rules, doing nothing that might evoke criticism, and, as it were, serving their time.

If public workers *want* to do good, meaningful, engaging work, but are actually applying only part of their energy and creativity, then giving them opportunity and scope creates a reward for them and a boon to the agency. How do workers perceive productivity improvement efforts? What is their stake in change?

Worker Perceptions. Public sector workers are often jaded and alienated. They are trapped between a system they did not design and a public that is often frustrated and blames them for the problems. Managers do not listen to them, even if they are better educated and closer to the problems. Co-workers teach them to survive by not making waves, and they adapt, rewarded by job security.

Job security is a prime concern. Workers need to be reassured that no one will lose a job. Workers also fear being exploited. They are concerned that measures of productivity will not reflect fairly or completely what they do and might be used to create onerous work standards. They may fear that change will break up a familiar work group.

Whether or not they are conscious of it, workers have a tremendous stake in productivity improvement. Motivation is a two-way street: To get a worker to change inside, you must offer something the worker values. Chapter 7 is devoted to the question of motivation. At this point, it is sufficient to suggest that what workers value most—what causes them to "buy in" psychologically and invest their energy and emotion into making operations and services better—is the chance to participate, to be listened to, and to have a voice and some degree of control over the workplace.

Vision, in the sense of specific, unambiguous goals, may be difficult to achieve in the political arena; but vision, in the sense of seeing one's own work as part of something intrinsically worthwhile and therefore important, is inherent in most public sector work (Kee & Black, 1985, p. 32).

Workers attest to that:

Workers have a lot of pride, and they do not want to come to work looking behind corners to see where the boss is. They would rather just do a day's work and go home. Just give them what they need, and do not bother them (Contino & Giuliano, 1991, p. 190).

Managers attest to that:

You have to get to know [government employees] and use them. If you come in and simply try to impose change, they'll kill you every time. But if you involve them, they can be extremely responsive (Ted Gaebler, quoted in Walters, 1992, p. 36).

Getting from here to there is not easy: Overcoming cynicism and creating a new work culture is not done overnight. But success enriches everyone.

The Politics of Change

It is a fact of life that productivity is improved by making changes: changes in what people feel and know, changes in work routines and tools, changes in how resources are acquired and configured, changes in the way services are structured and delivered. The objective of doing more and better with less is achievable only by disturbing what is. Even the measurement of productivity creates change by introducing a new unit, new procedures for generating and collecting data, new analytical skills, and a shift of power into the hands of those who generate and exploit the information.

If it is true that productivity improvement means change, it is also true that change brings resistance. That is implied by the open systems model. Practical experience confirms that people do adapt to their routines and to one another. Organizational units depend on the routines of other units. When the system and the people are all "broken in," things flow smoothly and habitually. Change deprives people of comfort with expectations and requires them to learn new routines and adapt to new norms. It is therefore unsettling; consider the Japanese manager who is asked to work as an equal with female executives or the American worker asked to sing the company song and do exercises on the factory roof in the morning.

Productivity improvement is an exercise in inducing change in the face of this natural resistance. Success depends on maintaining pressure for change, recognizing and dealing with constraints, and motivating actors to cooperate.

There must be a strong and continuing source of pressure. One or more actors must provide sufficient clout to convince key individual and group decision makers that change cannot be forestalled or avoided. For this reason, the support of top management or labor unions or both is particularly vital. Given the short tenure of most top managers and the short time frame built into most budget systems, this favors, in general, those undertakings that can be accomplished in a relatively short time.

Who will provide the pressure for change? At bottom, it has been the public, rebelling against higher taxes and voicing its disapproval of government. Policy makers doubtless welcome any evidence that government is efficient and effective, but they are unlikely to rally under the productivity banner as many did in the 1970s. They are, however, searching about for new options, and that creates a favorable climate for change. Evaluators, auditors, comptrollers, and financial control boards are by their quantitative and analytical nature attuned to the relationships of resources and results. They will continue to spur specific projects by pointing out cases of evident waste or mismanagement.

Specific constraints have to be recognized and overcome. It is vital to identify possible impediments: anyone whose approval or cooperation is needed, a law that must be changed, a special funding allocation, a union contract stipulation. Politics is about power: gaining allies and neutralizing opposition in order to achieve one's purposes. The politics of productivity improvement involves building support and overcoming roadblocks.

Productivity improvement means changing the way that people behave. People act in terms of their interests and perceptions. Accordingly, it is important to ascertain what it is that various actors value and fear and to offer whatever information, reassurance, and rewards may prove necessary to persuade them. The process of meeting, explaining, listening, and discussing can be time-consuming, but it makes for viable, more easily implemented changes.

The politics of productivity improvement has to do with diagnosing the context within which the organization moves and recognizing the perceptions and motivations of all relevant actors. It is a matter of recognizing barriers and finding ways around or through them. The barrier may be a civil service rule, the union, a middle manager with political ties who cannot be persuaded or removed, or lack of money to hire a needed skill. Any proposed innovation comes with a set of requirements; it is feasible only if these already exist or if they can be finessed. We will argue throughout the book that the technical and the political are equally necessary in public productivity improvement. The choice of innovative technique should be guided by the question, "Will it work?" Deciding to adopt it should be guided by the question, "Is it feasible?" Politics is the art of the possible.

References

Ammons, D. N. (1985). Common barriers to productivity improvement in local government. *Public Productivity Review, 9*, 293-310.

Aronson, J. H., & Skancke, S. I. (1983). White House Conference on Productivity: An opportunity for change. *Public Productivity Review, 7*, 313-323.

Balk, W. L. (1975). Toward government productivity bargaining policies. *Public Productivity Review, 1*(2), 8-18.

Balk, W. L. (1977). Why don't public administrators take productivity more seriously? In M. Holzer, E. D. Rosen, & C. Zalk (Eds.), *Local government productivity* (pp. 45-51). Washington, DC: Academy in the Public Service, Georgetown University Graduate School.

Balk, W. L. (1984). Productivity in government: A legislative focus. *Public Productivity Review, 8*, 148-161.

Behn, R. D. (1980). Can public policy termination be increased by making government more businesslike? In C. Levine & I. Rubin (Eds.), *Fiscal stress and public policy* (pp. 249-280). Beverly Hills, CA: Sage.

Carroll, N. L. (1992, February 1). State and locals fighting fiscal crises. *PA Times*, p. 8.

Chicago just one of 6,627 local governments. (1992, March 1). *PA Times*, p. 2.

Cohen-Rosenthal, E., & Burton, C. E. (1987). *Mutual gains: A guide to union-management cooperation.* New York: Praeger.

Contino, R. A., & Giuliano, J. (1991). Productivity gains through employee participation at the New York City Department of Sanitation. *Public Productivity & Management Review, 15*, 185-190.

Cottman, E. M. (1980, October 1). Federal, state mandates erode local flexibility. *PA Times*, p. 1.

Easton, D. (1965). *A systems analysis of political life.* New York: John Wiley.

Epstein, P. D., & Fass, S. (1989). Comprehensive productivity programs: A leveraged investment. In E. C. Hayes (Ed.), *The hidden wealth of cities: Policy and productivity methods for American local governments* (pp. 111-131). Greenwich, CT: JAI.

Fosler, R. S. (1980). Local government productivity: Political and administrative potential. In C. Levine & I. Rubin (Eds.), *Fiscal stress and public policy* (pp. 281-301). Beverly Hills, CA: Sage.

Gotbaum, V., & Handman, E. (1978). A conversation with Victor Gotbaum. *Public Administration Review, 38,* 19-21.

Hayes, F. O'R. (1977). *Productivity in local government.* Lexington, MA: Lexington.

Hodes, N. (1991). Achieving quality through labor-management participation in New York State. *Public Productivity & Management Review, 15,* 163-168.

Kee, J., & Black, R. (1985). Is excellence in the public sector possible? *Public Productivity Review, 9,* 25-34.

Lewis, C. W., & Logalbo, A. T. (1980). Cutback principles and practices: A checklist for managers. *Public Administration Review, 40,* 184-188.

Long, N. E. (1987). Power and administration. In J. M. Shafritz & A. C. Hyde (Eds.), *Classics of public administration* (2nd ed.) (pp. 203-212). Homewood, IL: Dorsey.

Mann, S. Z. (1980). The politics of productivity: State and local focus. *Public Productivity Review, 4,* 352-367.

Mann, S. Z. (1989). Labor-management cooperation and worker participation: A public sector perspective. *Public Productivity Review, 12,* 229-236.

McGowan, R. P. (1984). Improving efficiency in public management: The torment of Sisyphus. *Public Productivity Review, 8,* 162-178.

Methe, D. T., & Perry, J. L. (1980). The impacts of collective bargaining on local government services: A review of research. *Public Administration Review, 40,* 359-371.

Naff, K. C. (1991). Labor-management relations and privatization: A federal perspective. *Public Administration Review, 51,* 23-30.

National Center for Public Productivity. (1982). *The National Directory of Centers of Productivity and Quality of Working Life.* New York: Author.

Newland, C. A. (1972). Personnel concerns in government productivity improvement. *Public Administration Review, 32,* 807-815.

Newland, C. A. (1980). Labor relations. In G. J. Washnis (Ed.), *Productivity improvement handbook for state and local government,* (pp. 503-529). New York: John Wiley.

Petersen, J. E. (1992, January). The property tax revolt: Here we go again. *Governing,* p. 64.

Poister, T. H. (1983). Monitoring the productivity of a state highway maintenance program. *Public Productivity Review, 7,* 324-343.

Rivlin, A. M. (1971). *Systematic thinking for social action.* Washington, DC: Brookings Institution.

Ryan, R. (1978). The impact of three years of experience and a new governor on the State of Washington's productivity program. *Public Administration Review, 38,* 12-15.

Steisel, N. (1984). Productivity in the New York City Department of Sanitation: The role of the public sector manager. *Public Productivity Review, 8,* 103-126.

Sullivan, H. (1987). Privatization of public services: A growing threat to constitutional rights. *Public Administration Review, 47,* 461-467.

Thompson, J. D. (1967). *Organizations in action: Social science bases of administrative theory.* New York: McGraw-Hill.

Usilaner, B. L. (1981). Can we expect productivity in the federal government? *Public Productivity Review, 5,* 237-246.

Walters, J. (1992, March). The shrink-proof bureaucracy. *Governing,* pp. 32-38.

3

Productivity Concepts and Applications

The influence of our fragmented, short-time-frame political system on public productivity improvement, first raised as an issue in Chapter 1, was examined in Chapter 2. Another issue, raised in the same discussion, concerned the youth of the public productivity field. Two of the consequences of that youth form the subject of this chapter: (1) the need to nail down the basic concepts that we talk about, including just how productivity differs from policy making, with which it is often confused and because of which productivity often receives a "bum rap"; and (2) the desirability of integrating productivity findings into the data systems that inform management decisions. When it becomes clearer to all what productivity means, what it measures, and the many valuable uses to which its component measures can be put, the way will be clearer for general application of the many sensible, feasible improvement ideas that have been developed in various corners of the field and that are reported in Chapters 6 through 10.

Concepts

Introduction

Much of the confusion over public sector productivity comes from confusion about definitions (Quinn, 1978, p. 41). As Bouckaert (1990) has phrased it, people approaching the study of productivity from different disciplines or perspectives operate in different "clusters," using different terminology and methodologies, and they tend not to interact. "All these differences put researchers into intellectual ghettos" (p. 83). An even more insidious source of confusion comes into play when people do interact and communicate under the illusion that they are attaching the same meaning to words when, in fact, they are not. A famous story is told of an argument between Roosevelt and Churchill at one of their meetings during World War II. They agreed an issue was important, but disagreed about whether or not to table it. Churchill wanted to table it; Roosevelt did not. The key was in the meaning of "to table": to an Englishman, it meant to bring the issue forward for immediate action; to the American, it meant to put it aside for later action.

Many public productivity terms are vague, ambiguous, and laden with implicit assumptions, and that has undercut progress in the field. "We are often speaking on different wavelengths—using 'efficiency' when we mean 'effectiveness' or 'service quality' or 'productivity' " (McGowan, 1984, p. 177). Differences in usage have caused us to talk past one another; broad, free-floating terms have become rugs under which we can sweep unsorted ideas. We need to reexamine our most basic vocabulary and put it into better working order.

The following propositions are set out as a way of establishing some crucial distinctions and to help reduce misunderstanding and stimulate conceptual rigor. They are designed to deal with particularly ambiguous basic terms by disentangling two meanings of "effectiveness" and suggesting a specific relationship between "quality" and "effectiveness" as they relate to productivity.

Before moving ahead, it is worth remembering that all definitions encounter, at the boundaries, nagging exceptions that test, or prove, the rule. This in itself does not negate the utility of the core concept. For example, it is undoubtedly useful to distinguish "living" from "dead." But what if the heart beats while the brain is inert? At what point does life begin? When we define a body, do we include the symbiotic, but independent, bacteria without which the body could not digest its food? Do we include dead tissue—sloughed skin, hair ends, fingernails? These boundary issues may assume real importance in debates over moral or medical issues, but they do not undercut the usefulness of recognizing an essential difference between life and death. The core meaning is not nullified by the ambiguities at the periphery. So let it be with the productivity field. Exceptions should be viewed in proportion and not become the basis for eliminating useful major distinctions.

Propositions

Proposition 1: Woodrow Wilson's distinction between "politics" and "administration" is a useful one. Politics has to do with choices among competing preferences and what David Easton has called "the authoritative allocation of values" (1959, p. 129). The struggle for political power is a struggle to obtain the power to determine policy—that is, to decide what issues will be addressed and by what means. Now, it is true that the political and administrative domains do become less distinct at the boundaries: The appointed heads of administrative agencies are as political as administrative, and it is true that public administrators do influence the political policy process by drawing attention to issues, giving expert opinion on options, and choosing to implement vigorously or suppressively. But public administrators' central focus, their reason for being, lies in a process that can be distinguished as beginning only after the (political) decision has been made to undertake a program.

The process of administration starts upon the granting of authorization and funds to some implementing agency. An agency can be regarded as a "black box" for converting resources into a set of services. Viewed that way, a fire department is nothing more than a way of converting money (and, in many communities, volunteer labor) resources into fire suppression and fire prevention services. Administration centers on that conversion process: on the acquisition and deployment of space, people, and equipment to achieve the programmatic ends.

The importance of this distinction between politics and administration is that it suggests the distinction between the domains of program evaluation and productivity. Program evaluation assesses the effects of a program in terms of a political goal, a desired societal outcome, but productivity assesses the efficiency of the conversion process. Walter Balk has drawn this distinction repeatedly:

> Evaluation systems must exist in government which are more comprehensive than those centered around individual agency productivity. These are the "program evaluation" efforts of legislative and executive groups. Inevitably, evaluations of this type must give primacy to broad political and social value considerations, only one of which is productivity. . . . In a nutshell, productivity improvement efforts are necessary and vital because they are essential to squeezing optimal yield out of allocated resources; but they are only part of the political impact picture (Balk, 1975, p. 14).

> In my opinion, narrowing the definition of productivity to that of agency performance gives the term operational and control stability. This would make consideration of political consequences, or policy accountability, a separate field of inquiry (Balk, 1978, p. 47).

> Semantics is a major problem. Productivity is not a precise enough term—the word should relate directly to agency activities rather than to broad political policy decisions (Balk, 1980, p. 499).

Proposition 2: The success of a policy is contingent on two things: choice of undertaking (doing the right thing) and appropriate implementation (doing the thing right).

Obviously, implementation of a program is a necessary condition for its success. But there is another factor: The line of reasoning on which the policy is based must be correct. A counseling program for delinquents or inmates may be set up on the assumption that counseling will induce attitudinal changes and that changed attitudes will result in changed behavior. The program may be duly implemented, but if, in fact, counseling does not affect attitude or attitude does not determine behavior, then it will not succeed.

> If the program is unsuccessful, there are two general categories of reasons. Either it did not activate the "causal process" that would have culminated in the intended goals (this is a failure of program), or it may have set the presumed "causal process" in motion but the process did not "cause" the desired effects (this is a failure of theory). . . . Stated another way, program failure is a failure to achieve proximate goals; theory failure occurs when the achievement of proximate goals does not lead to final desired outcomes (Weiss, 1972, p. 38).

This recognition of the two necessary conditions for success helps further to carve out the distinctions between politics and administration, between the program evaluation and productivity fields. Productivity analysis and improvement are concerned with implementation, administration, and proximate goals. It is wrong to blame the bureaucrat or the productivity field for a failed policy if the failure was one of theory, not implementation. That is the "bum rap" referred to above.

Proposition 3: Ambiguity in the meaning attached to the term "effectiveness" has been a source of confusion in the productivity field and can be diminished by recognizing a distinction between program effectiveness and the effectiveness of the implementation process.

Clearly, a policy or program is effective if it results in the desired outcome: that is, if it has an impact on the situation or problem that was targeted for action. In this usage, "effective" pertains to "outcome" and, as Proposition 2 suggests, it reflects on both choice and implementation of means. Effectiveness in this sense can be determined by looking at the impact created by having done the right thing and having done it right. There are practical problems, such as ruling out other causal influences and assessing how much confidence to place in findings, but program effectiveness and outcome have a clear conceptual relationship.

Now let us consider another version of "effectiveness," as related only to the implementation issue. *Implementation effectiveness* reflects program actualization, the extent to which the mandated services have been produced and delivered. It focuses on outputs, not outcomes. For the purposes of the productivity field, it is implementation effectiveness that is of most direct relevance.

This distinction between different meanings of effectiveness is important because it is instrumental in clarifying the role of output quality. The productivity field has long assumed a close relationship between quality and effectiveness, but the relationship has remained poorly defined. "Common practice is to encompass both *service quality* and *program-effectiveness* characteristics within the term effectiveness and refer collectively to all of the performance factors" (Usilaner & Soniat, 1980, pp. 92-93).

Looking at effectiveness in this new and alternative way, by recognizing two different kinds of effectiveness, helps clarify a conceptual relationship between "service quality" (that is, the quality of outputs) and effectiveness. Service quality pertains to implementation effectiveness, and, because theoretical validity is an intervening factor, it can be expected to have only a partial and indirect influence on "program effectiveness."

To elucidate through a practical example, "good arrests" are of direct relevance to implementation effectiveness, but they are much more tenuously tied to outcomes—that is, to changes in the nature and amount of crime (see, for example, Downs & Larkey, 1986, pp. 72-74). The incidence of crime may be affected by many factors other than the operations of the police department; arrests may not lead to deterrence. Those are problems of pinpointing causality and failures of theory; they fall outside the realm of productivity, which takes the police mission as a given and seeks only to make more efficient and effective the process of implementation: producing and delivering appropriate quantity and quality of services such as patrol, arrest, traffic control, and response to emergency calls.

Proposition 4: The quality of output is directly related to *implementation* effectiveness. Conventional wisdom bears this out. When one looks at the way quality has been measured in practice, it is clear that the most common indicators have indeed related to implementation.

As will be discussed much more fully in Chapter 5, quality is generally determined in terms of attributes. Thus, the quality of a referral service may be determined according to how promptly, accurately, and courteously information is dispensed. The quality of a pothole-filling operation would be determined by looking at how promptly, quickly, and durably the filling is done. Note that all these attributes pertain to output, to the service itself. There are exceptions: One common criterion for gauging the quality of sanitation work is street cleanliness, which is indeed an outcome measure. But such exceptions are few in number and appropriate only in those situations where causality is not problematic.

Proposition 5: Output quantity and output quality are cofactors in determining implementation effectiveness.

> Effectiveness encompasses both *quantity* and *quality* of a service. For example . . . public transit effectiveness depends not only on the number of people who use it, but also on whether these people have safe, comfortable, rapid, convenient, timely, and reliable journeys (Epstein, 1992, p. 171).

A specific relationship between service quantity, quality, and (implementation) effectiveness needs to be established. We suggest that quantity and quality are codeterminants; that is, multiplied together (output quantity × output quality) they measure how effectively the implementation process is taking place. If either is a zero, implementation effectiveness is zero.

The usual productivity formula,

$$\text{Output quantity} \div \text{Input}$$

expresses the efficiency with which outputs are produced. When output quality is incorporated into the measurement system (as suggested below and in Chapter 5), then the productivity level,

$$\text{(Output quantity)(Output quality)} \div \text{Input}$$

also becomes a useful statement of the efficiency with which implementation is effectuated.

The incorporation of output quality into the output measure by means of a coefficient of quality has already been suggested, although the meaning of "effectiveness" was left unexplored:

> Let a quality coefficient, K, express the overall quality level of any output whose quantity is being measured. . . . Without entering the debate over just what effectiveness is . . . the following assumptions may be made: . . . that the more and the better the work, the more effective it will be (maximizing output quantity O and quality K maximizes effectiveness—OK work is effective work); and that 'more' and 'better' are codeterminants— neither an infinite supply of useless work nor an infinitesimal amount of elegant work will be effective (Rosen, 1981, p. 212).

One preliminary point needs to be made here. Service quality is taking on increased importance with the new "customer" orientation in management (see Chapter 10). It is important to be aware that client satisfaction with services may not correlate with programmatic success. It is possible, for example, that a new school program, with which parents are very happy, is not lowering the dropout rate, which it was intended to accomplish. Of course, if the programmatic goal is really only the political end of making a given group feel attended to, regardless of objective accomplishment, then happiness equals success. The point is that output quality is a factor in effective implementation but not a guarantor of impact.

Summary of Propositions

To summarize, this set of propositions attempts to specify the intuitively accepted, but as yet undefined, relationship between "quality" and "effectiveness." This is important because the productivity field has been impeded by ambiguities about what productivity covers (and does not cover), what effectiveness means, and how quality fits in.

The line of reasoning underlying the proposition sequence has been:

- By dichotomizing politics and administration, it is possible to differentiate the realm of program evaluation from the productivity field.
- By examining the implementational versus the theoretical factors for program success, it is possible to distinguish "implementation effectiveness" from "program effectiveness."
- Focusing on implementation makes plausible the postulate that output quality and quantity codetermine implementation effectiveness.
- Incorporating both quality and quantity into the output measure permits the productivity formula to express not only the efficiency with which outputs are produced, but also the efficiency with which implementation is effected.

Some of the assumptions built into the propositions have long and honored histories. Some are new to the field and certainly are not universally accepted. The reader is cautioned accordingly.

Applications of Productivity Measures

Introduction

Productivity improvement means more than a one-shot effort. It means a pervasive concern for conserving resources, for finding new ways to enhance efficiency, and for improving the level and quality of "product" delivered. This culture requires a work force that is tuned in and turned on and management that is open to insights and ideas from employees, clients, and anyone with information on problems and performance; it requires at least some people who are comfortable with measurement.

Perhaps the first general contribution the productivity improvement effort can make to the organization as a whole is capacity building. To achieve the attitudes and skills that support productivity improvement, managers and workers need to be trained in cooperative modes, group dynamics, problem-solving techniques, measurement, analysis, and drawing conclusions from data. Certain innovations may require learning new technology or upgrading old skills. The experience of working together to solve specific problems enhances communication and understanding throughout the organization and with the clientele. This general enhancement of sensibilities and skills, in a sense, builds the body tone of the entire organization, making it more capable of rational action and adaptive change.

Information collected in the process of measuring and improving productivity can, and should, be applied to fill managerial information needs of many kinds. The types of information generated for specific productivity measurement and improvement needs are listed below, along with typical applications.

Information From Productivity Measurement

Output Quantity Measures

Measuring productivity requires, first, specification of what the "products" or services are. Many public agencies operate on "automatic," not pausing to take stock of what they are doing. Everyone thinks that everyone knows the set of services produced and their relative importance. Simply identifying the major outputs can be an exercise in mutual education as representatives of different functional areas within an agency come together to decide on a list. Top agency policy makers can use this process and information to reexamine priorities and to develop within the organization the sense of unified purpose that underlies esprit de corps and the capacity for excellence.

Deciding on a fair way of measuring the quantity of a specified service also sets into motion a process of thinking through and fixing in everyone's mind what the objectives are. It requires defining precisely of what a unit of service consists and when it is completed. Shall we measure our output by number of people interviewed or number placed? Well, is our service interviewing job seekers or placing them in positions? In large organizations, process tends to become an end in itself; this exercise becomes a way of getting the organization's head straight.

In developing a system for measuring output quantity, decisions often have to be made about how to count units of work that vary in difficulty. Some clients are easier to place in jobs than others. The measurement system that is developed must take that into account, or, human nature being what it is, workers will tend to take on the easy cases. Open, representative discussion aimed at identifying and weighting such differences often stimulates exchanges on how to handle them in practice: "Let's get together after the meeting and talk about this some more!" Communication and exchange for the purpose of measurement enhances communication and exchange in general.

Once set, measures of output may be used to define objectives. Field studies show that setting quantitative goals leads on to superior output (Miner, 1980, pp. 184-185).

Input Measures

Productivity is a relationship between outputs and inputs. Inputs are resources, such as labor, equipment, space, energy, and supplies. To measure productivity, it is necessary to ascertain just how much of a given resource goes into producing the output. Learning how much overhead goes into maintaining one low-volume operation may suggest reorganization. Information on the longevity of a piece of equipment supports purchasing decisions and budgeting projections. The information on how much worker time it takes to process each unit of work can be used to deploy the work force more rationally, to plan labor needs for expanded operations, and to justify budget claims.

A determination of just which resources are used in producing a given service provides management with the capacity to establish accounting "cost centers" and to make informed decisions about the relative efficiency of different operations.

A focus on inputs may suggest the search for economies of scale. To take one illustration: A public hospital may want a diagnostic instrument whose cost per unit of output (patient treated) will be very high because it will be rarely used; that cost per unit calculation may induce the hospital to consider an alternative arrangement, perhaps joint purchasing and sharing with other hospitals in the area or perhaps contracting for that service from another hospital.

> Cost analysis might disclose whether one additional refuse collector increases or decreases the collection cost per unit. It might show an excessive cost for operating a particular truck or point out that a new truck will be cheaper than the cost of repairing an existing truck. Or it might show that modest increases in service delivery will result in dramatic increases in operating expenses (Kory & Rosenberg, 1984, pp. 8-59).

Output Quality Measures

As will be seen in Chapter 5, the quality of a service is determined by its usefulness to the client. A service is of better quality if it is more accurate, prompt, durable, reliable, comfortable, accessible, courteous, and so on. Different indicators modify different services, but the rationale is the same.

Deciding on the relevant indicators of the quality of a given service (and deciding on the relative importance of those indicators) involves ascertaining clients' needs and desires. That is done by asking them and by listening to the employees who deal with them. The very process of involving employees and clients empowers them and builds a sense of ownership and understanding that brings not only new ideas and insights, but also a tolerance and acceptance that facilitates implementation of routines and innovations.

Specific findings on client needs and level of satisfaction can be used to define the directions in which operations should be reshaped. Among Paul Epstein's (1992) suggestions are:

- Target programs or services to neighborhoods, regions, or clients with special needs. . . .
- Reallocate existing services according to need. . . .
- Learn about inexpensive changes that can make services more helpful to citizens or clients. . . .
- Learn how community or client conditions and perceptions change after a service delivery change has been in effect for a period of time (p. 192).

Findings on client satisfaction can also be used in dealings with others— as evidence of the administrative agency or unit's accomplishments, to defend it against inappropriate criticism and to back up requests for resources or authority. Claims of greater efficiency from privatization "may indicate a difference in service levels and quality and not greater efficiency or productivity" (Barnekov & Raffel, 1990, p. 140); measures of service quality can be used as controls in considering or monitoring contracts.

Information From Productivity Improvement

A productivity improvement undertaking involves collecting and analyzing information: to ascertain the existence and magnitude of problems, judge the probable payoffs of alternative approaches to those problems and then determine the effects of the selected interventions. Much of that information has other potential uses.

Productivity improvements that focus on the work process (see Chapter 6) produce such records as logs of worker activity, flow charts showing how the work proceeds, and demand curves that reveal patterns of fluctuation in the amount of work to be done. Such data, when analyzed, reveal such information as how much of a worker's time is spent on which tasks, how long a unit of work takes from beginning to end, how often a piece of equipment is idle or down for repairs, and what kind and level of resources will be needed in the future.

Improvements that focus on the worker's motivation and skill (see Chapters 7 and 8) develop information on subjects such as worker morale, assessed training needs, and the frequency and causes of absenteeism. In addition, specific feedback and suggestions arise from the participative management innovations (suggestion systems, task forces, quality circles, and joint labor-management committees) that form part of this approach.

Productivity improvements achieved by exploiting alternative options for obtaining resources and producing better service (see Chapters 9 and 10) generate attitudinal data on client needs and perceptions, as well as information on alternative costs for producing public services in-house, by contract, through interlocal cooperation, or by contracting out to another jurisdiction or the private sector.

Integrating Productivity Findings
Into Organizational Decision Making

Management Decisions

Capacity. Management requires information on the organization's capacities. Productivity data can tell how long a unit of work takes to complete, how much labor will be needed, the state of worker skills and morale, and what additional resources may be obtainable from nontraditional sources. Such information permits realistic judgments of the feasibility of expanding operations, meeting a new need, withstanding a potential disruption (strike, shortage, etc.) and more realistic estimates in goal setting, planning, and budgeting for future activities.

Operations. Information on the relationship between resources and production permits allocating staff and resources efficiently. Measures of productivity provide a gauge for testing alternative work methods, optimal team size, optimal scale of operations. Productivity measures can be used to predict periods of heavy workload and to set production standards for the control of operations.

Monitoring Performance. Productivity measurement, done over time, identifies trends in organizational performance and warns of the emergence of undercutting problems. A record of performance points up a "historical best" period and leads to asking "What were we doing then that was so right?" Comparison with productivity levels in other jurisdictions may reveal the need for improvement and lead to exploring the methods that make the other jurisdictions more productive. Measures of productivity "provide benchmarks from which progress in making improvements can be evaluated" (Hatry & Fisk, 1971, p. 7). "Productivity data can be used by staff analysts and auditors to question the causes of apparent progress or lack thereof" (Holzer, 1988, p. 2).

Setting Service Objectives. Information on outputs reveals shifts in the volume and priority of different types of output over time. Information on citizen satisfaction levels and what they look for in service quality affords feedback on organizational performance, serves as a test of policy, and points up the need to set new service directions and priorities. Paul Epstein has identified "forms of value associated with performance measurement and productivity improvement efforts," including "reallocation of resources to more closely meet community needs" and "making services more responsive to community needs" (1982, p. 164).

Politics and Public Relations. A reputation for poor performance robs an agency of its credibility.

> Because of a history of equipment neglect and poor performance, the [New York City Department of Sanitation] had little of the institutional and political credibility necessary to obtain the funds or the broad public support required to institute change. . . . In this environment, there was a natural reluctance to purchase large numbers of new vehicles just to see them destroyed through abuse and poor maintenance long before the end of their useful lives (Steisel, 1984, pp. 104-105).

Mitchell and Scott (1987) have made the theoretical point that "underlying notions of legitimate authority are grounded today in the ideas of expertise, entrepreneurship, and stewardship," adding that "administrators as a class . . . may want others to believe they are expert, visionary, and trustworthy, [but] little theoretical or empirical evidence supports these claims" (p. 446). Productivity measurement and improvement can enhance credibility by demonstrating administrators' expertise through their sure command of productivity theory and technique, entrepreneurship by their induction of change, and trustworthiness by their use of measures to back up their claims.

Personnel Management

Information from productivity measurement and projects can provide the human resources management system with such "inventory" information as status of employee morale; match of worker skills to job skills; work site, child care, drug, alcoholism, and other problems; schedule preferences; and tardiness, absentee, and turnover rates.

Productivity measurement provides the factual underpinnings for union negotiations and the process of productivity bargaining. Participative management programs, such as quality circles, provide a window on worker perceptions.

Productivity findings can serve the management of human resources by providing measures and standards as a basis for evaluating individual and group performance and for the design of reward systems tied to performance. "Ways in which productivity measurement results could be used effectively to fill program gaps . . . include: establishing incentive systems built around measures by providing rewards for meeting viable and valid standards" (Suttles, 1980, p. 148).

James Swiss (1983) has cautioned, however, that when the stakes get high, when salaries and budget are too directly affected by performance measures, the incentives to cheat are also high. "It is usually far better to use the system information as one input to be considered in all types of managerial decision making, without direct budget tie-ins, and thus lower the incentives for cheating and displacement to a level where counterincentives are feasible" (p. 33).

Finance and Budget

For the financial management system, information on levels of output, production time, and resources used in producing a unit of work provide a practical basis for estimating payback from a potential investment: in equipment, space, or training, for example. This refers to both the magnitude and the period of payback. Productivity data provide estimates that serve the process of making decisions about purchasing versus leasing, or producing in house versus contracting out. Knowing relative production costs provides a basis for estimating a reasonable user fee.

For the budget system, productivity measures are a major source of data to support justification of resource requirements (Hatry & Fisk, 1971, p. 7) and for making cost projections for different levels of effort. With productivity figures, budgets can be linked to performance—to evaluate and encourage it.

> A notable use of such productivity measures is Florida's "Agency Productivity Agreements" in which high-level officials establish specific performance targets, some of which relate to service effectiveness and others concern process and output targets. Detailed performance measures concerning workload, output, efficiency, and effectiveness for these targets are set out in the agreements in the departments' budgets to evaluate their achievements (Poister, Hatry, Fisk, & Greiner, 1985, p.18).

Despite the Florida example and others like it, the linkage between productivity and budget is far from adequately utilized:

> Budget reform proponents believe that the type of information presented in proposed budgets affects budget outcomes. . . . Performance budgets, program budgets, Planning Programming Budget Systems (PPBS), Management by Objectives (MBO), and Zero Base Budgeting (ZBB) are all budget reforms that require information about agency or program performance. . . .
>
> A sampling of budget documents from jurisdictions that have implemented one or more of these budget reforms will convince the reader that changing the budget's format is more often accomplished than changing the information presented in the budget. . . . A survey of 88 cities, for example, revealed that 74% used a performance budget format, but only 31% used efficiency information when making spending choices (Grizzle, 1985, pp. 328-329).

Conclusion

The discussion thus far has dealt with the benefits to an organization from integrating productivity information into its decision making. Balk, Bouckaert, and Bronner (1989) have urged the close integration of productivity and financial control systems as a way of benefitting the productivity effort. They suggest that "government productivity improvement programs will become more effective as they tie in systematically with other planning and strategic objectives of networks of agencies; as they are seen as important adjuncts to and rationalizers of financial controls" (p. 129). Dulworth and Taylor (1989) provide support:

> In 1984, GAO [General Accounting Office] issued the report *Increased Use of Productivity Management Can Help Control Government Costs*, which describes the Productivity Group's analysis of six private-sector, seven state and local government, and nine federal agency productivity improvement efforts. . . . They stated that the single greatest deterrent to sustained productivity improvement was the tendency to approach the effort as a . . . temporary add-on to regular activities. If a productivity improvement process is integrated into an organization's procedures, appraisal systems, goal-setting practices, budget process, management information systems, and human resource systems, it influences behavior in the organization and ultimately becomes part of the organization's culture (p. 148).

References

Balk, W. L. (1975). *Improving government productivity: Some policy perspectives.* Beverly Hills, CA: Sage.

Balk, W. L. (1978). Toward a government productivity ethic. *Public Administration Review, 38,* 46-50.

Balk, W. L. (1980). Organizational and human behavior. In G. J. Washnis (Ed.), *Productivity improvement handbook for state and local government* (pp. 477-502). New York: John Wiley.

Balk, W. L., Bouckaert, G., & Bronner, K. M. (1989). Notes on the theory and practice of government productivity improvement. *Public Productivity & Management Review, 13,* 117-131.

Barnekov, T. K., & Raffel, J. A. (1990). Public management of privatization. *Public Productivity & Management Review, 14,* 135-152.

Bouckaert, G. (1990). The history of the productivity movement. *Public Productivity & Management Review, 14,* 53-89.

Downs, G. W., & Larkey, P. D. (1986). *The search for government efficiency: From hubris to helplessness.* New York: Random House.

Dulworth, M. R., & Taylor, R. C. (1989). Assessing and improving organizational productivity. In J. S. Wholey, K. E. Newcomer, & Associates, *Improving government performance: Evaluation strategies for strengthening public agencies and programs* (pp. 143-161). San Francisco: Jossey-Bass.

Easton, D. (1959). *The political system: An inquiry into the state of political science.* New York: Knopf.

Epstein, P. D. (1982). The value of measuring and improving performance. *Public Productivity Review, 6,* 157-166.

Epstein, P. D. (1992). Measuring the performance of public services. In M. Holzer (Ed.), *Public productivity handbook* (pp. 161-193). New York: Marcel Dekker.

Grizzle, G. A. (1985). Performance measures for budget justifications: Developing a selection strategy. *Public Productivity Review, 9*, 328-341.

Hatry, H. P., & Fisk, D. M. (1971). *Improving productivity and productivity measurement in local governments*. Washington, DC: Urban Institute.

Holzer, M. (1988, November 1). Focus: Productivity improvement in New York State—the science and art of capacity building. *Managing New York State*, pp. 1-5.

Kory, R. C., & Rosenberg, P. (1984). Costing municipal services. In J. Matzer, Jr. (Ed.), *Practical financial management: New techniques for local government* (pp. 50-60). Washington, DC: International City Management Association.

McGowan, R. P. (1984). Improving efficiency in public management: The torment of Sisyphus. *Public Productivity Review, 8*, 162-178.

Miner, J. (1980). *Theories of organizational behavior*. Hinsdale, IL: Dryden.

Mitchell, T. R., & Scott, W. G. (1987). Leadership failures, the distrusting public, and prospects of the administrative state. *Public Administration Review, 47*, 445-452.

Poister, T. H., Hatry, H. P., Fisk, D. M., & Greiner, J. M. (1985). Centralized productivity improvement efforts in state government. *Public Productivity Review, 9*, 5-24.

Quinn, R. E. (1978). Productivity and the process of organizational improvement: Why we cannot talk to each other. *Public Administration Review, 38*, 41-45.

Rosen, E. D. (1981). OK work: Incorporating quality into the productivity equation. *Public Productivity Review, 5*, 207-217.

Steisel, N. (1984). Productivity in the New York City Department of Sanitation: The role of the public sector manager. *Public Productivity Review, 8*, 103-126.

Suttles, S. A. (1980). Filling the "gaps" in executive branch supporting activities. *Public Productivity Review, 4*, 146-150.

Swiss, J. E. (1983). Unbalanced incentives in government productivity systems: Misreporting as a case in point. *Public Productivity Review, 7*, 26-37.

Usilaner, B., & Soniat, E. (1980). Productivity measurement. In G. J. Washnis (Ed.), *Productivity improvement handbook for state and local government* (pp. 91-114). New York: John Wiley.

Weiss, C. H. (1972). *Evaluation research: Methods for assessing program effectiveness*. Englewood Cliffs, NJ: Prentice-Hall.

4

Measurement

The awful truth about measurement is that so many people are uncomfortable with it. They feel unjustified in devising measures: It does not seem right to assign numbers, to play God. It seems unfair to reduce complex, dynamic phenomena to a few statistics; so much is left out. They feel vulnerable as consumers of measurement. Statistics can be manipulated: "Figures don't lie, but liars figure." They feel especially vulnerable as the subjects of measurement. It puts power into the hands of people who may misunderstand the situation at best, and misuse the measures at worst. This is nowhere more true than in the public workplace.

Agency managers, in some cases, cannot provide productivity information because they are not up-to-date regarding measurement techniques. But, more commonly, the hesitancy exists because they recognize the inherent limitations of the data and the need for careful interpretation. They fear that precipitous decisions may be made by legislators and that information will be taken out of context in order to make political hay (Balk, 1984, p. 159).

And yet these same people use, and take for granted, all kinds of measures, including measures of performance. Consider baseball. Who had the right to decide that performance will be measured in terms of batting average, runs batted in, or number of errors? Are these the "right" measures? The measurement system distorts certain things: The batter's performance in making a solid hit may or may not count, depending not on the batter's ability but on the fielder's. Consider the economy. We confidently say that the market went up, or the cost of living dropped, or unemployment is stable. We have this information because someone, at some time, decided to begin by counting certain things (and disregarding others). The market level and the cost of living are measured by the average price of only selected indicators. Unemployment figures omit people who have given up trying to find work. A man's suit size is the number of inches around the chest—disregarding everything else. A shirt is measured according to the number of inches around the neck, disregarding chest size.

The point is that measurement involves choices and no measurement system captures everything. There is no objectively "right" measure of anything—although, as will be seen, there are rules of measurement. Every conventional measure began with someone's starting to count something. The meter is the length of a metal bar in a vault in Paris. The standard difference between shoe sizes is the length of three aligned barleycorns.

Measurement offers not a perfect but a consistent and mutually understood way of determining and comparing magnitude and of knowing with some confidence when that magnitude is going up or down. The only alternative is subjective impressions. It is easier to try on shirts from the "15½" bin than to search through all the shirts for those that look like the right size.

The Need for Measurement

The public productivity field requires measurement. Without measurement, it is impossible to know with any certainty how an agency is doing. For example, how does its efficiency stack up?

Just look at the wide variations in tons per man for solid waste collection from city to city, and you'll suspect that some are more productive in providing service than others. [The accompanying figure shows, for twice-a-week collections, a variation from a low of 334 to a high of 1645 tons per man!] (National Commission on Productivity and Work Quality, 1974, p. 7).

Is an office becoming more or less efficient? What has been its "historical best" performance? Is it doing less well today? Only measurement permits solid comparison.

How can the quality of public services be improved, if there is no clear understanding of what service quality is?

> We have . . . had a lot of discussions with the Civil Service Employees Association . . . , which is the largest state employee union, about the issue of QtP [Quality through Participation]. In planning our efforts with them, we agreed on some basic premises. One is that employee involvement must have top-level commitment from both labor and management for it to work. . . . Finally, we will have to determine (and in the public sector it is very difficult) just what quality means in the public sector and what it means in our various operations, in state agencies with different missions and goals. How do you measure quality? What does it mean? How do you know it when you see it? All of those things have to be determined in order to move to a successful quality effort (Hodes, 1991, p. 166).

If a productivity improvement project is undertaken, how can its effect be ascertained? Only by knowing the productivity levels before and after the change. The success of new methods can be judged confidently only if a system exists for measuring productivity.

> Unfortunately, there is not as much data on the actual effects of Quality Circles in United States settings as there should be. . . . This lack of an adequate data base is the greatest weakness of the Quality Circle program in the United States and poses the greatest threat to its continuation and expansion into other areas of the workforce (Roll & Roll, 1983, p. 140).

To sum up, measurement is essential in targeting productivity problems, identifying models of good performance, spotting trends, and judging the success of initiatives to improve productivity. In recognition of the importance of measurement, the National Academy of Public Administration passed a resolution in November 1991 that urged all agency heads and key program managers to develop and utilize measures of performance ("NAPA Speaks Out," 1991).

The State of the Art

We possess the potential to generate useful productivity information for most fields of public service. We have the techniques. Rough but serviceable measures of inputs have been available for almost 30 years. The measurement of the quantity of public sector outputs has been established for some 20 years. In the last decade, approaches to measuring output quality have been produced. We have general agreement on the proposition that productivity measurement should encompass considerations of both efficiency and service quality. Why, then, has so little systematic use been made of measures of productivity? For example: "The states reported little activity in the area of productivity measurement and evaluation such as monitoring of productivity improvement efforts by agencies" (Poister, Hatry, Fisk, & Greiner, 1985, p. 17).

At least part of the answer lies in the absence of a paradigm, a conventionally accepted measurement system. Practitioners need both guidance and the confidence that what they are doing is generally accepted practice and thus defensible from criticism. Given the risks of pioneering, the pandemic discomfort with measurement, and the lack of convention on procedure, it is not incomprehensible that public managers might be reluctant to initiate and deploy productivity measurement systems, important as they may be. While the productivity field is indebted to the many researchers and practitioners whose bold and creative work has produced a rich trove of techniques, criteria, and approaches, that very variety is a source of confusion to the nonexpert. Finally, variation between measurement systems makes it extremely difficult to compare agencies or jurisdictions (Hatry, 1980a, p. 271).

These arguments for the importance of building agreement in the measurement field have influenced this chapter and the next. Instead of describing the many approaches that have been developed over the history of the productivity measurement field, we will build on the definitions established in Chapter 3 to present one general model of a productivity measurement system that incorporates and synthesizes most of the important work done in this field. The reader should realize that this is not the only possible model. It is adopted because it offers a consistent methodology for quantifying the level of inputs, output quantity, and output quality and then integrating these factors into measures of productivity, efficiency, or operational effectiveness as desired. It meets the important criterion of being "simple enough so that lay people can readily command the rationale" (Rosen, 1981, p. 209).

Before we can get to the substance of how to measure productivity, it is necessary to lay a foundation by considering several important issues related to measurement in general and public productivity measurement in particular.

Issues in Public Productivity Measurement

The Political Context

Public-Private Differences

It is relatively easy to measure productivity in the private sector. Private sector outputs are often goods, such as shoes and automobiles, that can be counted. Services are more difficult to quantify, but the fact that private sector services (medical treatment, haircuts, etc.) are for sale means that dollar value can be used to measure them.

The public sector produces services, and they are not for sale on the open market. While "shadow" prices might be derivable for services with private-sector analogs (such as medical treatment), many public agencies (for example, the Department of State or the Department of Defense) have no market equivalent. Similarly, the major resource in the public sector is labor, but the cost of labor is usually a function of longevity. Using the dollar value of labor input would make it appear that productivity went up every time some retiring senior employee is replaced by a cheaper new hire. The dollar is therefore not generally serviceable as a measure of public sector input. In the private sector, costs of production are used to indicate output quality, a useless measure for the public sector. The result is that public sector productivity generally has to be measured without the convenient and universal dollar as a ruler.

Without the dollar as universal surrogate, each public sector output has to be measured directly by counting the actual amount of service delivered and gauging its quality in terms of selected criteria. Given the number of public services, this is a tremendously important fact. A different system must be developed for each service—and there is usually more than one per agency: fire fighting and fire prevention, tax audit and check issuance, garbage collection and street sweeping. "Each service area must be examined in depth. Very little knowledge or data can be transferred from one service area to another" (Mark, 1981, p. 42).

It is a vast understatement to say that measuring public sector productivity is complex. That complexity can be eased, however, by using one general procedure to guide the different agency initiatives.

The Politics of Measurement

The public, the media, and elected officials are fed productivity figures. Measures should provide answers to their concerns, such as what use is made of public resources or how the public work force compares in efficiency and quality with a private deliverer of the same service. On the other hand, they need to understand the measurement process if they are to support it and make intelligent use of its findings. Otherwise, political prejudices become the basis of judgments. The media, public, and elected officials have been made skeptical by distorted "facts"—such as the body count in the Vietnam conflict. To restore confidence, the entire society has a stake in credibly generated and credibly used information.

Top managers are ultimately responsible for the efficiency of the agency, department, office, or bureau, even though middle management handles operations. Good productivity data serve them in dealing with the public, in making the agency's case with elected officials, and in allocating resources internally. These managers also need to understand how the measures have been derived if they are to use the information responsibly.

Middle managers and workers have the largest, most personal stake in the productivity measurement system because their performance is judged on the basis of these figures.

> Their perceptions of the measures (as reasonable, realistic, and fair or as simplistic, biased, and unfair) will color their behavior. If the measurement system is perceived as realistic, fair, and permanent, labor and management will tend to accept it as legitimate. If it is perceived as unrealistic, unfair, and ephemeral, they will attempt to manipulate it by playing games with the numbers (Rosen, 1984, pp. 25-26).

The best way to ensure that a measurement system will be accepted and used appropriately is to include as many viewpoints as possible in its development. Participation generates more ideas, permits more interests to be accommodated in the measurement system, and facilitates the collection of good data and their constructive use as feedback.

Installing a measurement system is an organizational change. Like other changes, it requires backing to overcome resistance, which may be more easily done if it evolves through a series of steps. It requires new routines, such as keeping additional records (though it may make some old ones unnecessary). It is a move toward rationality and the constant monitoring of performance. A new power center emerges around those who know how to generate and present measurement information.

To sum up, a successful measurement strategy combines strong leadership with broad participation, utilizes communication and training, and takes the politics of the situation into account (Brinkerhoff & Dressler, 1990, chap. 8). To deal successfully with the politics of the situation, those who develop and install the measurement system need not only technical expertise, but also good interpersonal skills.

Siting the Measurement Effort

To measure the work of an agency, it is necessary to understand measurement and to understand the work of the agency. Measurement expertise and objectivity is usually found in a staff office, like budgeting. Knowledge of operations resides in line personnel. The individual or team responsible for measurement can be located in either place. Performing measurement out of the staff office reinforces and supports the technical purity of the process but isolates the measurer(s) from the work force and from the day-to-day realities of the work. Conversely, locating the measurement effort in the work unit makes for better knowledge of the work and closer rapport with the work force but isolates measurement experts from their professional base.

In the light of these forces, it is useful to structure the measurement process as the responsibility of a team that includes both measurement and line people. It could be structured as an ad hoc task force or a formal matrix project unit. In any case, the team is where the system would be developed by threshing out and reconciling technical and contextual imperatives. If client input is appropriate (for example, in deciding quality criteria), the team can include representation from that group.

> However developed and wherever located, the measurer is in a "staff" capacity—on tap but not on top. Although much can be achieved informally in tactful negotiation with the subject work force, the measurer must be backed up by serious, continuing support from the top of the line. Without such support the program becomes an exercise in window dressing (Rosen, 1984, p. 27).

The Nature of Measurement

Measurement Is Arbitrary

All measurement is arbitrary (meaning discretionary, not capricious). Even the most scientific units of measurement are the result of arbitrary decisions. The centigrade scale for measuring temperature takes the difference between the freezing and boiling points of water, and divides it into 100 even parts. The Fahrenheit scale sets the freezing point of water at the number 32 and then divides the difference between that and the boiling point into 180 even parts!

It is necessary to drive home this arbitrary nature of measurement, because practitioner reluctance to decide on measures constitutes a real psychological barrier to progress in the quantification of public sector productivity. As long as the decision on what to count, and how to count it, makes sense to the people who will use and be judged by the figures, and if the agreed-upon measures meet some basic criteria (to be spelled out below), then a useful system exists and can legitimately be put into use. The role of operations people (and possibly clients) is to make sure the system makes sense in terms of the work; the role of the measurement experts is to make sure the system meets the basic criteria for good measures.

The one immutable obligation is to provide a clear written record so that everyone who contributes to or uses the data, and anyone who wants to borrow the system, will know exactly what each measure represents and exactly how it is derived. Then, and only then, will measurement be uniform and reliable and comparisons fair and informative. Is the input of a worker's time counted as number of workdays per year or only as days present? Does "delivery time" start when the letter is posted or when it is postmarked? Does the output count include all arrests or only those that survive a first screening? While it is legitimate to choose either method of counting, the method must be specified along with the figures.

"Measures" Versus "Standards"

The productivity literature contains many instances where standards and measures have been confused. They are different. *Measures* present an indication of what *is*: 20 worker days were used, 50 arrests were made, average delivery time for a letter is 2.3 days. *Standards* provide an indication of what *should be*: The average letter should take 1.5 days to arrive; the investigator should make eight site visits per day.

Standards may be derived from measures; that is, knowing "what is" does provide a reasonable basis for deciding "what should be." Standards can then form a rational basis for judging performance, exercising control over operations, and planning resource needs. Worker misgiving about measurement is often rooted in the fear that measurement is an opening wedge to the unilateral imposition of higher standards. That is another reason for worker participation in the measurement process.

Measures Evolve

It is better to start with a few simple measures and modify or augment them over time. Proceeding one step at a time permits experience to reveal the usefulness and limitations of measures: Are data reliable and easy to collect? Is something important being left out of the count? Do the findings fill the needs of users? Proceeding slowly also allows everyone time to adapt to the idea of measurement and the measurement system itself.

> Finally, be opportunistic. Do what you can when you can. Most of the cities you look at that have fine comprehensive measurement systems did not start out with a master plan and put it all in at once. They bit off a little piece here, two years later they got an opportunity to start another piece (Ken Steil, testimony in Legislative Commission on Economy and Efficiency in Government, 1981, p. 16).

Even crude preliminary measures can provide useful information, as long as their limitations are understood by everyone.

> Where rapport between labor and management is good, where analysis and interpretation are already accepted as necessary complements of measurement, and where it is already agreed that the monitoring system is evolutionary, even crude numbers can be constructively and harmoniously used (Siegel, 1980, p. 13).

The danger to guard against at this stage is letting crude measures degenerate into simplistic ones by forgetting the tentative and limited nature of simple, early findings. They should not, for example, be used for setting standards.

> The development of performance standards from scratch can be tricky. Errors may have adverse consequences. Standards set too high may frustrate employees; standards set too low may be difficult to change. Poorly

devised standards may lead to perverse responses. For example, sanitation workers judged only on the weight of garbage collected may "water down" their loads before having them weighed, or police officers judged solely on number of arrests may become overzealous and thereby generate complaints of police harassment (Ammons, 1991, p. 65).

As a general rule, measures should be as simple as possible without disregarding important dimensions of the work. The tendency to overmeasure out of an eagerness to leave nothing out should be overcome.

> The next important thing to keep in mind when you are talking about application of the system is that quantity of numbers is not so important as the quality of numbers. Producing a large report is not necessarily producing a good report. One thing to keep in mind is that producing reports adds to the workload of the department. . . . You have to keep things in perspective and when you identify numbers, you should identify them with a purpose in mind. What are the questions we are trying to answer? What do we want to know? What is this number going to tell us? If you don't know what it's going to tell you, then you shouldn't be asking for it. And you shouldn't be counting it (Joseph Vitteretti, testimony in Legislative Commission on Economy and Efficiency in Government, 1981, p. 21).

Too many data provide noise, not information:

> Overabundance of data, multiple sources of data, redundancy in data collection, . . . and complexity of data collection procedures and technologies have created situations in many agencies where there is more confusion or "noise" than useful data. Stacks of printouts sit on desks, shelves, and other less obvious places. . . . Managers lack time or simply find it too difficult to try to identify good signals from the mass of numbers (Wholey, Abramson, & Bellavita, 1986, p. 141).

Managers can be the source of the trouble, and participation the cure:

> What is it that you the managers need to know? The answers to that question in our experience always have been eyes bigger than the stomach answers. Managers . . . will make unending lists of the things that they think they would like to know. We found that a very good corrective for that is to make those managers come out with us in the field to try to collect that information to see how much they really need to know. We were able to reduce that to one-tenth usually (Greg Farrell, testimony in Legislative Commission on Economy and Efficiency in Government, 1981, p. 9).

Attributes of a Good Measure

How does a good measure differ from a bad one? Of the 22 criteria for choosing good measures that have been cited more than once in the literature (Grizzle, 1985, p. 331), a few are preeminently important. A good measure has validity and is reliable, clear, relevant, accurate, sensitive, and affordable.

Validity and Reliability

These are essentials (O'Sullivan & Rassel, 1989, p. 82). A measure is valid if it really measures what it ought to measure. If, for example, we want to determine how long it takes for the average letter to be delivered, it would be invalid (although it has been done) to use as the measure of "how long" the period from postmark to delivery. Such a measure tells only part of the story: It leaves out the period between mailing and postmarking. Infrequent pickups and backlogged processing would not be reflected in this measure: It does not measure what it was intended to measure.

A reliable measure is one that is consistent, giving the same readings at different times or by different measurers. For example, Operation Clean Sweep in Washington, D.C., used four pictures, exemplifying "clean," "moderately clean," "moderately littered," and "heavily littered" alleys, as a way of enhancing consistency of judgment among observers (Hatry, Winnie, & Fisk, 1981, pp. 100-101). The pictures help reduce variations in judgment attributable to different individual perceptions and norms about cleanliness; they make the measure more reliable.

Clarity

Measures should be clear and understandable if they are to be used and used properly. "Generally, esoteric measures that are overly technical or that involve complex combinations of elements have limited use, at least for higher level officials" (Hatry, 1980b, p. 313).

Relevancy and Controllability

A good measure is one that "provide[s] information needed to make a decision about the performance of the program or agency" (Grizzle, 1985, p. 334). A good measure is controllable: That is, "the person or group being measured should have control over all aspects of performance that go to make up the measure" (Hurst, 1980, pp. 43-44). It is of no help to a productivity improvement effort to measure things that play no part or cannot be changed.

Accuracy and Sensitivity

An accurate measure is one that has no built-in bias or distortion. The mail-delivery example above provides an illustration of bias: The measure made the delivery time appear consistently shorter. A sensitive measure has "the discriminating power . . . sufficient to capture the variation that occurs in the object, event, or situation being measured" (Grizzle, 1985, p. 333). If streets were measured only as "clean" or "not clean," the system could not record changes between the two extremes.

Practicality

This criterion includes the cost of data collection or analysis and the ease of obtaining the needed data (Grizzle, 1985, p. 333). A good measure is not prohibitive in cost or effort. However, the mere availability of a measure does not in itself make it a good measure.

If good measurement requires such care, is it worth the effort? Hatry's advice in 1980 still holds:

> Finally, a word of caution. There is a great temptation to local governments to cut corners on performance measurement procedures and not to worry about the accuracy and validity of the information. Thus far, because of the limited use made of performance information, this may have been justified. But as more important use of performance measurement is made (such as to guide major program and policy choices, provide performance incentives to employees, as well as for performance contracting), then much more care will be needed. Good information does not come from nothing. You get what you pay for. Sound data collection practices and quality control of the data will be required and should be provided (Hatry, 1980b, pp. 338-339).

Dysfunctional Measures

It is important to be aware that measures can do harm. They can lead to perverse behaviors. This is not an argument against measurement, but rather a caution to guard against pathologies.

In the 1950s warnings were being sounded that "judicious use of a tool [measurement] requires awareness of possible side effects and consequences" (Ridgway, 1976, p. 506). Using a single criterion (such as number of interviews conducted) to measure employment-agency performance motivated workers to complete interviews but to spend less time on locating jobs. Multiple measures can create confusion because "the individual is forced to rely upon his judgment as to whether increased effort on one criterion . . . may [be offset by] a reduction in performance on some other criterion which will outweigh the increase in the first." Composite measures that first weight and then combine individual measures can help lead to "obtaining a balanced stress on objectives" (Ridgway, 1976, pp. 506, 512, 513).

Swiss has pointed out the problem of cheating (misreporting data) as "symptomatic of a system that was designed or installed without proper concern for systemic incentives" (1983, p. 27). He suggested three lines of approach for providing disincentives. One is the imposition of sanctions to offset the potential benefits of cheating (p. 28). The second is developing cross-checks through alternative sources of data:

> One of the most important attributes of most productivity systems is that the operating unit reports on its own progress toward the goals. The unit is not likely to wish to report bad news. . . .
> Sometimes this problem can be surmounted through a formal, parallel reporting system that taps different sources and thus serves as a double check. . . . [One can utilize] contacts "down in the ranks" who would blow the whistle on any attempt to cover up difficulties (pp. 29-30).

The third approach is simply to lower the stakes by using the measures anonymously or in aggregate form (p. 31). Deliberate cheating on measures must be punished, and spot checks using alternative sources makes sense as a "reality check." However, the most effective way to build and employ a valid measurement system is to use measurement data as feedback toward making improvement, not as a high-stakes basis for punishment or reward.

Writing more recently, Bouckaert and Balk (1991) have stressed that even "neutral" measures have organizational effects, and that should be taken into account.

> For too long we have been focusing on the intrinsic measurement requirements, the so-called scientific elements required to be a good measure.

Measures have to be mutually exclusive, process oriented, mission oriented, and so on. They have to be time controlled, comprehensive, and reproducible. Now we must direct more attention toward the extrinsic requirements, that is, the impact on the organization of the use of measurement. We must search for optimal measures, those that minimize dysfunctional effects and maximize functional effects, allowing us to focus on the extrinsic requirements of the organizational purpose (p. 232).

Doing Measurement

What to Measure

Like a camera, measurement can take in the whole picture or zoom in to focus on some part of the whole. The first measurement decision is the choice of subject to be studied, the unit of analysis. In organizational life, the unit of analysis might be an entire agency, one regional office, one department within that office, or one work unit within the department. The unit of analysis can even be one worker, although that moves us into the realm of individual performance evaluation. In principle, productivity analysis can be done at any organizational level; in practice, usefulness determines the choice.

In the department [of Agriculture], one of the many organizations furnishing productivity information is the Soil Conservation Service. The outputs and associated inputs for the entire Department of Agriculture are collected, processed. . . . This measure is useful for analyzing the Department of Agriculture, but the executives of the Soil Conservation Service felt additional information would be more useful. . . . [Bureau of Labor Statistics] met this need by developing productivity measures for individual programs such as flood prevention service, snow forecasts, and soil mapping. Because the Soil Conservation Service now has its own detailed set of productivity measures, it is possible to analyze the specific programs of the service as well as the overall performance of the Department of Agriculture (Mark, 1981, p. 35).

New and different entities can be targeted for measurement but, once a unit of analysis has been set, it defines what belongs: what labor and other resources are included, what outputs are produced, and who the clients are.

When to Measure

The purpose of measurement is to permit valid comparison. Performance cannot be judged as absolutely good or poor; it is comparisons of performance, over time or between organizations, that provides useful information on trends and alternative production systems.

Comparison across jurisdictions or between organizations must be made using the same measurement system (or restating the findings of one in terms of the other). For example, if in one jurisdiction typists work 35 hours a week while in another they work 37 ½ hours a week, the total amount of work they turn out has to be restated in common terms, such as number of pages typed per worker hour. It is also important to compare under like circumstances. Ambulance response time in high-traffic areas cannot be compared to response time in open streets. Select typical time periods; avoid start-up periods, for example.

Before-and-after measurement is usually done to detect trends or to assess the results of a productivity improvement effort. Care should be taken that such measurement is made under equivalent conditions, on similar workloads, and for comparable periods (if there is seasonal or other systematic variation).

Avoiding Pitfalls

Strive for typical readings. Whatever the data to be collected—amount of time to complete a given operation, percentage of workday lost to lateness, number of telephone inquiries answered—it is impossible, and unnecessary, to count every single instance. If information is collected on only a sample, the figures can be extrapolated to the entire operation. The key is that the sample must indeed be representative: chosen at random, large enough to drown out the freakish cases, and as free as possible from the distortions of the Hawthorne effect (abnormal behavior resulting from attention as the subject of a study). The measurement expert will know the rules and procedures for proper sampling.

Make proper use of the findings. Findings about the behavior of a group of Boy Scouts may not translate to office workers; a small improvement in the output of a pilot group may not justify claims of a significant innovation. The role of the measurement expert is to know the rules and procedures for sampling and for interpreting data. Details of the procedure should be provided for users of the information.

Use of Measurement Teams

Measurement can be done by one person: a resident measurement expert or someone hired as an outside consultant. It may be faster to proceed that way, but the disadvantages are clear. The outside expert will be unfamiliar with the intimate details of operations, and line workers will be suspicious of an imposed system. A measurement team produces a better system because it incorporates many insights and facilitates the acceptance and institutionalization of the final system because its members are networked into many parts of the organization. The team process may be relatively slow and clumsy, but its product is more likely to work well.

A typical measurement team might comprise a measurement expert (from in-house or outside), an in-house trainee in measurement, representatives from major segments of the unit to be analyzed (including managers, first-line supervisors, shop stewards, and other key workers) and, possibly, client representation. Different participants will become particularly important at different points in the process.

Like other participative groups, the team will probably need some preparation, some orientation to the philosophy and techniques of group decision making. One particularly useful instrument for the measurement process is nominal group technique, which is described in Chapter 5.

Data Sources

Data are collected in only a few ways.

Physical evidence is of limited use, except for solving crimes, but wear and tear can indicate usage, for example. *Observation* can be a good source (especially if people do not know that they are being observed). Using careful observation, a measurer can chart the work process in order to determine such facts as how long a process takes or what percentage of the day is wasted in walking from one place to another.

Existing *records and documents* are an important and common source of information about resources and operations. Records reveal, for example, how many licenses were issued last month, how many workers were assigned to a given project, how many grievances were filed, or the repair history of a bus. Record systems should be studied to see whether they need to be added to, reorganized, or "cleaned up" (to correct omissions or overlap, for instance). Special records may be necessary to provide specific information; for example, personal logs may be needed to determine who does what kind of work and for how long.

Some facts cannot be seen from the outside; they are matters of attitude and perception. *Surveys* (personal interviews or written questionnaires) serve as a way of determining such facts as worker morale, client satisfaction, and what the public looks for in a particular service area.

The measurement expert should know the proper way to employ all of these techniques.

The Productivity Formula

Background

There is no one, generally accepted definition of public productivity. In 1981, Jerome Mark of the Bureau of Labor Statistics wrote:

> The public sector literature variously defines productivity measurement as measurement of efficiency, effectiveness, cost reduction, input-output, management improvement, performance, methods improvement, work standards, and program evaluation (p. 21).

In 1986, the introduction to a volume presenting "The Best of *Public Productivity Review*, 1975-1985" began:

> The lack of general consensus or endorsement of one specific definition of productivity in the *PPR* or elsewhere in the literature suggests conceptual turmoil.

The introduction included, in a footnote, a sampling of definitions:

> "Productivity" is defined for our purposes as output per employee hour, quality considered. . . . "optimal output per unit of input" . . . "to me, it is dollar input (both direct and indirect).". . . "[P]roductivity can be more correctly stated as the relationship between achieving a result and the time it takes to accomplish it" (Halachmi & Holzer, 1986, p. 5).

The definition that has best stood the test of time and that is most often cited as a reasonable one (see, for example, Hatry & Fisk, 1980, p. 124) was presented in 1976 by Nancy Hayward of the National Center for Productivity and Quality of Working Life:

> Governmental productivity is the efficiency with which resources are consumed in the effective delivery of public services. The definition

implies not only quantity, but also quality. It negates the value of efficiency, if the product or service itself lacks value. It relates the value of all resources consumed—human, capital, and technological—to the output of public services or results achieved (Hayward, 1976, p. 544).

The formulations used here build on this definition. Two new features are added: (1) the specification of "effectiveness" to mean only "effectiveness of implementation" (leaving program effectiveness to the program evaluation field); and (2) the suggestion that "effectiveness of implementation" can be measured as the product of output quantity and output quality.

Summary

A lot of material has been presented thus far in order to create some familiarity with approaches and issues in productivity measurement. This familiarity is important if public administrators and policy makers are to become comfortable and knowledgeable about using hard data to learn more about what they are doing. The following summary lays out the underpinnings of the "how to measure" procedure that will be described in the next chapter.

1. For purposes of defining and measuring productivity, the organization (work unit) is treated as if it were a black box. What goes on inside the box is irrelevant for measurement: Whatever the differences in process, *productivity* measures only the relationship between what goes in (resources) and what comes out (services). Productivity improvement does tinker with the process, but that is another issue. Improvement is not measurement.

The relevant concept of output for a given organization is its final products or services—that is, the products or services that left the organization or were for use outside the organization. Thus, all other activities are intermediate and viewed as part of final output measurement; they are not counted separately (Mark, 1979, p. 21).

2. Productivity is measured indirectly by first measuring outputs and inputs and then calculating the ratio:

$$\text{Productivity} = \text{Outputs} \div \text{Inputs}$$

$$P = O \div I$$

As Ross and Burkhead (1974) phrased it some time ago,

> In examining productivity in the public sector, the output concept closest to that used in the private sector is output directly produced. . . . These are the activities actually performed by the public sector; they are quantities that come out of the production pipeline (p. 53).

3. Outcomes are not included, for the reasons spelled out in Chapter 3: They are affected by too many other (nonprogrammatic) influences, and disappointing outcomes may result from flawed policy assumptions, not the implementation process.

4. Efficiency is the same as productivity, *if* the quality of outputs is disregarded:

$$\text{Efficiency} = \text{Output quantity} \div \text{Inputs}$$

5. The effectiveness of program *implementation* is the product of output quantity and output quality:

$$\text{Implementation effectiveness} = \text{Output quantity} \times \text{Output quality}$$

6. Productivity includes considerations of both efficiency and the quality of outputs:

$$\text{Productivity} = (\text{Output quantity})(\text{Output quality}) \div \text{Inputs}$$

7. Productivity is improved when more or better output or both is produced with the same or less input.

> It was agreed that . . . productivity means more than a mere striving for greater efficiency. It must embrace in some mix the concepts of efficiency, effectiveness, and quality of working life. In government, particularly, it must conceptually include the notions of responsiveness, timeliness, and service to the public. It cannot be considered as merely a set of efforts to reduce costs. If there is an improvement in the quality of a delivered governmental service with the cost remaining the same, it must be concluded that there has been a productivity gain (Washnis, 1980, p. 152).

Integrating quality into the productivity formula makes it possible to calculate the change in productivity induced by changing quality.

Productivity Index

One final item: the productivity index. The use of a productivity index is well established and uncontested. An index permits easy comparison of productivity over time. It is constructed by taking the productivity figure (however measured) for one stipulated base year and setting that figure at 100. The productivity level for each succeeding year (measured the same way) is stated in terms of the base year. So, for example, if productivity in 1997 is 2% higher than in the base year (say, 1990), the index reads 102. If productivity in 2001 is 5% lower *than in the base year*, the index is 95.

We are ready to start measuring.

References

Ammons, D. N. (1991). *Administrative analysis for local government: Practical application of selected techniques*. Athens: Carl Vinson Institute of Government, University of Georgia.

Balk, W. L. (1984). Productivity in government: A legislative focus. *Public Productivity Review, 8*, 148-161.

Bouckaert, G., & Balk, W. (1991). Public productivity measurement: Diseases and cures. *Public Productivity & Management Review, 15*, 229-235.

Brinkerhoff, R. G., & Dressler, D. E. (1990). *Productivity measurement: A guide for managers and evaluators*. Newbury Park, CA: Sage.

Grizzle, G. A. (1985). Performance measures for budget justifications: Developing a selection strategy. *Public Productivity Review, 9*, 328-341.

Halachmi, A., & Holzer, M. (1986). Introduction: Toward strategic perspectives on public productivity. In M. Holzer & A. Halachmi (Eds.), *Strategic issues in public sector productivity* (pp. 5-14). San Francisco: Jossey-Bass.

Hatry, H. P. (1980a). Current state of the art of state and local government productivity improvement—and potential federal roles. In C. H. Levine (Ed.), *Managing fiscal stress: The crisis in the public sector*. Chatham, NJ: Chatham House.

Hatry, H. P. (1980b). Performance measurement principles and techniques. *Public Productivity Review, 4*, 312-339.

Hatry, H., & Fisk, D. M. (1980). Measuring productivity: Issues and needs (Sub-theme Session Report, National Productivity Conference). *Public Productivity Review, 4*, 124-128.

Hatry, H. P., Winnie, R. E., & Fisk, D. M. (1981). *Practical program evaluation for state and local governments* (2nd ed.). Washington, DC: Urban Institute.

Hayward, N. (1976). The productivity challenge. *Public Administration Review, 36*, 544-550.

Hodes, N. (1991). Achieving quality through labor-management participation in New York State. *Public Productivity & Management Review, 15*, 163-168.

Hurst, G. E., Jr. (1980). Attributes of performance measures. *Public Productivity Review, 4,* 43-49.

Legislative Commission on Economy and Efficiency in Government. (1981, March 4). *Proceedings of a seminar on the development, implementation, and use of performance measurements in the public sector.* Albany, NY: Author.

Mark, J. A. (1979, January/March). Measuring federal productivity. *Civil Service Journal,* pp. 20-23.

Mark, J. A. (1981). Measuring productivity in government: Federal, state, and local. *Public Productivity Review, 5,* 21-44.

NAPA speaks out on performance monitoring. (1992, February 1). *PA Times,* p. 9.

National Commission on Productivity and Work Quality. (1974). *So, Mr. Mayor, you want to improve productivity. . . .* (Stock No. 5203-00049). Washington, DC: Government Printing Office.

O'Sullivan, E., & Rassel, G. R. (1989). *Research methods for public administrators.* New York: Longman.

Poister, T. H., Hatry, H. P., Fisk, D. M., & Greiner, J. M. (1985). Centralized productivity improvement efforts in state government. *Public Productivity Review, 9,* 5-24.

Ridgway, V. F. (1976). Dysfunctional consequences of performance measurements. In R. T. Golembiewski, F. Gibson, & G. Y. Cornog (Eds.), *Public administration: Readings in institutions, processes, behavior, policy* (3rd ed.) (pp. 505-514). Chicago: Rand McNally.

Roll, J. L., & Roll, D. L. (1983). The potential for application of quality circles in the American public sector. *Public Productivity Review, 7,* 122-142.

Rosen, E. D. (1981). OK work: Incorporating quality into the productivity equation. *Public Productivity Review, 5,* 207-217.

Rosen, E. D. (1984). Productivity: Concepts and measurement. In M. Holzer & S. S. Nagel (Eds.), *Productivity and public policy* (pp. 19-43). Beverly Hills, CA: Sage.

Ross, J. P., & Burkhead, J. (1974). *Productivity in the local government sector.* Lexington, MA: D.C. Heath.

Siegel, I. H. (1980). *Company Productivity: Measurement for Improvement.* n.p.: The W. E. Upjohn Institute for Employment Research.

Swiss, J. E. (1983). Unbalanced incentives in government productivity systems: Misreporting as a case in point. *Public Productivity Review, 7,* 26-37.

Washnis, G. (1980a). Rationalizing current federal efforts. (Sub-theme Session Report, National Productivity Conference). *Public Productivity Review, 4,* 151-158.

Wholey, J. S., Abramson, M. A., & Bellavita, C. (1986). *Performance and credibility: Developing excellence in public and nonprofit organizations.* Lexington, MA: Lexington.

5

Measuring Productivity

The Unit of Analysis

This is the description of one way "how to" measure the productivity of any public sector work unit. The first task is to decide on the unit.

In the public sector the output is always some kind of service that is produced by an organization and delivered across its borders to clients outside. If the organization is a teaching hospital, it delivers treatment to patients and training to doctors. If the organization is the hospital's purchasing unit, it delivers purchasing services across its boundaries to its clientele, which consists of other departments in the hospital.

In the first example, the unit of analysis is the hospital; in the second, it is the purchasing unit. The first step in measuring productivity is to choose: to decide clearly just *whose* productivity is to be measured. If, for example, it is the purchasing department, then purchasing services constitute the output, and only those resources that are used in producing purchasing services constitute the relevant input. The quantity of purchasing service and the quality of purchasing service are of significance. No other part of the hospital counts.

It will be remembered that productivity is measured indirectly by measuring outputs and inputs and then calculating the ratio. Let us start with inputs.

Measuring Inputs

Introduction

Inputs are resources—the resources consumed in producing outputs. Resources include labor, equipment, supplies, space, and utilities. Of these, labor is the major public sector resource, the biggest budget item for most agencies. Measuring and improving the productivity of labor is of primary importance in the public sector, because it is such a major resource and also because it represents so much potential that is untapped by traditional management systems.

The first point to note again is that the input measure should include only those units of resource that are associated with the relevant output. For example, if a quality assurance officer in a state social services agency performs both investigative and auditing work, only the portion of the officer's work that is devoted to investigation would be counted in measuring the productivity of the investigative services; conversely, only the contribution to auditing would be counted in measuring the productivity of the auditing service. If the relevant output is "quality assurance," including both investigation and auditing, then the officer's full time would be counted as the relevant input. The same principle of matching input to output also pertains to any other kind of resources.

The usual practice in public sector productivity measurement is to deal with only one kind of resource at a time. This makes it possible to focus on the productivity of one factor, and it also simplifies the measurement process. For example, looking at the relationship between the output (services produced) and only the labor input used to produce it gives a clear measure of the productivity of labor. It can provide an uncluttered picture of the impact of a labor-specific innovation (such as a new training program) on productivity. On the other hand, if the point is to determine how new technology (such as a new type of sanitation truck) affects productivity, then only equipment (and not labor) would be the single type of resource considered. Thus it is possible to take the same output (such as tons of garbage collected) and, by measuring one resource or another, make specific findings about management options.

Sometimes, however, it is necessary to aggregate different inputs. For example, new word processing equipment may save labor resources but increase equipment resources consumed to do the same amount of work. How to calculate the net effect on productivity? Because labor is measured one way (usually, worker time) and equipment another (perhaps, number of machines), the only way to aggregate them is to convert both to estimated dollar values. The dollar is the lingua franca, the universal medium that turns apples and oranges into fruit salad. However, it has its limitations for measuring public sector productivity, as we shall see.

Measuring Labor Inputs

To return to the more usual situation of considering one type of resource at a time, the most important and most commonly measured public sector input is labor. The dollar is not usually used for measuring labor in the public sector, because managers do not control labor costs—civil service categories and rules do. The dollar measure does not meet the measurement criterion of controllability. It gives misleading results: A new agency with many young people at the bottom of the civil service ladder would appear more productive than a unit with more old-timers.

Starting with the 1960s productivity measurement initiative by the Bureau of the Budget, the tradition has been established that public sector labor is measured in terms of worker time (Bureau of the Budget, 1964).

> The foremost example of current use of these indicators is the federal government. . . . The focus is entirely on labor productivity—that is, output related to the number of *employee-years* (and not to dollars expended) (Hatry, 1978, p. 29).

"Time" need not be expressed in years. It can be specified in any time unit—whatever is convenient and sensible in terms of the work. Writing checks might be expressed in minutes, closing court cases in weeks or months. "Number of" and "time" have two measurement virtues we have not mentioned. They can start at zero, and they increase evenly: The difference between 1 and 3 workers is the same as the difference between 135 and 137 workers. Not all measures are so neat.

The amount of "worker-time" is calculated very simply:

$$\text{Worker-time} = \text{Number of workers} \times \text{Time per worker}$$

Thus,

$$
\begin{aligned}
\text{6 worker-hours} &= \text{2 people working 3 hours each} \\
&= \text{6 people working 1 hour each} \\
&= \text{24 people working } \tfrac{1}{4} \text{ hour each} \\
&= \text{1 person working 6 hours}
\end{aligned}
$$

The one stipulation for calculating and presenting these figures is that the units must be carefully labeled: "6 worker-hours," "5 worker-years," etc. It is also important to specify how a "worker-year" or "worker-day" is determined. There are choices, which is acceptable. That is how measures are developed. But the method for stipulating must be made clear to those who will use or borrow the figures. For example, what does 1 worker-year include? All calendar days? Only official working days? Vacation days? Leave days? Sick days?

A useful way to approach this decision is to return to the measurement criterion of "controllability." As a manager, I cannot hope to make better use of my workers by requiring them to come in on Sundays or on holidays. I can influence when a vacation takes place, not whether; it is generally an entitlement. Those days can be left out of the count; they contribute nothing to the productivity picture. Leave days and sick days are different; they may be taken or not. They may lie within the influence, if not the absolute control, of management. A productivity innovation, such as paying a cash bonus for unused leave days, might result in being able to produce more with the same work force. If leave days are included in the count of worker-days, the improvement will show up in the productivity figure because the same input (number of work days, including leave days) can be compared with the output before and after the innovation. For this reason, it is recommended that the "number of worker-days" should exclude weekends, holidays, and paid vacations but include sick and personal leave days.

Worker-time is a simple and rough count. It counts an entire day whether the worker is late or not (which is good, because cutting down on lateness or overextended lunch hours will show up as improved productivity: same number of days, more work done). It disregards the nature of the "worker": salary, education, skill level, type of work, and so on. This may also be a virtue. If the same number of worker-days can result in more or better service or both because, for example, skills have been upgraded through a training program or a better employee recruitment and screening process, then the productivity figure, if measured this way, will appropriately show an increase: same input (that is, same number of worker-days), but more and better output.

Data on the amount of worker-time should be available from existing personnel records. The labor of each worker who is on payroll, but not on vacation, any working day counts as one worker-day, as long as the individual is assigned 100% to the relevant output. If not, the time must be prorated.

Measuring Other Inputs

Convenience is the guide to choosing counting units for nonlabor resources. Equipment input may be counted as "number of" something (copying machines, garbage trucks, railroad cars). The effect of an insulation or energy conservation program may be measured using as input measure the number of kilowatt-hours or the energy costs (corrected for inflation for purposes of comparing over time). Space resources may be measured in footage or in rental costs, for example. Improved productivity of these resources will be reflected as more production per truck, per kilowatt-hour, or per square (or cubic) foot.

Measuring Output Quantity

As we will see, output quantity ("how much") and output quality ("how good") are measured by totally different strategies, but they are attributes of the same thing—some kind of output. How much of what? How good is what? The first step is to decide on the "what"—the output to be measured.

Step 1: Identify the Outputs

List the Major Outputs

What is the mission of the unit? Some organizations produce only one or two kinds of service. Most complex organizations perform several or many functions. A state college registrar's office maintains student records, provides transcripts, registers students for courses, and certifies eligibility for graduation. A sanitation department removes garbage, maintains landfills, sweeps the streets, conducts inspections for sanitary code violations, and plows and sands the streets when it snows. Garbage removal services constitute one kind of output, street sweeping services another, and so on.

Our measurement team might start by brainstorming a list of the major functions. Representation from different parts of the organization and from clients is particularly important here. It is astonishing how, in practice, team members from one part of an organization are unaware of some of the services produced by other sections of the organization. Make a full list.

Prioritize and Simplify

One or a few services will probably be of major importance—that is, they constitute a major part of the work load and consume most or a large part of the resources. Others may reasonably be grouped together as aspects of the same function; for example, conducting fire safety inspections and giving talks at schools can be grouped together as "fire prevention." Some services are patently trivial, candidates for the bottom of the list.

Select

One cannot, and should not, try to measure many kinds of output at the outset. Typically, one or two of the most important outputs are selected to start with. Later the system can be made more sophisticated by including more functions. The selection criteria that Jerome Mark laid down in 1979 are still helpful:

> In determining final output indicators, managers have to identify specific units of service that are countable, are fairly homogeneous over time . . . and reflect a significant proportion of the agencies' workload (p. 21).

Step 2: Decide on Output Indicators

Select Indicators

How will the selected output(s) be measured? The quantity of output is usually measured as "number of" units. (These are units of counting, not units of analysis.) What should the counting unit be? For example, will the output of "placement service" be measured by counting "number of interviews" or "number of placements?" Either is reasonable, each leaves something out, and each will have an effect on people's behavior. The decision of a team, rather than an individual, will decrease the likelihood of adopting egregiously partial or perverse indicators.

Notice that the output of every kind of service is measured in different terms:

> The nature of the indicators varies substantially. They include such diverse items as trademarks disposed, tanks repaired, weather observations made, square feet of buildings cleaned, electrical power generated, and deportable aliens located. The output volume ranges from several hundred units completed per year (e.g., river basin studies) to billions (e.g., pieces of mail delivered) (Mark, 1979, p. 21).

Adjust for Workload Difficulty

Some units of output may be significantly more difficult than others. Some investigations are brief background checks, others take a lot of digging; some job seekers are easily placed, others lack skills or personality; a fire in a one-family house is not the same as a fire in a 40-story office building. Differences in work difficulty can be dealt with several ways. If the "mix" of easy, moderate, and difficult work remains fairly constant over time or between agencies, then differences in difficulty can be disregarded: The difficulty of the "average" unit stays the same, and comparisons will be fair.

If workload differences are real and cannot be assumed to be consistently mixed in the same proportions, then the different work can be grouped into two or three classes, with each class counted separately; for example, one figure can be derived for number of residential fires suppressed and another figure for number of commercial fires suppressed.

Finally, work of varying difficulty can be counted together by taking the least difficult unit of work (let us say, a one-family residential fire) and setting that as "one standard unit of work." The average apartment house fire may be judged to be three times as much work to put out: Each apartment house fire would be counted as three standard units. Each downtown office building may be counted as seven standard units. In this way, the total amount of fire-fighting service can be expressed in one figure. That has the virtue of simplicity, along with validity.

How can the relative weights be determined? An analysis of the fire department records may indicate the relative amount of time or effort each kind of fire demands. A group of individuals knowledgeable about the work might be called on to arrive at the figures, perhaps by use of the nominal group technique described below.

Attention to differences in work difficulty is important in enhancing the validity of the measurement system. More important, it serves as a very important way of controlling "creaming"—that is, the selection of easy cases and neglect of more difficult ones in order to pile up the output numbers. In the public sector, this practice is not only an unfair way of measuring, but also a denial of equity and a betrayal of the organizational mission when, for example, a state employment service neglects those who are most in need of help so that it can look good on the placement figures.

Measure the Outputs

Collect the Data. Like input data, output information is often already at hand. Agencies usually keep records of the number and type of units of service produced in any given time period: number of clients seen, applications processed, passengers carried. These records may have to be adapted or reclassified or augmented, but lack of this type of data is not a barrier to measurement of the output of most agencies.

Total the Output. The total number of output units for the selected time period is the output figure. The measurement expert can provide guidance on selecting a time period that is long enough and representative enough. For comparison over time, similar seasons should be measured.

Aggregate Outputs (Optional). If several different types of output have been selected for counting, it is possible to aggregate them using the same strategy as for aggregating work of varying difficulty.

> A question had come up when the program was initially involved in the changeover and work redesign. For the purpose of individual staff performance evaluations by the program director, a measure was needed to compare the amount of work that an investigation entailed, to the work of counseling a client. . . . After discussion of this issue it was determined by the staff, at the time of the changeover, that the two services were *not* equal; therefore, the two services were weighted. . . .
>
> The staff had determined that a case under counseling supervision would carry a weight of 0.5 per month, while an investigation would earn a staff member 1.0 during the month in which it was completed. . . .

In summary, the quantity of output = (1) × (number of investigations) + (.5) × (number of counselee months) (Muniz, 1982, pp. 43-44).

Calculating Efficiency

If the quality of outputs is put aside (disregarded, presumed to remain constant over time, or presented independently of the output quantity figures) then

$$\text{Output} \div \text{Input} = \text{Efficiency}$$

Because output (O) is expressed as "number of units of service" and input (I) is most usually expressed in terms of worker-time or equipment units, the most common public sector efficiency figure (and productivity figure, if quality is disregarded) reads something like "75 licenses issued per worker-week" or "1,200 passenger miles of transport per bus-day."

> To summarize, output (rather than process or outcome) is generally measured and related to input to derive the productivity figure. There is no universal measure of output quantity; each kind of good or service is measured in units appropriate to it. Choices are made by measurers: which good or service to count, whether to differentiate levels of difficulty of work, how to aggregate different kinds of output. . . .
>
> The typing pool produces thirty letters . . . per worker-day. Its productivity can now be compared with its own performance last year, or with that of another typing pool. But what if one pool produced clean, accurate, attractive copy, while the other produces messy, error-ridden work? Before these outputs can be compared usefully, the quality of the work must be considered (Rosen, 1984, p. 34).

That is the subject of the next section.

Measuring Output Quality

The Need for Quality Measures

Public sector productivity measurement systems began by measuring efficiency, the ratio between quantity of output and quantity of input. Output quality was disregarded or assumed to be a constant. For pioneering efforts, simplifying assumptions like this make it possible to concentrate on first things first—and, clearly, the question of "how much" precedes "how good."

But the question of "how good" could not be ignored for long. As early as 1971, Harry Hatry of the Urban Institute, in collaboration with Donald Fisk of the Bureau of Labor Statistics, urged that quality be taken into account in measuring efficiency (Hatry & Fisk, 1971, p. 3). Hatry has consistently argued that including quality is important to the validity of the measurement system:

> How meaningful can the "cost per ton of waste collected" be unless it pays attention to the quality of the output? A reduction in unit cost achieved at the expense of a reduction in service quality is not a true efficiency improvement. Has the service degraded, through excessive spillage, for instance, or a shift from backdoor to curb collection? Another example: Increases in the "number of arrests per police officer" may not mean increased efficiency if the percentage of arrests failing to lead to conviction because of police error (i.e., the quality of arrest) is worsening (Hatry, 1978, p. 28).

The importance of output quality gained in recognition, even when it was not yet included in practice:

> The report recognizes problems with the nature and scope of the current measurement system which is based on a definition of productivity which compares outputs to inputs. This is expressly an efficiency measure. . . . Productivity measurement must take into consideration the quality and effectiveness of the goods and services that are delivered as well as the irresponsiveness to public needs ("Measuring Federal Productivity," 1980, p. v).

Hatry and co-workers did more than exhort. They began to develop methods for measuring the quality of services. They identified criteria (such as cleanliness, comfort, timeliness, and accessibility) that could be used as quality indicators, and they proposed methods for collecting this kind of data for substantive fields (Hatry, Blair, Fisk, Greiner, Hall, & Schaenmar, 1977).

Today, as a result of two developments, output quality has taken on new and greater importance. One factor has been the influence of the private sector's emphasis on quality (for which the Japanese success had been a goad and a model). Quality-centered management requires an ability to measure quality because, as the brochure describing the award-winning total quality management initiative of the U.S. Air Force's 1926th Communications-Computer Systems Group says, in large letters: "You cannot manage what you do not measure!" (Federal Quality Institute, 1991, p. 10).

The second source of contemporary interest in quality comes by default from the current fiscal crisis and popular dissatisfaction with government. Efficiencies are already happening, not so much by managerial design as by the reality of having to maintain services in the face of severe budget cuts. Managers can still maneuver with regard to quality, however. Added to that, low workforce morale and public discontent with agency performance combine to suggest a more participative, customer-oriented approach to improving productivity by improving quality. Productivity measures that reflect quality gains give managers a way of demonstrating their achievements with solid numbers. The external influence of the private sector model coupled with this internally felt need to shift focus put quality and its measurement high on the agenda.

Quantifying Quality

The Strategy

The strategy for measuring quality is totally different in the public and private sectors. In the private sector quality is considered to be improved when labor is added as, for example, in hand-finished garments. Some early public sector measurement work did adopt this private sector approach:

> Definitions of quality are quite ambiguous and measuring these changes can be difficult. For our purposes, changes in output quality can be viewed as changes in the characteristics of the output associated with differences in the labor requirements to make these changes. For example, in a data processing unit where the output indicator is number of forms keypunched, redesigning a form to provide more information, which requires more key strokes, is a quality change (Mark, 1979, p. 22).

That approach has several disadvantages and has long since been superseded for the public sector. It has no capacity to convey the result of providing objectively better service with less labor. It is really not a valid measure, because it does not measure what it is intended to measure—the quality of the "product." A much more useful method has been developed for measuring the quality of public agency output. It hinges on the use of quality indicators.

Use of Indicators. Ask several people, "How can you tell a high-quality train service from a poor one?" The answers are almost certain to take the form, "A good train service is reliable, fast, safe, comfortable, prompt, accessible." Some people may list a few attributes, some may list many. There may not be total agreement on whether every item belongs on the list. There would certainly be disagreement on the relative importance of each criterion. But the use of attributes or criteria as indicators, if not definers, of quality makes intuitive sense. It has face validity. If a panel of riders creates a weighted list of attributes, a list incorporating their different judgments, that list acquires content validity as well. That is, one can "demonstrate that the measure involved includes all the identified elements and assigns to each the proper weight" (O'Sullivan & Rassel, 1989, p. 92).

Can a list of attributes be developed? Clearly, yes. The nominal group technique, described below, is an excellent way to proceed—for compiling a list, narrowing the list down to a few key indicators, and deciding the relative importance of each so that they can be weighted. Theoretically, an individual "expert" could do the job, but having a representative group increases the validity, as we have seen. Getting such a group to identify and weight criteria is entirely feasible and not particularly costly in time or in effort. It also makes sense in terms of public relations: People understand and accept what they have had a hand in creating.

Nominal Group Technique. Sometimes it is necessary to make decisions where there is no objective way of knowing what is a "correct" or even a "good" answer. In such a situation, a practicable decision can be derived from the best judgments of a group of people. However, the usual group, especially if it contains people of differing ranks, presents the problem that some people will be inhibited and unduly influenced by the opinions of others.

The nominal group technique developed by Delbecq, Van de Ven, and Gustafson (1975) is a useful instrument for producing group consensus without the social dynamics. "It has been found to be particularly effective in areas where there are many intangibles, little past history, large people involvement, and semistructured or unstructured processes" (Presnick, 1980, p. 28).

Here is how it works. Members of the group generate ideas by writing their judgments silently and privately. Then, in round-robin fashion, each member reads out one idea while a leader or facilitator lists the ideas (no criticisms allowed). People may volunteer to clarify ambiguous items. Next, everyone votes privately for a certain number of "most important" or "best" items. The results of the voting are made known to the group by the leader; everyone then votes again and again in a series of rounds. Unpopular ideas tend to be abandoned, and consensus builds over time.

Step 1: Choose Quality Indicators

What makes for a good mail service? Perhaps speed, accuracy, and courtesy (Rosen, 1981, p. 215). For a good counseling service, garbage-collection service, tax-collection service, pothole-filling service, or park service? Alas for measurement, there is no one, universal measure of the quality of everything. Each kind of output, each service, is "qualified" by its own particular, customized set of indicators. What they all have in common is only the idea that quality implies "fit for use by the customer" (Brinkerhoff & Dressler, 1990, p. 48).

Identify Indicators. Measuring quality starts by developing a list of quality indicators for the particular output that is being measured. This involves "brainstorming" a list and then narrowing it down to perhaps two or three key attributes. Remember that trying to measure everything is a trap: As compared with the most important attribute(s), each additional item will probably take equally long to produce and but yield only marginally more insight.

Which group might produce this list? One possibility is the measurement team itself, possibly with additional "customer" representation. Alternatively, the identification of quality criteria might be turned over to a special task force or even to an existing quality circle.

Decide on Relative Weights. If some quality criteria are significantly more important than others, they should be incorporated into the measurement system. The idea of weighting some elements as more important than others is well established in the productivity field; as early as 1964 the Bureau of the Budget discussed the weighting of outputs:

> Such weights should represent the relative importance of different outputs with respect to the purpose for which the outputs are to be combined.

It should be stressed that the weights do not represent any "ultimate" or unique value of the individual outputs (p. 46).

As an example of weighting, consider a mail delivery service. Speed may be deemed twice as important as accuracy, and accuracy twice as important as courtesy. To reflect this, speed would be weighted at 4, accuracy at 2, and courtesy at 1, which means that speed would be counted four times, accuracy twice, and courtesy once in computing a weighted quality "average:"

$$\text{Quality} = [4(\text{speed}) + 2(\text{accuracy}) + 1(\text{courtesy})] \div 7$$

Weights do not have to be expressed in round numbers, but round numbers are obviously simpler to use, as long as they do not create undue distortion. It is generally wiser to begin simply and then refine as time goes on.

Step 2: Measure the Quality

How can each relevant attribute be scored? How can a number be assigned to show the level of performance with respect to any particular criterion? Alas, again, the type of score depends on the method used to collect the data. Each score is derived in its own way. Methodologically, this is all right, as long as the units are clearly labeled, but practically it makes for a more complicated procedure. The logic is straightforward, but the procedure has several steps.

Collect Data on Achieved Quality. One way data on quality can be collected is through the process of observation. We have seen how observers, using a set of pictures as a guide, rated the cleanliness of alleys. To take another example, one could mail test letters and observe how long it takes for them to arrive. If an adequate sample of mail is sent from several representative parts of the country to a representative set of destinations, then a useful number could be derived: "average time for a letter to arrive." (Any subsequent comparisons should be based on the same procedure.) The method just described has some loaded words: *adequate, representative, useful.* The measuring expert should know how to deal with these.

The same observational approach could be used to judge speed of service by noting the travel time between set points. A complication: "speed" or "rate" is calculated as the inverse of time. It seems familiar when expressed as "miles per hour," but less so when expressed as "average letter per number of days." Just notice that the longer the letter takes, the smaller the score will be: If it takes 1 day, then the score is $1 \div 1 = 1$; if it takes 4 days, then the speed score is 1/4.

Data on quality may also be obtainable from records. Quality may be reflected in such figures as the number of complaints, the number of reversals from above, or the number of units that have to be redone because of error. These would usually be expressed as percentages of units that are correct (error-free, unreversed, or unprotested): for example, 99.7% of letters were delivered to the right address; 82% of arrests survived a first screening; 60% of the planted trees survived the first year. The fewer the flaws, the higher the scores.

Quality data may be obtained from user surveys. For example, a survey might indicate how quietly the sanitation crew worked, how courteously the unemployment office staff behaved, how comfortable the bus seats were, how clear the instructions were. Questionnaires often ask respondents to rate items on a Likert scale (usually in five steps from "agree strongly" to "disagree strongly"). The resulting score might be: "On a 1-5 scale, with 5 being the most favorable opinion, seat comfort received an average score of 4.3." The better the quality, the higher the score.

This phase of measurement has consisted of choosing the means for collecting data and then measuring the actual performance level by the most appropriate means, even though the resulting scores for different criteria may take different forms.

Scores that remain expressed in different ways can be combined into one composite measure, but the resulting figure becomes prohibitively difficult to interpret and compare, as Hatry and Fisk (1971, p. 19) acknowledged in their early effort to incorporate quality into the measurement of solid waste-collection service by calculating: tons of solid waste collected × average street cleanliness rating on a 1-4 scale × percent of survey population expressing satisfaction with collection.

Compare Achieved to Desired Levels. There is a way around that situation. Each of those scores can be converted to a common system, permitting these various scores to be added together, averaged, and generally manipulated mathematically. This is done by taking each actual, achieved score and comparing it with an ideal, or desired score.

> Under the assumption that there are two dimensions of . . . service perform-
> ance—quantity and quality—the focus of this case analysis is on quality.
> Quantity of performance relates to amount of products and services produced;

quality of performance relates to the degree to which products and services meet standards for attribute and variable characteristics (Hershauer, 1979, p. 75).

For example, if 100% accuracy is the desired level, and only 99.2% has been achieved, then:

$$\text{Actual} \div \text{Ideal} = 99.2\% \div 100\% = .99$$

If a two-day delivery time for the average letter is the goal desired, but it actually takes four days, then (hang on here, for the division of fractions):

$$\text{Actual} \div \text{Ideal} = (1/4) \div (1/2) = (1/4) \times (2/1) = 1/2 = .50$$

If an average 4.5 courtesy rating on a Likert scale is the goal (set in the knowledge that total satisfaction is not humanly possible), but a rating of 4.3 has actually been attained, then:

$$\text{Actual} \div \text{Ideal} = 4.3 \div 4.5 = .96$$

The important thing to notice is that because, in each case, the actual and the ideal are both expressed in the same units, the units cancel out. What is left is a number somewhere between 0 and 1.

Exceptions are possible but unlikely. It is conceivable that work can exceed the quality goal, which would produce a number greater than 1. That would suggest that the standard has been set too low or, as a less likely scenario, that too much effort is being invested in perfection. Those responsible for the measurement system will need to explore the question of whether to count or credit quality that exceeds standards.

At the other extreme, it is theoretically possible, but difficult to imagine in practice, that the output would do more harm than good and result in a negative number. As a general rule, neither of these things should happen, and the score should lie between 0 (if everything is done wrong—for example, if every letter is misdirected) and 1 (if all the output meets the ideal set for it in every dimension of quality).

Weight and Aggregate Scores. The use of the achieved-to-ideal ratio has two great advantages. First, because all scores are expressed the same way, the quality level is easy to read and communicate, no matter what the criterion: A .99 on speed and a .50 on durability tells the public works agency in a clear way just how it is doing on each quality dimension of a pothole-filling service. It is easy to spot a drop or rise in performance with respect to any single criterion and to track performance on each dimension from year to year.

Second, scores on several different attributes of quality can now be weighted and aggregated, thus producing a single overall quality score. For example:

$$\text{Quality} = [4(\text{speed}) + 2(\text{accuracy}) + 1(\text{courtesy})] \div 7$$
$$= [4(.50) + 2(.99) + 1(.96)] \div 7$$
$$= .71$$

As long as all of these variables are measured in a consistent way from year to year and as long as the ideal or desired scores remain unchanged, it is possible to track quality performance over time. If the assumptions (such as desired level) and the measurement procedure are clearly spelled out, other agencies or jurisdictions can compare their performance to this one by correcting for any differences between measurement systems. For example, if another jurisdiction also takes four days to deliver the average letter but has set three days as the desired delivery time, it will get a .75 reading, instead of a .50 reading for the same performance on the same aspect of quality.

The foregoing example points up the chief disadvantage of this measurement system. The score depends on the desired level; the lower the goal set, the better one looks on the score sheet. Unless the premises are clearly conveyed and clearly understood by potential users of these figures, there is the possibility that the system can be misused.

Using the Quality Measures

Applications of Quality Data

Individual or aggregate measures of service quality are of value and interest in their own right. They focus and reinforce organizational goals by specifying quality objectives, both qualitatively and quantitatively. Quality measures can be used in the control process: for example, as mentioned earlier, creaming (selecting only easy units of work) can be controlled by using "equitability" as a criterion of service quality.

Creaming is an inequitable phenomenon if the program's intention is to serve the hardest to employ. An indication of equity, therefore, would be found in the characteristics of the trainees as compared to the characteristics of potential trainees in a community. Equity can be measured before a problem develops, and good management as well as public interest would seem to require such measurement (Buntz, 1981, p. 308).

Measures of quality can be used as formative feedback into the production process, pointing out areas in need of improvement and measuring the effect of improvement efforts. Quality measures, like other performance measures, may form the basis for a system of rewards. Conversely, if "public sector practitioners . . . contend that . . . how much they do is far less important than how well they do it" (Ammons, 1985, pp. 301-302), measures of quality can provide a reality check. Data on quality may be used in the budgeting or policy debates as evidence of high-quality performance. In the current emphasis on managing for quality, performance on the quality dimension becomes the lodestar by which to steer the organization.

However, for our purposes, the importance of quality measurement lies in its contribution to the measurement and improvement of productivity. Relating only the quantity of outputs to inputs gives an efficiency measure, which has been generally regarded as an incomplete picture of productivity. Quality must be considered.

Quality in the Productivity Formula

Just how to "consider" quality is a question as yet unsettled. There have been essentially four approaches.

1. *Disregard quality.* If quality is assumed to be unchanged, a constant, it can be disregarded in calculating productivity. For example, the federal government for many years simply made the assumption that quality did not vary and omitted it from the productivity picture. That was equivalent to not considering quality.

2. *Present quality information separately from efficiency measures.* Measures of the quality dimension of performance have been presented alongside, and independently of, measures of the efficiency dimension. Presumably, decision makers internalized both sets of information and somehow integrated both factors into their subsequent actions and poli-

cies. The City of San Diego (1983) pioneered such use of citizen satisfaction data as an adjunct to productivity measures: "Through the use of employee attitudinal data, citizen satisfaction data, and productivity data, TPM identifies the human and scientific factors that relate to work performance" (p. 1).

3. *Use quality measures as a screening device.* One or more quality criteria may be established for a given kind of output. A minimum acceptable standard can then be set for each. When the output is measured, any unit of work that does not meet the standards can simply be excluded from the output count. This is the strategy adopted by Harry Hatry (1980):

> Efficiency measures are generally defined as the relation of the amount of resources applied to a service or input to the amount of output. . . .
>   Units of output are measures of the amount of workload accomplished. Unfortunately, the readily available workload counts often say little about the real product of the activity. For example, the number of park acres maintained says little about how they look, the number of gallons of water treated does not indicate the quality of that water. Whenever possible, defective outputs should be identified and should not be counted as output (p. 317).

However:

> The problem with eliminating defective units from the output count is that services can be inferior (slow, grudging, etc.) but not entirely useless. Such outputs should be counted, but not given the same value as activities that are fast, courteous, or otherwise satisfactory (Rosen, 1981, p. 211).

4. *Use quality measures to discount output.* The fourth approach, the one adopted here, is not to eliminate, but rather to discount those units of output that fall below the desired standard.

We have seen that different quality indicators can be put into the same form (a number between 0 and 1). Several indicators can be aggregated into a weighted average, yielding one number between 0 and 1 that expresses the overall level of quality of an output. That overall number can be used as a coefficient of quality, K. If the output is multiplied by K, it is reduced in value according to the level of the quality. If the quality meets all desired standards, K will equal 1, and the output will be credited in full, undiminished. But as the quality level, the value of K, moves down, the output will be discounted—diminished proportionally. If $K = .9$, for example, the output will be counted as only 90% of the number of units.

Multiplying the output, O, by the coefficient, K, results in "OK work." Assuming, as we did in Chapter 3, that quantity of output times quality of output determines the effectiveness of implementation, then "OK work is effective work" (Rosen, 1981, p. 212). And OK/I equals productivity, with quality taken into account.

Despite disagreement over the term *effectiveness*, which we would have called *quality*, this formulation conforms to the conception that Walter Balk (1978) saw many years ago:

> If the production process is defined in conventional systems terms, two fundamental control ratios appear. The first is that of output to input—or efficiency. The second is output to standards—or effectiveness. Frequently, improving productivity is a question of optimizing these ratios by keeping them in balance, one with the other (p. 46).

Summary: Measuring Productivity

The process of measuring public sector productivity is recapitulated below. Some services lend themselves easily to the complete process. Other services are difficult to specify. For example, it is no coincidence that sanitation work has been measured and analyzed so fully. The mission is unambiguous, resources are clearly identifiable, the output is readily measurable, and criteria can be derived for directly indicating quality. On the other hand, the mission of the Department of State is ambiguous; resources available to the Central Intelligence Agency are not clearly identifiable; the output of a university is difficult to measure; the quality of research and development work lacks obvious criteria. Not every kind of service can be readily measured, but many, if not most, can be with a little imagination and confidence. The methodology exists.

Step 1. Decide what work unit or organization is to be measured.

Step 2. Make preliminary assessments. Is measurement expertise available? Is support available to impel the enterprise? Who will be involved? Is a measurement team feasible? Reporting to whom? Made up of whom?

Step 3. Lay the groundwork by discussing it with everyone involved and assemble the measurers.

Step 4. Think about the mission and identify the major mission-related services produced by the work unit. Select one (or a few) of the most representative to start with.

Step 5. Decide how to count the amount of output: in what units? for what time period?

Step 6. Decide what type of input will be used. (The productivity of labor? of equipment? It is difficult to measure total factor productivity. Consider one resource at a time; labor is most usual.) Is it clear which input units go into producing the output?

Step 7. Decide by what method data will be collected on quantity of input and quantity of output. (The measurement expert is important here.) Collect the data.

Step 8. If only an efficiency measure is desired, stop here and calculate Output ÷ Input.

Step 9. If quality matters, decide what criteria to use, what weight each criterion will carry, and what the ideal or standard level will be for each.

Step 10. Decide how to collect data on each criterion and collect them.

Step 11. For each criterion, calculate the achieved-to-desired score. If one overall quality rating is desired, aggregate the weighted scores.

Step 12. To calculate productivity, quality considered, multiply the output figure, O, by the overall quality rating, K, and divide by the input figure.

References

Ammons, D. N. (1985). Common barriers to productivity improvement in local government. *Public Productivity Review, 9*, 293-310.

Balk, W. L. (1978). Toward a government productivity ethic. *Public Administration Review, 38*, 46-50.

Brinkerhoff, R. G., & Dressler, D. E. (1990). *Productivity measurement: A guide for managers and evaluators*. Newbury Park, CA: Sage.

Buntz, C. G. (1981). Problems and issues in human service productivity improvement. *Public Productivity Review, 5*, 299-320.

Bureau of the Budget. (1964). *Measuring productivity of federal government organizations*. Washington, DC: Government Printing Office.

City of San Diego. (1983, February). *The City of San Diego organization effectiveness program*. San Diego, CA: Financial Management Department.

Delbecq, A. L., Van de Ven, A. H., & Gustafson, D. H. (1975). *Group techniques for program planning*. Glenview, IL: Scott, Foresman.

Federal Quality Institute. (1991). *Quality improvement prototype: 1926th Communications-Computer Systems Group*. Washington, DC: Office of Personnel Management.

Hatry, H. P. (1978). The status of productivity measurement in the public sector. *Public Administration Review, 38*, 28-33.

Hatry, H. P. (1980). Performance measurement principles and techniques. *Public Productivity Review, 4*, 312-339.

Hatry, H. P., Blair, L. H., Fisk, D. M., Greiner, J. H., Hall, J. R., Jr., & Schaenmar, P. S. (1977). *How effective are your community services? Procedures for monitoring the effectiveness of municipal services*. Washington, DC: Urban Institute.

Hatry, H. P., & Fisk, D. M. (1971). *Improving productivity and productivity measurement in local governments*. Washington, DC: Urban Institute.

Hershauer, J. (1979). The quality dimension of police service productivity: Village of Tinley Park, Illinois. *Public Productivity Review, 3*(3), 75-86.

Mark, J. A. (1979, January/March). Measuring federal productivity. *Civil Service Journal*, pp. 20-23.

Measuring federal productivity: A report and analysis of the FY78 productivity data. (1980, February). Washington, DC: Office of Personnel Management.

Muniz, E. (1982). *Improving productivity through job redesign*. Unpublished master's thesis, John Jay College of Criminal Justice, New York.

O'Sullivan, E., & Rassel, G. R. (1989). *Research methods for public administrators*. New York: Longman.

Presnick, W. J. (1980, May). Measuring managerial productivity. *Administrative Management*, pp. 26-28, 46-48.

Rosen, E. D. (1981). OK work: Incorporating quality into the productivity equation. *Public Productivity Review, 5*, 207-217.

Rosen, E. D. (1984). Productivity: Concepts and measurement. In M. Holzer & S. S. Nagel (Eds.), *Productivity and public policy* (pp. 19-43). Beverly Hills, CA: Sage.

6

Improving the Work Process

Adam Smith was writing in 1776, but he stated then, better than anyone has since, the advantage of working smarter, not harder.

> To take . . . the trade of pin maker, a workman not educated to this business could scarce, perhaps, with his utmost industry, make one pin a day, and certainly could not make twenty. But in the way in which this business is now carried on . . . one man draws out the wire, another straights it, a third cuts it, a fourth points it. . . . I have seen a small manufactory of this kind where ten men only were employed. . . . But though they were very poor, and therefore but indifferently accommodated with the necessary machine, they could . . . make among themselves about twelve pounds of pins in a day. There are in a pound upwards of four thousand pins of a middling size (1937, pp. 4-5).

Adam Smith was describing the historic change to division of labor and the synergism it produced. The principle is still in force. Improvements in the work process can make better use of resources, improve service to clients, and remove sources of worker frustration.

The term "work process" refers to the way operations are structured and conducted. It includes such elements as organization, technology, routines, schedules, and work assignments. Restructuring the work process can be done in minor ways, such as by letting custodial workers load their own carts instead of waiting at a supply window, or in major ways, such as by computerizing an agency's information system,

This kind of effort represents a technical, engineering, or management science approach to productivity improvement. It is quantitative in nature and not too far removed from the tradition of the scientific management era. It seeks an optimal match of organizational capacity to demand, of labor and skills to the needs of the work. It seeks to streamline work flow, minimizing waste and delay. The object is to produce services promptly, reliably, and economically.

The point has been made already that, while having a technical solution is necessary for improvement, some issues of a political nature also must be considered before any change in the work process is attempted. What are the implications of the change for the work force? Will people need to be reassigned, retrained? What do they stand to gain? Can the change be made more rewarding? What permissions, resources, and concessions will be needed in order to make the change possible? How can these be obtained? Such behavioral and political issues are the subject of other chapters, but their importance is stressed here in order to reinforce the point that although the technical and behavioral dimensions of productivity improvement can be separated analytically, they are inseparable in practice.

Returning to productivity improvement through changes in the work process, the first question is, how can such opportunities be recognized?

Recognizing Problems With the Work Process

Symptoms

Problems with the work process manifest themselves in observable symptoms. One is idleness of labor, equipment, or space. Another is slowness, delays, or bottlenecks. Accidents and danger constitute a third set. Finally, periodic or chronic overload—of individual workers or of the entire system—is a cue that an opportunity exists for making an improvement by modifying the work process.

Idleness

Does a computer, a garbage truck, or a piece of special equipment sit unused several hours a day or several days each month? This raises the question of how more use can be made of the resource. The answer might be to change the work process: Relocate the computer so it can be shared; initiate a preventive maintenance program for the garbage truck; "contract in" additional work from another agency (see Chapter 10).

Is a building utilized only 8 hours a day or only 10 months of the year? Consider a flexitime schedule, creating a longer day by permitting some workers to start and end the day earlier and allowing others to arrive and stay later. Make a school building available to the parks department for its busy summer season.

> Government organizations have large staffs and budgets. Even a small percent increase in our productivity can free up large numbers of people or money for new tasks. The EPA employs 16,000 people. If each person managed to eliminate [20] hours of wasted effort a year, the EPA would recover the equivalent of 160 new people (Cohen & Brand, 1990, p. 104).

Are mail-room workers idle at midday, after the morning run and before the afternoon pickup? They can perform other tasks, such as stuffing envelopes, during their idle period. Do police officers just sit around for hours until their courtroom appearances? They can be issued walkie-talkies and assigned to patrol the neighborhood of the court until they are needed.

Delays

If the work is delayed as it flows along, that is a clue that productivity can be improved by rearranging the work process. Do clients complain about how long it takes to get service? Do backlogs of unfinished work build up? Are there perceptible "bottlenecks" where everything gets slowed down—awaiting supplies, transport, or an approval? New technology may be the answer; so may a simple reassignment of tasks.

Danger

Another clue suggesting a change in the work process is an unsafe task: bullets, fumes, and traffic are among the threats to the safety of public sector workers. These conditions spur the search for new technology in the form of protective devices and clothing. Can the operation be automated so that the human being can be removed from a dangerous situation? Such a question gave rise to the development of the robot for bomb removal.

Overload

Does work flood in at certain times of the day, certain days of the week, or certain months of the year? Do some workers carry more than their share of the burden? What of the increasingly common condition in which the demand simply exceeds the capacity of the organization? Periodic overload can be solved by charting the pattern of demand for service and using that data to design changes. Excessive demand for services can be dealt with rationally by the use of some clear system of prioritization: Principles already used by emergency medical units can be applied also to overloaded detective bureaus and child protection agencies.

Finding the Symptoms

Some symptoms may be evident, recognizable to anyone who cares to look around. Blatant idleness is clear. Other symptoms may not be as evident as a worker's spending the day, feet up on the desk, reading the newspaper on a "turkey farm." Such symptoms have to be discovered.

One inexpensive, readily available source is the files. Complaint records may reveal one bus route or driver as the object of a disproportionate number of complaints. Worker grievances may cluster around one routine. Safety records will show which operations or employees are most vulnerable to accident. The work force is often overlooked as a source of information about what is going poorly and where the problems lie. Worker insights can be evoked through dialogue, "town meetings," surveys of opinion, and such participative vehicles as task forces, quality circles, and joint labor-management committees. Managers can position themselves to see things through workers' eyes, as in the Tennessee program described by Francis Guess (1984):

The Governor has instructed all members of his cabinet . . . to, at least once a month, work at the lowest levels of their department. This can be most instructive! As Commissioner of General Services, I often worked in our State Employees' cafeteria, bussing dishes, cooking food. This allowed me to learn some things first hand. . . . One day, I was cooking breakfast, and I asked the ladies who were helping me, "Why is it so hot in here?" And they said, "Well, we tried for several years to get a ventilation fan, and we haven't been able to get it." Needless to say, after my experience, ventilation fans were soon installed in their kitchen. But I think it points out the fact that it took my personal experience to bring that about (p. 17).

Observation, records, and worker perceptions do not reveal all problems with the work process. More deliberate efforts to generate and analyze data may be in order. Some common techniques, including process flow charting, demand analysis, and plotting job travel, will be discussed later in this chapter.

Improvement in the work process can be achieved through a number of devices. One is reorganization.

Reorganization

Every jurisdiction structures its administrative machinery in some way. Some patterns are fairly universal: Most local governments assign the law enforcement function to one agency, a police department, and fire suppression to another, a fire department. Some patterns vary; in one city, every agency operates its own maintenance unit; in another, one centralized department of maintenance serves all of the city's agencies.

Similarly, each agency has its own formal structure: its unique configuration of job design, number and type of departments, number of levels in the hierarchy, number and hours of shifts, and the degree to which it is centralized or scattered geographically. These are not set in stone. The present structure of any organization reflects not only an initial design, but also an ongoing series of modifications, as when a police department creates a specialized drug enforcement unit or a state department of social services adds a new regional liaison level to the hierarchy.

While some reorganization is always taking place in the natural course of things, consciously applied reorganization becomes a means for deploying limited resources to better effect. The possibilities include:

- redesigning jobs,
- redistributing work,
- changing the number of levels or units,
- centralizing or decentralizing operations, and
- changing work shifts.

A word of caution is in order here. Reorganization looks good. It conveys the sense that someone is in charge, taking visible action to correct a problem with the basic structure. That can be a seduction. All too often, reorganization is undertaken in the blind faith that shaking things up will somehow make things better. Reorganization should be undertaken only where there is clear reason to believe that: (1) it will solve a specific problem and (2) what is gained by the change will outweigh what is lost by it.

Redesign Jobs

A "job" is one person's share of the organizational enterprise. It is the basic building block on the organization chart, and it is a key organizational point—the locus where the needs of the work and the needs of the worker come together. The design must make sense from both perspectives. The assembly line job, one cog in a smooth-running "machine," may represent the ultimate in efficiency from the standpoint of the work. But if it frustrates an adult personality, as Charlie Chaplin showed so poignantly in the film *Modern Times*, then it does not make sense from the standpoint of the worker.

Jobs can be redesigned to make the work process smoother, as when patrol officers take on the responsibility for keeping the gas tank filled in the patrol car. Jobs can be redesigned to produce greater satisfaction for the worker, as when a clerk is given freedom to make a decision that used to require the supervisor's approval. One major achievement of the productivity movement has been the recognition that the quantity and quality of a worker's output reflects not only on the technology, but also on the worker's psychological feeling of ownership. In this section, we will focus on the use of job redesign to improve the efficiency and effectiveness of the work; we will leave its use to enhance worker motivation for discussion in Chapter 7.

A job has two dimensions: scope and depth. A job is made up of a set of tasks, and it carries a given amount of authority or discretion. Job redesign typically involves varying the scope (the kind and number of tasks), the depth (the amount of authority), or both.

Some jobs may be too broad by containing too many tasks. Having to move back and forth constantly from one to another gives rise to errors and wastes time. The answer is to shed some tasks by farming them out to other workers or, where possible, by transforming one complex job into several simpler jobs:

> When the Ocean County [New Jersey] [pretrial intervention] program began . . . its staff consisted of four probation officers and a program director. Each officer processed a number of cases all the way through, from the initial investigation to conclusion. . . . [A]fter a number of months, case loads increased to the point that investigations became backlogged. Paperwork was being neglected and it seemed that counselees were not receiving adequate supervision. . . .
>
> The staff discussed its options and decided to redesign the administrative structure of the program by creating two specialized jobs: investigator and counselor. . . .
>
> The data showed that . . . before the work redesign, .72 units of work were produced per worker day [1 unit = 1 investigation completed or 2 months of counseling per client]. During the comparable time period a year later, after the work redesign, productivity increased to 1.2 units, quality . . . increased slightly . . . [and] all . . . preferred the new, specialized work design (Muniz, 1982).

Some jobs may be too narrow, containing too few tasks. Boredom with the limited routine is not the only negative consequence. One "specialist" has to wait for the other. A classic caricature of the public service depicts a street repair crew: One person works while three others wait, leaning on their shovels. Making a job more varied and interesting can also save money:

> To ensure that all dogs in Pico Rivera, California, . . . receive rabies vaccinations, the city annually canvassed the community to determine which residents owned dogs. The task was assigned to part-time personnel or contracted out . . . at costs as high as $23,000. . . . The city worked out an agreement with the postmaster to have mail carriers compile lists while on their daily mail routes. . . . In exchange, the city's paint crew . . . painted a dozen mailboxes for the post office. . . . Since the program is maintained for public health and safety reasons, the public and especially the mail carriers benefit (International City Management Association, 1990, MGT-14).

Finally, if only one worker understands the filing system or knows how to perform a particular procedure, that worker's absence causes delays if everything is "put on hold" or errors if someone else attempts the unfamiliar.

Redistribute Work

Is the work indeed assigned so that the absence of one person cripples operations? Does the work of a skilled specialist include hours spent on menial tasks?

> Rep. Patricia Schroeder (D-Colorado), chair of the Subcommittee on Civil Service, charged recently that the federal government wastes hundreds of millions of dollars in payroll costs by requiring professional employees to perform work which could be done less expensively by lower graded employees. . . . [The Government Accounting Office] found that, in . . . four agencies, the amount of work which should be delegated to lower level workers amounted to the equivalent of 8,274 full-time professionals ("Payroll Waste," 1981).

Is the work force as a whole expending a disproportionately large amount of time on relatively unimportant aspects of the work? The answers to questions such as these can be found by the technique of charting the distribution of work.

As a simplified illustration, let us consider a hypothetical small personnel office. Let us assume that Joan heads the office, Jean is the office clerk, and Sam, Flora, and Bill are personnel specialists. The first step in the charting process is to classify all the tasks into a few major categories: for example, "time and leave" (processing time, absence, and salary data for use by payroll), "recruitment" (preparing job descriptions, running advertisements, and arranging interviews), "benefits" (health and retirement plans), "personnel files," "office" (reception, telephone, and office files), and "administration" (making and administering personnel policy). The next step is to have each worker keep a log, perhaps for one typical week, recording the category, task, and amount of time. The final step is to construct a chart, which might look something like Table 6.1.

The chart provides some answers and suggests some new questions. First, it is clear that only Flora deals with benefits; presumably, only she has reason to keep up with the latest rules and procedures. Flora's vacation, illness, or resignation will deprive the office of the capacity to handle these matters. Second, Joan, who is the supervisor, spends 35% of her time

Table 6.1 Work-Distribution Chart for Personnel Office

		Number of hours per week				
Process/Task	*% Staff Time*	*Joan*	*Sam*	*Flora*	*Bill*	*Jean*
Time and Leave						
Time Sheets	9		8		9	1
Absences	7		4	6	4	
Salaries	2	3				1
Recruitment						
Descrips/Ads	5	3	2		3	2
Correspondence	6		5		5	2
References	4		5		3	
Interviews	2		2		2	
Benefits						
Health	11			22		
Retirement	4			8		
Personnel Files						
Files	8		2		2	12
Appraisals	5		6		4	
Reports	12		6		8	10
Office	10	8				12
Administration	15	26		4		
Total	100	40	40	40	40	40

on telephone inquiries and writing up records. Perhaps some of this activity can be assigned to a less highly paid worker. Third, does this office really want to devote 17% of its time to meetings? Can the length of time spent on the telephones be cut by adopting new procedures, such as using recorded messages or mailing out prepared information sheets?

The Pennsylvania Department of Transportation (PennDOT) offers an illustration of this kind of introspection. Faced with the need "to revitaliz(e) a department which was notorious for waste, poor management, and corruption," the new administration made sweeping changes (Poister, 1982, p. 325). As part of the process, it examined the relationship between organizational purpose and job assignments.

> Further reductions in personnel were achieved by reviewing the manpower of each unit in light of current priorities. While some units were allotted more personnel . . . many units were found to be relatively over-staffed for the department's missions in the 1980's. For example, since January 1979,

right-of-way activities have been curtailed in keeping with the department's philosophy of maintaining the existing road and bridge system first, and limiting new construction to vital projects; some [40] right-of-way personnel have been reassigned (Scheiner, 1981, p. 15).

Change the Number of Units or Levels

Organization charts locate every job in a two-dimensional diagram. Jobs are grouped horizontally into administrative units (departments, sections, offices, or precincts) and vertically into hierarchical levels (from worker to first-line supervisor and on up to agency head). Productivity can sometimes be enhanced by changing that chart, by reorganizing to match the structure to new conditions.

An underutilized, inactive unit can be eliminated and perhaps a new one added. With the passage of time, some services are in less demand, while new needs arise. For example, as a neighborhood profile ages, prenatal health units are utilized less but a need grows for senior citizen centers; the parks need fewer swings and more checkers tables; there is less need for monitoring truancy and more for monitoring scams against the elderly.

Unprecedented problems may require the creation of new specialized units in police, health, educational, and other agencies.

> Prosecutors in Milwaukee County, Wisc., say that the county's Speedy Trial Project, which established two courts that handle only drug cases, has cut the time it takes to process felony drug defendants from an average of over 300 days to less than 90 days, and the project's success may allow for its expansion to other courts ("Single-Focus Courts," 1990, p. 5).

Even in the absence of radical demographic or social change, attention should be paid periodically to the possibility that existing units might be split or merged to achieve better operation.

> With the goals of improved public service and lower costs, the City of Kalamazoo, Mich., has inaugurated a program that will completely merge the city's police and fire departments within five years. . . . The program is expected to save $4.5 million during the transition period alone because of reduced staffing . . . and will put as many as three times the number of officers on the streets. . . . (T)he program has won the enthusiasm of many police and fire officers because dual-service officers receive more free time, 10 percent more in pay, and greater variety in their work ("Kalamazoo Police/Fire," 1983).

The number of levels in a hierarchy is not set in stone. Adding layers is a common tendency in public sector agencies. In times of financial constraint, it becomes particularly important to consider a less popular option: the removal of administrative levels.

> The first step in reducing the size of the work force was eliminating unnecessary administrative positions. Top department managers immediately inventoried the department to find cases of: "desk" administrators in line units who had no field supervision responsibilities; . . . "one-on-one" organizations where only one assistant reported to the unit manager; and full-time workers who carried out functions that the line manager could handle in addition to his regular duties (Scheiner, 1981, p. 15).

Centralize or Decentralize

Productivity can be enhanced through the geographical restructuring of operations. Centralization brings common services together into one place, under one roof. Conversely, decentralization scatters operations across territory. Each has its advantages and disadvantages. Centralization enhances uniformity, agency control over policies and operations, and full utilization of specialized personnel and equipment, but clients have to travel to the central location and managers lose intimate contact with the field. Decentralization brings services closer to the clients and permits tailoring to suit local needs, but it requires providing managers, experts, and equipment at many locations where they may be underutilized.

All too often, present arrangements reflect ancient history, not present conditions. From the standpoint of improving productivity, it is valuable to reexamine the current organizational arrangement to see whether further centralizing or decentralizing might solve existing problems. Centralize?

> Two municipal hospitals in the Bronx are to be merged under a single administration in an effort to reduce costs and provide more efficient medical care. . . . Besides administrative changes, medical services will be consolidated. . . .
> The introduction of physicians in private practice at North Central Bronx would "maximize the utilization of currently underutilized operating suites." . . . Conversely, . . . obstetric and gynecological services were underutilized at Bronx Municipal, a situation which could be improved through a rationalization of resources in the area (Sullivan, 1982, B1, B11).

Or decentralize?

About once a month, Deborah S. Miskovich, Pittsburgh's housing court magistrate, dons the robe and hits the streets.

The city is trying a novel way to put pressure on landlords who fail to maintain their properties: Send the city housing magistrate out to hold hearings on site. "Well, it certainly alleviates the need to take testimony as to what the exact situation is," says Miskovich, who has been playfully dubbed "Have Gavel, Will Travel" (Walters, 1991).

Change Work Shifts

Most public sector agencies operate on one daytime shift. This is probably true of a licensing agency, a bureau of records, or a personnel office. Other agencies utilize a second shift, possibly to serve clients who work during the day, such as a school offering evening classes. A night shift for the custodial function is very common in public buildings. Still other agencies operate around the clock, typically using three shifts. These include police and fire departments, prisons, hospitals, residences for the mentally ill, and transportation systems. Some are on fixed shifts, others on rotating shifts.

As with the other aspects of organization, some redeployment of the present shift configuration should be considered as a way to improve operations or conserve resources.

The post office, which is limited by union contracts to 10 percent part-time employees, has three full-time shifts. Two of them cover two peak periods—four hours in the early evening and four in the early morning. [Elmer] Cerin would like to see these peaks covered by part-time workers, filling out either end of one full-time shift. At the Morgan facility, at 4 P.M., postal workers play cards in the cafeteria; the letter-sorting machines sit idle; supervisors chat by their stations. Three hours later, the din and bustle are overbearing, like a mid-Manhattan traffic jam (Judis, 1988, p. 54).

Conclusion

As we have seen, reorganization can take many forms. One morning invested in playing "what if" reorganization games may pay off in better productivity. What if tasks were reassigned? What if these two units were merged? What if we created a new unit, centralized an operation, or moved from rotating to fixed shifts? As with so much of the productivity improvement effort, the key factor is not one magic technique, but rather some awareness of possibilities for change and a willingness to consider them.

Charting

Demand Analysis

How much trash is put out for collection and when? How many 911 calls come in at different hours of the day, days of the week, or months of the year? Is this predictable? Demand analysis is a technique based on measuring and charting the level of demand to ascertain any regular patterns or trends.

There often exist strong and predictable regularities in the pattern of ups and downs in demand for service. Demand may vary by hour of day: Citizens use a lot of water in the early morning, pick up application forms during lunch hour, and swamp the toll booths at 5 p.m. Demand may vary by day of the week, time of the year, or section of the jurisdiction: All of the weekend's complaints come in on Mondays, the IRS is swamped in the spring, and most calls for hazardous waste removal may come from just a few districts. The pattern may shift over time.

Projections of long-range trends in demand serve planners and others involved in decisions about opening or closing facilities and preparing new programs to meet new needs. From the productivity improvement perspective, demand analysis is particularly useful as a technique for providing good service while making optimal use of labor resources—having workers available when needed but not idle when demand is low.

The use of demand analysis is indicated where workers are alternately overburdened and underutilized or when backlogs of uncompleted work accumulate periodically or even chronically. Without a deliberate effort to detect misfits between demand and staffing levels, waste of labor may go undetected; not every irrationality is this obvious:

> Air-conditioning units on New York City buses, both old and new, require such a high degree of maintenance that transit officials say they are fighting a losing battle to keep buses cool this summer. . . .
>
> Under the labor contract, air-conditioning mechanics are allowed to take vacations . . . during July and August (Goldman, 1982, p. B1).

The Demand Analysis Process

The process of demand analysis is not complicated or difficult. It begins by counting the demand. How many buses come in for repair each week of the year? How often does a given block become "somewhat littered"?

The demand is then charted by plotting the level of demand against the hour, day, month, season, or locale, whichever seems appropriate.

The demand for service from a hypothetical college bursar's office provides an example. It appears that demand may vary according to the time of day. The manager needs the facts. A student aide is assigned the task of counting over several weeks the number of students who come to the office during each hour of the day. Average figures are computed, and a demand curve (sometimes a bar graph) is drawn that shows number of students appearing versus time of day. The curve makes it clear that there is indeed a pattern: It starts very low at 9 a.m., rises very slowly from noon to 2 p.m., and jumps very high from 2 p.m. until closing. The pattern is the same every day of the business week.

Dealing With Demand Patterns

Match the Demand Curve. One option for the manager is to make sure that the resources of the office are deployed to match the demand curve. This means having the staff available in maximum force at the peak periods. For example, no paperwork, outgoing calls, or other postponable tasks would be done after 2 p.m., and personal leave would be confined, as much as possible, to the mornings. If the staff needed for the peak period is not fully utilized during the slow period, some creative alternatives should be considered.

> [In Fort Collins, Colorado], we took crew people during snowy winter days when it is too cold for sewer work, and with very little training, moved them to be drafting technicians' aides. They loved it. A "sewer rat" comes in; he has tremendous experience in map reading, he realizes that our maps are not updated; he brings to the person in the office a lot of knowledge of the field (Bachmann, 1984, p. 133).

The hypothetical bursar's office might arrange with another unit whose peak period is the morning to convert one or two employees to "floaters" who spend mornings in that unit and afternoons in the bursar's office. When a member of the bursar's office staff resigns, instead of hiring one full-time person, the office could pursue a "job-sharing" arrangement in which the one position is shared by two permanent part-time employees, both working afternoons only.

Level the Demand Curve. Before accepting the demand pattern as immutable, a manager would do well to explore the possibility of changing it—that is, leveling the demand. A city transportation system may offer discounted fares for off-peak travel. The parks department could charge lower fees for using recreational facilities during slack periods. A state motor vehicles bureau may change the driver's license application date from four times a year to the applicant's birthday, thus smoothing a four-bump curve into a horizontal line. An over-the-counter operation may be converted to a mail-in procedure, permitting clerks to process requests at a steady, uninterrupted pace. In our example, more students might be encouraged or required to come to the bursar's office in the mornings—by being reminded that there is less waiting in the mornings or by being assigned alphabetically.

Demarket or Prioritize. In some cases, measuring the demand level may establish the fact that demand is simply too high for the capacity of the organization: Even optimally deployed, the available resources could never handle the workload. Such quantitative evidence strengthens the manager's recourse to new strategies. One is demarketing: persuading clients to make less use of the service, as when a water department urges the public to repair leaking faucets and grow fewer water-hungry plants in their gardens.

> Underlying demand management is the shift *away from the supply mentality*. Landfills provide an illustration. In California some 65% of all county landfills will be filled to capacity by the year 1996. The supply mentality would argue that California is running out of capacity and should invest in more landfills. The demand management psychology argues that California has *too much waste*, and looks at ways of reducing the volume. These ways include trash-to-energy plants, recycling, composting, and reducing the amount of waste generated by home and businesses (Hayes, 1989, p. 222).

Another strategy for dealing with excessive demand is to prioritize: to deal with demand, not in the order in which it arrives, but according to predetermined criteria of selection. MASH unit doctors classify incoming wounded according to a triage system: Those whose wounds can await treatment go into one class, those who are so badly wounded that treatment is unlikely to help go into another, and those for whom intervention is both vital and promising are given priority. This principle finds other applications:

> The [Rochester, New York, police] department developed a case screening procedure called a "solvability factor." The department analyzed 500 criminal cases that have been solved to determine what factors had led to their solution. . . . If none of the solvability factors can be found, a case is not further investigated. The city's clearance rate in 1980 was 37% for Part I Offenses, compared to the national average of 19% for cities of similar size (International City Management Association, 1981, No. 123).

Prioritization systems go against the grain of the expectation that everyone is entitled to service and no one should be denied it. However, the reality is that in a situation where resources cannot cover all the demand, some kind of de facto selection system already operates, usually the order in which requests are received. Prioritization recognizes the impossibility of meeting all demand and attempts to make optimal use of resources by basing selection on rational criteria, such as urgency of need and ability to help.

> Oregon's plan to ration benefits . . . amounts to nothing short of a revolution. Oregon wants to alter the scope of Medicaid coverage in a way no state has done before. . . .
> The revolution is in the roster of illnesses and problems that would *not* be covered. . . . The common cold gets ranked low because it gets better by itself or with home remedies. Several forms of advanced cancer ranked low because they rarely get better at all. . . .
> What Oregon is saying is that it is working in a world of finite resources. It can no longer pay for all the medical procedures science has to offer. A line has to be drawn somewhere. Rather than shade it at various levels of poverty and classes of people, Oregon wants to make distinctions among services (Lemov, 1991, pp. 49-50).

Flow Charting

Deliberate, careful observation of how work proceeds can be a powerful instrument for eliminating wasted effort. Although appropriate for factory-type operations, time-and-motion studies and computerized routines have only limited applicability to public sector operations, because public agencies generally operate under conditions of variety and change. No two arrests or trials are the same. Social service, education, health, environmental protection, housing, veterans, job safety, and diplomatic agencies all deal with heterogeneous clienteles and changing realities.

However, while such conditions and routines may be uncertain, they certainly are not random. These operations may be far from ready for automation, but they can be managed using something better than the traditional tools of "experience," intuition, and impression. The situation calls for techniques that are quantitative, but simple and feasible. Process flow charting is a popular choice.

Flow charting is an industrial engineering technique for tracking, depicting, and analyzing the steps through which work proceeds. It typically provides a running record of how much time is spent in various work operations and in transit, delays, inspections, or storage. The point, of course, is to discover opportunities to improve the work flow by eliminating steps and reducing the time spent on anything but operations. As an illustrative example, let us consider the placement of hospital "boarder" babies into foster care.

It is patently impractical to chart all of the work done by all of the employees in any sizable agency. The procedure usually begins, therefore, with work sampling—the selection of some portion of the work that will be considered indicative of the entire operation.

> The laws of probability provide the basis for work sampling. These state that a large number of observations made at random intervals and classified into distinct activities will provide a fairly reliable account of how often specific activities occur. A requisite of a work sample study is that observations must be made randomly, if unbiased results are to be obtained (Weiss, 1986, p. 58).

In our example, the decision might be to chart the placement of 10 infants. It is vitally important that the sample be carefully chosen to be as typical as possible of the normal work of the organization, including kind of subject, routines followed, and prevailing conditions.

The work is now observed, timed, and labeled in terms of the five categories listed above. *Operations* would include such activities as interviewing potential foster parents. *Transport* or *travel* would include riding from the hospital to the foster home. *Delays* are periods spent waiting for anything: a nurse, a vehicle, the copying machine, a supervisor. *Inspection* refers to the process of approving work done, such as a superior's review of the placement plan. *Storage* covers the periods when work is put aside to be acted on later, as when the court suspends the removal of a child pending an assessment of parental competency. Figure 6.1 depicts a simplified version of part of a process flow chart.

Time (mins.)	Chart Symbols	Process Description
12	D	Waiting to use telephone
15	O	Telephone with foster parents
48	→	Travel to hospital
35	O	Signing papers
25	D	Awaiting supervisor
15	□	Supervisor approves papers
35	O	Receiving infant
45	D	Awaiting transport van
45	→	Travel to foster home
40	O	Talk with foster parents on care
20	O	Writing instructions for parents
55	→	Travel to office
20	D	Waiting to use computer
85	O	Writing up report

Figure 6.1. Process Flow Chart, "Boarder Baby" Placement

The value of work process charting lies in the documentation it provides and the answers it suggests.

A study of the operations entries suggests how the work might be expedited. What operations are listed on the chart? What takes the most time? Does one process delay others? For example, could the approval be obtained in advance so that it does not hold up receiving the infant? What steps could be cut? For example, instead of writing out all the instructions, the social worker might use a generic "instructions for foster parents" sheet and simply check the relevant items. The list of operations may also reveal whether all of the operations make appropriate use of the workers' skills.

When attention is turned to categories other than operations, new insights emerge. In our example, the chart reveals that 1.7 hours of this day were wasted in waiting. Another 2.5 hours were used for travel. In fact, less than half the day went to operations. Some waits might be eliminated: Perhaps the social workers could use their own cars and not have to call for department vans. Waiting time might be converted to operations time: Perhaps a laptop computer or tape recorder would allow the social service worker to use waiting time by preparing reports. There may be ways to cut travel time; for example, the foster parents might receive the child at the hospital (an example of coproduction, which is discussed in Chapter 10).

Mapping Travel

In many public agencies, particularly those in the social service, inspection, or criminal justice areas, there may be a considerable amount of outside travel. Even in the office, considerable time may be spent in walking to and from equipment, files, and other offices. When process flow charting points up travel time as a costly item, then mapping travel patterns and charting trip frequency (Ammons, 1991, chap. 5) can suggest ways to combine trips, rationalize routes, or both. This can save more than money, as the San Antonio city manager reported:

> We had recently added two fully equipped emergency medical service units to our [ambulance] fleet of 19. . . . But that cut only 12 seconds from the average response time. So our in-house data processing staff got to work . . . [and] developed a program for our computer-aided dispatch system that anticipates—by location, time of day and day of the week—where the next call for emergency medical service is likely to come from. We position the ambulances nearby, instead of sending them back to the fire stations between calls as we used to. The result has been the reduction of an additional minute and a half in average response time, down to 5.2 minutes. That can make the difference between life and death (Briseno, 1991).

Technological Change

By far the most familiar and attractive option for improving the work process is changing the technology. "Changing the technology" means more than computerizing or automating or buying heavy equipment. Technology includes all methods and know-how by which work is done. Going from automobile to foot patrol constitutes a change in technology; so does substituting plastic bags for garbage cans.

Of course, much technological change does involve the acquisition of computers or other major hardware. Like reorganization, this kind of change is inviting because it is exciting and highly visible. But, like reorganization, it should be undertaken only if it serves a real purpose and the payoffs will clearly outweigh the costs. New hardware comes with its own set of problems—including financing, the need for new expertise, and the displacement of workers.

The Search for New Technology

Technological change can provide answers to certain problems. Repetitive, boring jobs that permit little discretion or judgment are candidates for automation. Mail sorting is such a job. Dangerous or difficult work stimulates the search for safer alternatives: new fire suits, bullet-proof vests, or machines to mark highway lanes, for example.

> For normal public sector work, robotry does not seem suitable. . . . The New York City Department of Sanitation, however, breaks the mold and is actively exploring the introduction of a programmable Trallfa robot into its truck-painting operation. . . .
>
> The job of painting one of the eighteen different vehicle types used by the Department of Sanitation is . . . messy, hazardous, and time-consuming. . . . The health hazard is obvious and pressing. Although the department uses the best masks and coveralls, and a wall of water runs down the rear wall of the room to pick up paint particles, the job is still one of the worst in the shop (Hughes, 1983, pp. 118-119).

The very existence or availability of new technology may invite its application. When a law enforcement official reads about a computer program that can take available crime data and create an area map showing geographical relationships and trends, he or she will probably ask, "Can we use this?" ("The MIDAS Touch," 1987). When a solid waste director hears about a process for mining old landfills, the first question might be, "Could we, too, make money and extend landfill life by extracting and selling metals and dirt?" ("There's Gold," 1990). When a recession in the aerospace industry impelled the Boeing company to seek diversification by developing new technology useful to cities, the city of Tacoma, Washington, took advantage of the situation and cooperated in innovative projects (Hayes, 1977, pp. 171-203).

Information Technology

Uses of Information Technology

Computerization and the management of information is the leading form of technological innovation in the public sector.

Today the federal government, all 50 states, and virtually all city and county governments utilize computers. At the city and county levels alone, computers are used for some 450 different computer applications including paying employees, sending utility bills, analyzing demographic data, routing vehicles, and allocating manpower (Northrop, Kraemer, Dunkle, & King, 1990, p. 505).

The advantages of the computer arise from its capacity and speed. The ability to store vast quantities of information and to manipulate data quickly and accurately makes it valuable for many public purposes and fields. Common applications include the following.

Data files: keeping, searching, and providing records (such as personnel files, crime and health statistics, geobased profiles of city blocks). For example:

> Imaging technology can enable a government worker to locate immediately the digital equivalent of a given document, reproduce it in paper form for a citizen who has requested it and return that information to its indexed slot in computerized archives within minutes.
>
> In a government office, it is not unusual for a number of staff members to need the same file at the same time. By permitting simultaneous use of the file electronically, imaging technology avoids the problems of incomplete or misplaced files. . . .
>
> A 12-inch disk holds enough information to fill 18 file-cabinet drawers with paper documents (Richter, 1992a, p. 42).

Analysis: manipulating and presenting data (often in graphic form) to support management and the decision process (such as planning, staff deployment, predicting need for capacity). For example:

> CITE (Court Information Tracking Environment) performs docketing, indexing, scheduling, calendar preparation, formatted notice preparation, revenue and trust accounting, and statistical and management reporting for civil, criminal, traffic, probation, domestic relations, and small claims cases ("Projects in Progress," 1991, p. 3).

Word processing: writing and editing letters, reports, and other documents. For example:

> HPD [the New York City Department of Housing Preservation and Development] pilot tested the use of radio-based handheld computers by having

inspectors . . . use them on apartment inspections in response to heat and hot water complaints. The handheld computers and radio system eliminates the need for inspectors to report to the office at the start of each day to complete and file paperwork from the previous day's inspections. Instead, they save office and travel time by completing required forms on the computer while in apartments (Epstein & Leidner, 1990, p. 217).

Control: monitoring and "flagging" key variables (such as inventory level, sewer flooding). For example:

> In a courthouse, the PLC [programmable logic controller] controls the interior and exterior door locks, cameras and monitors, intercom systems, intrusion alarms, fire/life safety devices, card-key access, and other security devices. . . .
> If a problem arises in a courtroom, the module will either automatically sense the problem or be prompted by a panic/duress situation alarm. It instantly switches the monitor to the problem, locks the necessary doors, initiates preprogrammed elevator operations in the zone, and secures the area (Fitzgerald, 1992).

Simulation: vicariously testing the effect of varying elements in a system (such as the effect on traffic flow created by retiming traffic signals or reversing road lanes). For example:

> The radically innovative aspect of Metro's new computer system lies in its ability to model the impacts of land use and transport system alternatives interactively. . . . The kind of information available includes highway and transit network characteristics, data on trip-generating land use, traffic volume on highway network links, intersection turning movements, and patronage on segments of the transit network. The interactive system permits planners to "window" in on a subset of the region and to model the impact of alternative configurations of land development and transport systems (Adler & Edner, 1988, pp. 155-156).

In addition to speed and capacity, computers and related information technology innovations provide the significant advantage of overcoming time and distance. Electronic message systems make it easier to reach people and to deal with messages at one's convenience (Swain & White, 1992, p. 649). The fax machine and teleconferencing permit discussion, information exchange, and decision making in a real-time framework. Teleconferencing and televised workshops and training sessions avoid travel time and expense. For a large state such as Alaska, where winter travel is difficult, teleconferencing is a particularly valuable option. The Federal Emergency Management Agency (FEMA) held its first such conference there in October 1981, recognizing that "FEMA's large and geographically dispersed field constituency, and FEMA's vital communications mission to its constituency, made video-conferencing an ideal medium" (Wesley, 1983, p. 5).

Arie Halachmi (1991) has pointed out the importance of information technology to employees with special needs. New information technology makes it possible to work at home (the alternative workplace will be discussed in Chapter 9). More fundamentally, it just makes it possible to work:

> Scanners, fax machines, speech synthesizers, optical imaging, and robotics remove some important constraints on the employment of individuals with special needs. More important, they allow such employees to function on the same level as other workers, to be subject to the same evaluation procedures, and to vie for the same careers. Accommodating individuals with functional impairment is not only the law but an economic necessity for dealing with the shrinking labor force (p. 334).

Issues in Using Information Technology

Centralization Versus Decentralization. This has been called "one of the major debates regarding information policy" (Overman, 1985, p. 144). Central information systems, usually based on mainframes programmed and run by data processing professionals, can bring together, into one common system, information on an organization's capacity, clientele, and operations, regardless of how physically dispersed the organizational subunits may be. It offers uniformity and the capacity for manipulating large amounts of data and making analyses that smaller data bases could not warrant or support.

Microcomputers offer the advantage that they are flexible, easily tailored to individual and local needs. They are less "foreign," more trusted; users develop a more personal interest in the integrity and validity of the data generated (Adler & Edner, 1988, pp. 153-154). However, they make it difficult to integrate information:

> Exchanging files among different word processors and spreadsheets may require commands and manipulations with which most users are not familiar. Moreover, incompatibility among data formats can result in costly

delays and impede the sharing of information. In short, microcomputer technology stimulates many centrifugal forces (Rocheleau, 1988, p. 170).

Historically, there has been tension between central computer office staffs and those who adopt microcomputers. Those who "built their careers on programming in standard languages on mainframes" were disquieted by the advent of microcomputers and concerned about their disadvantages (Rocheleau, 1988, p. 169). The "acrimonious and contentious relationship" has "smoothed" in recent years (Richter, 1992b, p. 37). A typical system today might include a combination of central mainframe and user-specific microsystems, with the central office perhaps providing support for developing microcomputer networks.

Integrating Information. An important issue is the integration of information from the individualized microcomputers into "one overarching system that will solve a particular problem or support a specific application" (Richter, 1991, p. 38).

> State and local governments can no longer afford a balkanized approach to information resources. Operating between the rock of added responsibilities and the hard place of restrained budgets, they know they cannot meet the need for shared information by throwing more equipment or people at the problem. . . .
> In recognition of that fact, governments now are focusing on squeezing higher performance from solutions already in place (Richter, 1991, p. 40).

For example, it is possible to devise hardware and software to integrate purchasing and other accounting records so that "from one terminal, you can do accounts-payable, accounts-receivable and general ledger transactions, and enter them only one time" (Richter, 1991, p. 43).

> Most people have access to [the Justice Information Management System] through some 2,000 terminals in offices all over [Harris County, Texas]. More and more people, however, are using personal computers operating on local area networks (LANs) instead of terminals. The Justice Internet links these individual LANs in what one observer calls an "electronic nervous system." . . .
> Internet seeks to link the county court's LAN with the community supervision and corrections department, pretrial services agency, dispute resolution center, and the administrative office of the district courts ("Doing More," 1991, p. 1).

Interagency sharing of information raises questions of deciding just what should be shared and how to control access to what should not be shared. For example, police and prosecutors' offices have common need to know criminals' histories, but some information "will not be shared for reasons of agency policy . . . or statutory and legal requirements concerning access to information" (Goldsmith, 1990).

Another problem is that systems integration plans are expensive and usually require considerable outside help. From the productivity standpoint, the important considerations are whether the elimination of present barriers would save resources, eliminate duplication, and improve service. The point at which existing technology needs upgrading is a good time to consider adopting an integrated system.

Errors and Recovery. As public agencies rely more and more on computerized information systems, it becomes increasingly important to have that information correct and available. Errors can have devastating impact on the quality of services:

> When someone trying to describe, say, a 35-year-old mother of five instead entered the code for a 20-year-old male high school dropout, the system would check the profile against existing city and state records, and find out that the worker's entry contradicted information about the recipient in those other data bases. Until the discrepancy could be cleared up, which might take weeks, no payment would go out.
>
> Advocates for the poor say that welfare centers recorded error rates as high as 30 or 40 percent (Gurwitt, 1989, p. 63).

As more people make direct entries into central data banks, the risk of error increases. This can be minimized by dealing with factors (such as fatigue and lack of proper training) known to increase the chance of error. Appropriate programming can help catch clearly anomalous entries (Halachmi, 1991, p. 336).

"Only one in five state and local governments has a comprehensive plan for restoring its information networks in the event of disaster" (Richter, 1991, p. 37). Although consequential, such plans are expensive, and elected officials are faced with other, more visible needs for funds. Short of a full plan, there are some things that can be done to help ensure that a system can be sustained or at least restored more quickly. Among the recommended policies:

- keep a list of where software is kept and how data processing technicians and management authorities can be reached at night or on weekends;
- prepare some likely scenarios, together with a set of instructions as a working plan for restoring the system; and
- build in diversity and redundancy so that everything does not rely on one medium (for example, Madison, Wisconsin, owns fiber-optic cables and also leases some telephone company lines into the same sites) (Richter, 1991, pp. 39, 41, 44, passim).

Human Problems. We have already noted the problem of controlling data quality in the face of human capacity for error. There are other human problems as well, and their effects need to be weighed in the productivity balance.

The advent of computerization presents difficulty for workers who have invested psychologically in their accustomed jobs. Some go through "some or all of the four stages of bereavement that ideally culminate in acceptance: denial, resistance, anger and depression" (First, 1990, p. 48). Although there is no definitive conclusion on the matter, considerable concern has been voiced by researchers about the possible health risks posed by prolonged exposure to computers: radiation emissions from video display terminals, screen glare, dust and allergens, postural difficulties to the hand and neck (Halachmi, 1991, pp. 341-343).

Computers affect organizational structure and processes. The distribution of computer knowledge does not conform to the hierarchy of formal authority, so managers may have to depend on subordinates and be called upon to take responsibility for decisions for which they lack expertise (Rocheleau, 1988, p. 174). Working via the computer offers none of the social and psychological supports and satisfactions of the work group. It does not create team spirit. And reliance on computer analysis deteriorates, rather than develops, human diagnostic and social skills (Halachmi, 1991, pp. 328, 333).

The emergence of gurus—experts to whom others turn for computer instruction and guidance—is all but inevitable. The advantage of this phenomenon is that these people lead the way and smooth the path to innovation (Rocheleau, 1988, p. 173). But it can distract such a guru from other duties and into what is often obsessive tinkering and advising. Then the experts may tend to leave because they are in demand.

Other Problems. Privacy is an important issue; protecting the rights of the individual may require careful control of access to data on a "need to

know" basis. The accidental or deliberate computer "virus" threatens operations. Care must be taken to guard against a system's being broken into
for the purpose of doctoring information (such as college grades). The
anonymous nature of data entry and retrieval opens a door to new kinds
of fraud and makes thievery difficult to detect.

Most fundamentally, the computer is no better than the data and programs fed into it: garbage in, garbage out. Its capacities invite "data pollution" (too many data, too little information). It can provide only those insights
that have been programmed for—and modifying an existing program to
answer new questions may be prohibitively difficult, especially in the case
of large systems. This recital of possible problems should constitute a
caution, not a discouragement for those considering computerization.

> The overall message of the study reported here is that the implementation
> of new information technology does not automatically lead to improved
> productivity. New information technology creates new problems besides
> helping to solve existing problems. Managers need to deal with the new
> issues if the new information technology is to meet their expectations
> (Rocheleau, 1988, p. 177).

John A. Worthley (1980) has offered some guidelines: Managers must be
thoroughly involved in the computerization process, careful planning is
required, communication between technicians and users must be continual, and a "people" strategy must be developed (pp. 16-17).

Other Technology

The productivity literature is rich with examples of the use of many
other kinds of new technology to achieve better efficiency and quality in
a wide range of public sector settings. The following are just a few examples.

> Newark, New Jersey, changed its method for handling discarded tires and
> now recycles them into rubberized asphalt, a superior paving material
> (International City Management Association, 1990, PW-1).

> Hazelwood, Missouri, added an electronic recording system to provide
> surveillance of the police department's booking process, creating an objec-
> tive record to use in dealing with the problem of complaints that "usually
> came down to the complainant's word against the officer's" (International
> City Management Association, 1990, PS-3).

The Ramsey County, Missouri, Community Human Services Department no longer issues benefits checks. Recipients receive plastic cards, to be used in regular automatic teller machines. Clients do not have to travel and wait for checks, and can manage their money better, by making withdrawals as needed ("For People on Welfare," 1990).

The Florida Department of Transportation films its 23,000-mile road system. "The video is used to monitor water drainage, corrosion, potholes and the general safety of Florida's state-maintained roads. It is also used in court, when road conditions influence a case" (Coburn, 1990).

At bridges and tunnels from California to New York, "drivers whose cars have bar-coded stickers on their windows can drive through specified lanes in toll plazas without stopping while lasers scan the stickers and debit the account" (Sylvester, 1990).

The Minnesota Department of Revenue, which receives some five million pieces of mail every year, installed a mail sorting machine that reads bar codes from the envelopes. This eliminated the unpleasant job of manual sorting, freed up labor, and increased both the accuracy and speed of mail processing, so that incoming monies get into the bank and start earning interest sooner ("New Machine," 1986, pp. 1, 4).

The list of technological innovations goes on. It includes one-person garbage trucks, remote-controlled automatic sprinkler systems, electronic water-meter-reading equipment. The journals or magazines devoted to each particular applied area are generally a good source of information about emerging technology specific to the field.

Deciding About New Technology

Where visible problems exist or where new possibilities are clear, a change in technology should be considered. However, between the concept and the action, considerable thinking needs to be done. Some of the issues to be considered are:

1. Will it work? Is the proposed new technology really appropriate to the operations of this work unit in terms of such factors as the scale and nature of operations? Will available equipment fit the need, or will adaptations be necessary and at what cost in time and money? Will the environmental or operating conditions be significantly different from those under which the model operated successfully?

2. Is it worth the investment? What will the innovation cost, all things considered? What are the anticipated benefits in terms of saving resources, improving outputs, or both?

3. Can funding be obtained? Major technological changes, such as computerization or acquiring a new truck fleet, create a major "lump" in the budget. (See Chapter 9 for a discussion of some alternatives for dealing with this problem.)

4. Can the necessary expertise be made available? Does it already exist in-house? Or will it be necessary to acquire it from outside via new hires or consultants?

5. What will be the impact on the work force? Will people have to be retrained or reassigned? Will they see this as an opportunity or as an affliction?

The New York City Department of Sanitation's experience with its automation of spray painting, described earlier, is instructive. The robots cost considerably more than was first estimated. Originally designed to be stationary, they had to be adapted to move laterally and vertically. For operational and budgetary reasons, the volume of vehicle-painting work has not always kept the robots busy full-time, resulting in the need to clean them of the quick-dry paint at the end of each shift. When the volume of work is very low, it does not pay to use the robots at all, and the work is done by hand (Conroy, 1991).

The point to be made is that unpredictabilities, complexities, and variabilities exist, and thus there is always some risk in undertaking change. No decision is guaranteed to be successful, but thoughtful discussion and consideration of factors and alternatives beforehand will improve the likelihood of success.

Avoidance of change is also a decision—often not the best one.

References

Adler, S., & Edner, S. M. (1988). Technological change in urban transport organizations. *Public Productivity Review*, *12*, 151-163.

Ammons, D. N. (1991). *Administrative analysis for local government: Practical application of selected techniques.* Athens: Carl Vinson Institute of Government, University of Georgia.

Bachmann, R. (1984). Applications of Theory Z to American public institutions. *Public Productivity Review*, *8*, 128-135.

Briseno, A. E. (1991, October). Managing local government with your back to the wall. *Governing*, p. 11.

Coburn, K. A. (1990, November). DOT engineer measures videos by the mile. *Governing*, p. 73.

Cohen, S., & Brand, R. (1990). Total Quality Management in the U.S. Environmental Protection Agency. *Public Productivity & Management Review, 14*, 99-114.

Conroy, F., Deputy Director, Bureau of Building Management for Sanitation, New York City Department of Sanitation. Personal interview, July 15, 1991.

Doing more and doing it better. (1991, November/December). *Court Technology Bulletin*, pp. 1, 5.

Epstein, P., & Leidner, A. (1990). Productivity forum for computer technology. *Public Productivity & Management Review, 14*, 211-219.

First, S. E. (1990, April). All systems go: How to manage technological change. *Working Woman*, pp. 47-48, 52, 54.

Fitzgerald, D. (1992, January/February). Security technology goes from keys to computers. *Court Technology Bulletin*, p. 3.

For people on welfare, no more checks. (1990, October). *Governing*, pp. 41-42.

Goldman, A. I. (1982, July 22). City losing battle to cool buses. *New York Times*, pp. B1, B8.

Goldsmith, S. (1990, October 15). Information bridges to breach interagency barriers. *Law Enforcement News*, p. 7.

Guess, F. (1984). Keynote speech, Second National Public Sector Productivity Conference. *Public Productivity Review, 8*, 13-20.

Gurwitt, R. (1989, May). Happy machines, unhappy people: How to ease the pain of the computer transition. *Governing*, pp. 63-66, 68.

Halachmi, A. (1991). Productivity and information technology: Emerging issues and considerations. *Public Productivity & Management Review, 14*, 327-350.

Hayes, E. C. (Ed.). (1989). *The hidden wealth of cities: Policy and productivity methods for American local governments*. Greenwich, CT: JAI.

Hayes, F. O'R. (1977). *Productivity in local government*. Lexington, MA: Lexington.

Hughes, A. J. (1983). Robotics: Effects on Japanese and American labor and a practical application in the New York City Department of Sanitation. *Public Productivity Review, 7*, 112-121.

International City Management Association. (1981). *The guide to management improvement projects in local government*. Washington, DC: Author.

International City Management Association. (1990). *The guide to management improvement projects in local government*. Washington, DC: Author.

Judis, J. B. (1988, September 25). U.S. mail: Mission impossible. *New York Times Magazine*, pp. 30-33, 50-51, 54.

Kalamazoo Police/Fire Department merger underway. (1983, March 1). *Public Administration Times*, p. 3.

Lemov, P. (1991, October). Climbing out of the Medicaid trap. *Governing*, pp. 49-50.

The MIDAS touch: Push-pin maps catch up to computer age. (1987, August 18). *Law Enforcement News*, pp. 1, 7.

Muniz, E. (1982). *Improving productivity through job redesign*. Unpublished master's thesis, (pp. 8, 9, 10, 34, 58, 60, 61, 62), John Jay College of Criminal Justice, New York.

New machine helps solve taxing problems. (1986, September-October). *STEP Update*, pp. 1, 4.

Northrop, A., Kraemer, K. L., Dunkle, D., & King, J. L. (1990). Payoffs from computerization: Lessons over time. *Public Administration Review, 50*, 505-514.

Overman, E. S. (1985). Decentralization and microcomputer policy in state government. *Public Productivity Review, 9*, 143-153.

Payroll waste laid to failure to delegate jobs. (1981, March 1). *PA Times*, p. 12.

Poister, T. H. (1983). Monitoring the productivity of a state highway maintenance program. *Public Productivity Review, 7*, 324-343.

Projects in progress. (1991, March/April). *Court Technology Bulletin*, pp. 2-3.

Richter, M. J. (1991, September). Staying connected: Disaster recovery for government telecommunications. *Governing*, pp. 37-39, 41-44, 46-47, 49-50.

Richter, M. J. (1992a, April). Image processing: Streamlining the paper chase. *Governing*, pp. 41-55.

Richter, M. J. (1992b, August). Managing information: The county study. *Governing*, pp. 31-32, 37, 39-46.

Rocheleau, B. (1988). New information technology and organizational context: Nine lessons. *Public Productivity Review, 12*, 165-178.

Scheiner, J. I. (1981). Productivity improvement in the Pennsylvania Department of Transportation. *Public Productivity Review, 5*, 14-20.

Single-focus courts bring swifter justice for Milwaukee drug offenders. (1990, October 15). *Law Enforcement News*, pp. 5, 7.

Smith, A. (1937). *The wealth of nations*. New York: Random House.

Sullivan, R. (1982, March 29). City will merge 2 hospitals in the Bronx to save money. *New York Times*, pp. B1, B11.

Swain, J. W., & White, J. D. (1992). Information technology for productivity: Maybe, maybe not: An assessment. In M. Holzer (Ed.), *Public productivity handbook* (pp. 643-663). New York: Marcel Dekker.

Sylvester, K. (1990, November). Laser toll collections are speeding up traffic. *Governing*, p. 19.

There's gold in that county landfill. (1990, October). *Governing*, pp. 36-37.

Walters, J. (1991, November). Slumlords take note: Court makes house calls. *Governing*, p. 22.

Weiss, W. H. (1986). How to work-sample your employees. In J. Matzer, Jr. (Ed.), *Productivity improvement techniques: Creative approaches for local government* (pp. 58-63). Washington, DC: International City Management Association.

Wesley, M. (1983, January 15). Teleconferencing aids agency operations. *PA Times*, pp. 5, 15.

Worthley, J. A. (1980). Computer technology and productivity improvement. *Public Productivity Review, 4*, 10-20.

7

Training and Motivating the Worker

The public sector is labor-intensive. Government services are produced by people and often delivered in person, face-to-face. The client's perception of the government worker's knowledgeability, competence, commitment, understanding, and efficacy contributes to public satisfaction or dissatisfaction with government service. Client opinion also feeds back directly to the public worker, reinforcing a sense of accomplishment or futility.

If workers are poorly prepared, locked into meaningless routines, and powerless to make improvement, then they will retreat emotionally. If they see themselves as skilled professionals, in command of resources, part of a team doing meaningful work, able to use discretion and influence change, then they will be free to become emotionally engaged in the work.

Satisfaction does not in itself lead to increased productivity. Neither does commitment. "Contrary to common assumptions, committed employees are not automatically disposed to maximize their productivity or to make extra effort on behalf of the organization" (Balfour & Wechsler, 1991, p. 366). There has to be added some creative tension in the form of a climate in which productivity matters and is measured and in which rewards are related to performance.

To the extent that individual competence and dedication can be improved, productivity can be improved. That is the point of this chapter. There is another point: Just as the public deserves honest and competent service, the millions of people who work in the public sector deserve a humane and fulfilling workplace. That is also the subject of this chapter and the next; there it will become more clear how intimately a more rewarding workplace and better public service are related, two sides of the same coin.

To see why so much potential for the worker to do better and enjoy it more has been lost, we need to review some history.

The Classical Perspective

The previous chapter treated productivity improvement from the viewpoint of the engineer. That perspective concentrated on diagnosing the production mechanism and then changing it to eliminate sources of inefficiency. The worker was taken for granted as a cog in the machinery.

The pioneers in diagnosing and prescribing for modern work organizations early in this century began with that very viewpoint. Frederick Taylor, father of scientific management, was an engineer; so was Henri Fayol, the early proponent of general principles of management. Taylor and Fayol were not unaware that the people who work in organizations are thinking, social human individuals, but in their efforts to concentrate on just how organizations make sense as efficient instruments of production, they made simplifying assumptions about the work force. Taylor assumed that workers would obey management and perform their duties in the manager-determined "one best way" because it was in their economic interest to do so (Taylor, 1978, p. 19).

Similarly, in 1922 sociologist Max Weber, who first identified the bureaucratic form of organization, made the assumption that workers could and would put aside personal considerations when exercising their vocational roles (Weber, 1987, p. 54). It facilitates analysis to be able to conceptualize an organization as an enduring structure, with replaceable parts in the form of depersonalized role actors—clerks, fire fighters, or budget officers. But this approach assumes away the complexity of the human beings in the organization.

Historically, we made the mistake of treating these assumptions as if they were true. The Taylor idea of management came to prevail: Managers do the thinking, and workers do as they are told. We lost sight of the fact that, even in the workplace, people remain human, complex, adult, and individual—thus missing the point that individual differences in competency, style, and dedication have real consequences for organizational effectiveness:

> A small number of police officers make a majority of the arrests which end in conviction, according to the findings of a recent study.
> For the seven jurisdictions examined, the study report stated, a total of "12 percent of the 10,205 officers who made arrests . . . accounted for more than half of all the convictions, while 22 percent produced not a single arrest that ended in conviction." . . .
> The high conviction rate . . . officers indicated that they tended to focus greater attention on locating and dealing with witnesses . . . expressed more interest in follow-up investigation . . . reported success in improving the cooperativeness of an existing witness by locating additional witnesses in order to create an atmosphere of mutual support . . . [and] also emphasized the importance of persistence of "follow-through" in various aspects of post-arrest activity ("Study Links Conviction," 1981).

The significance of the famous Hawthorne studies, undertaken two decades after Taylor, is that they confirmed the influence of psychological and social, not just economic, factors on job behavior. It has been half a century since the human being in the worker was rediscovered in those studies, but the influence of the Taylor assumption still pervades the management of many public sector organizations. Because they are expected to behave like cogs, often under systems that do not work and over which they have little or no say, too many workers become alienated, turned off, even uncaring.

Changing Perspectives

Worker dissatisfaction with traditional management has increased with the changing nature of the work force:

> The first inescapable conclusion from reviewing labor force trends is that *more employees, at all levels in organizations, need and want more power and autonomy.* . . .

The huge influx of younger people into the labor force in the 1970s was accompanied by a key generational experience different from that of the past. In earlier decades, many of those who led large organizations were veterans, with military service as a prime formative experience. More recent newly minted managers tend increasingly to have their attitudes formed on the college campus . . . [which] breeds expectations about rights to participation as well as discomfort with authoritarian styles of management. . . .

There is, in short, a rise of "rights consciousness"—among employees of all kinds (Kanter, 1981, pp. 3-4).

The worker's importance cannot be exaggerated. Even a perfectly planned operation would depend for its implementation on the skill and willingness of human workers. But there are no perfectly planned operations in today's ever-changing world of public administration: Programs must often be undertaken without certain advance knowledge of how, why, and whether they will work; unpredictable operating conditions arise; changes occur in the nature of the clientele and its needs. In addition, the size and complexity of modern systems make detailed central planning and detailed direction impractical, if not impossible. The classical "machine model" has reached its limits of utility.

Modern organizations must deal with uncertainty and change by becoming more open, alert, and flexible—more organic (Burns & Stalker, 1978). Information and decisions are not confined to "channels" but flow from various points and via shifting networks, according to the needs of each problem. It is often not the managers but the workers, at every level and sector of the organization, who discover that things are not working as it was assumed they would, who first encounter the unexpected difficulties, and who are the first to hear from the clients about needs that the program is not meeting. In short, workers know the operations most intimately and are in the most immediate contact with the clientele. Workers are not only the natural source of feedback on how things are going, but also the natural source of ideas and insights into the specifics of operations.

We have seen two general arguments for attention to the worker: The workers of today seek more autonomy and, to function effectively under today's conditions of uncertainty and change, organizations need worker input.

With its focus on the worker, this chapter takes the viewpoint of the psychologist or human relations expert. It reverses the thinking of the engineer by taking the task for granted and concentrating instead on how the skills and attitudes of the workers affect the productivity of the work unit. The ultimate goal in improving productivity through changing the worker is to provide more and better service through a better-managed, more efficient organization that becomes, at the same time, a more humane and fulfilling workplace.

Recognizing Problems With the Worker

There are basically only two reasons that workers are not doing a job well: They do not know how to or they do not care to. The two elements often go hand in hand: A 1991 survey of senior federal executives revealed a decline in employee quality, attributed to decreased commitment to public service and reduced willingness to work hard, along with declining communication skills, analytical ability, and interpersonal skills ("Federal Employee Quality," 1991).

Without appropriate knowledge, the most enthusiastic worker can make costly mistakes—funny as a premise for comedy, but not really funny in the workplace. On the other hand, boredom, alienation, and resentment can lead even knowledgeable workers into foot-dragging, inappropriate "games," and even sabotage.

Lack of Knowledge

Worker "knowledge" includes understanding of the purpose, rationale, techniques, materials, and context of the work. Lack of knowledge manifests itself most noticeably in errors, poor decisions, shoddy quality, and complaints.

> Thousands of older Americans eligible for government help with their Medicare costs are being denied aid in many government offices across the country. . . .
> Complaints are pouring into AARP [American Association of Retired Persons] and other advocacy groups from individuals who clearly qualify for aid but who are being turned away. . . .
> According to complaints filed with AARP, many people around the country are being told the QMB [Qualified Medicare Beneficiaries] program doesn't exist or that their state doesn't participate. . . . Other individuals are being deemed "ineligible" because they have too much income or other assets—when they are actually are below the levels set by law. . . .

> What seems to be happening: occasionally willful, occasionally inadver-
> tent government misinformation. Not long ago Families USA, which
> originally highlighted the problem, got a phone call from an intake worker
> in New Jersey asking what the QMB program was. . . .
> "We told her to send the applicant to the local office of Social Services."
> . . . "She said, 'I *am* a Social Services case worker and I don't know it
> [QMB] exists' " (McLeod, 1991, pp. 6, 7).

One clue to a problem, then, is complaints. Another is an excessive
number of errors and the need to redo too much work. Particular attention
should be paid to patterns: Do errors emerge from one person's work, one
step in the process, one hour or day of the week? Is there a tendency to
avoid assigning certain tasks to certain workers because they always mess
things up? Is work being sent back, rejected from higher authorities,
auditors, or other agencies outside the unit?

Worker lack of knowledge may be inferred from the nature of client
complaints. Incorrect advice suggests the worker needs to be made familiar with new rules or routines, as in the Medicare case above. The recep-
tionist may be disconnecting callers because he or she does not understand
the telephone system. Rudeness may mean the worker has not internalized
the service character and norms of the program; insensitivity may arise
from a worker's unfamiliarity with cultural differences.

One of the distinctions between the U.S. and Japanese systems is the
amount of time given over in Japan to preparing people for their posts,
not only by training in specific skills and familiarity with the system, but
also by inculcating attitudes, such as pride in being part of something
larger—like a social tradition and a worldwide fraternity of caregivers:

> Someone at a ward-level government in Tokyo invited me to come over to
> a training session for their home helpers, for taking care of old people. It
> is a very low-level job. They have a monthly session where they bring them
> all together, and I went over, expecting to hear them instructing on how to
> house clean, or how to give an old person a bath, or some technical sort of
> thing. What was there, was a professor, from a second-ranked university,
> giving a lengthy and very abstract lecture about the social welfare system
> of Japan and how it differs from the development of social welfare in
> Europe! And I thought, how can these home helpers, these middle-aged
> ladies of not much education, be interested in this? I looked around the
> room, and they seemed to be snoozing away. My immediate impression
> was, well, this is really stupid, Japanese bureaucracy at its worst.

> Afterwards my wife and I talked with these ladies, and they thought the lecture was terrific. Thinking about it, it struck me that the function of the lecture was not the information that was being imparted. Rather, it was the status of having a university professor come and talk with them and take them seriously as being part not only of the local administration of their own city, but also of social policy in Japan, social policy around the world (Campbell, 1984, pp. 137-138).

Poor decisions may result from incomplete or erroneous knowledge of conditions, factors, options, and probabilities.

The New York City blackout of July 1981 was caused by a system operator's belief that a feeder line was in service; he should have known— and others should have told him—that it was not. Thinking he knew the facts, he ignored appeals to save the system by shedding load ("The Control Room," 1981, p. 88). A parallel utilities catastrophe occurred a decade later when the Federal Aviation Administration lost computer control over air traffic at major eastern airports when the telephone lines failed because "no one [at American Telephone & Telegraph] noticed that the equipment was being powered by backup batteries alone, despite a series of alarms" (Schwartz, 1991).

Knowledge, skills, and attitudes are amenable to improvement through training, which will be discussed in more detail later in this chapter.

Lack of Motivation

Training is the cure if a worker wants to do a good job but does not know how to. But what if the worker does not care? The subtle but pervasive problem of worker motivation is a key issue for productivity in the public sector.

Poor worker motivation manifests itself in feelings of low morale, alienation, lack of ideas, hostility and resistance, as well as in pedestrian performance. These internal feelings become part of the organizational climate and may not be immediately obvious, although they can be detected by careful observation or through surveys of employee attitudes. Quantitative indicators of what Rupert Chisholm has called "withdrawal behavior" (1983, p. 16) do exist: the number of grievances, the absentee rate, the turnover figures. As the axiom goes, "First they gripe, then they stay out, then they quit." If this is true, the public sector has been warned: In 1981, the average daily absenteeism rate was 11% in New York state and 8% for federal employees, compared with 5% in the private sector (Roll & Roll, 1983, p. 124).

Motivation is undoubtedly a major key to improvement in public sector productivity. There is a great deal to learn about this approach from the experts in human relations and from those practitioners who have actually put new reward systems into place. As we will see, the opportunity to participate in decision making is a particularly rewarding experience for most workers, and many productivity improvement techniques focus on "participative management," which will be discussed in the next chapter.

Productivity and the Personnel Process

Before considering other approaches, it is worthwhile to pause to reexamine the existing personnel process with an eye to how some problems with the worker may be prevented, or at least minimized, by judicious use of ongoing opportunities to recruit, select, orient, evaluate, promote, and discharge workers.

The personnel process has often been a barrier to productivity. Narrow job classifications provide little scope for job enlargement or enrichment. Compensation scales reward everyone equally, regardless of performance. Inadequate appraisal systems make it difficult to certify true merit. Tests and training have often lacked job relevance. Promotions and layoffs are often based only on seniority. Let us consider how the personnel process might be conducted to enhance worker productivity.

Job Classification

Improvement can begin with the very first step in the personnel process. Narrow job classifications do have the virtue of specificity: a Clerk Grade 1 or Typist Grade 3 can safely be presumed to possess a certain skill at a certain level of competency. The cog can be snapped into the machine easily and surely: The system is reliable, and everyone knows what to expect.

But such narrow classifications impose a cost. Because it falls outside their job description, workers become deaf to the unanswered telephone and blind to the waiting client. Service suffers, as does the quality of the workplace and the worker's pride in identifying with it. Narrow job classifications deny managers the ability to assign people to a variety of duties, whether for the sake of efficiency or as a means of helping a worker find a better niche or a new skill. Managers are unable to upgrade workers in recognition of superior performance.

"Broadbanding" refers to the reclassification of jobs into fewer, broader categories. For example, our Clerk Grade 1 and Typist Grade 3 might both be reclassified into the broader title of Office Worker. While broadbanding gives managers greater freedom to deploy personnel efficiently, provides workers the opportunity to develop additional skills, and makes it easier to reward merit, it is often opposed by employees in general and unions in particular out of fear that it may cost jobs and give managers too much discretionary power. Those misgivings are not insurmountable, however:

> Managerial flexibility was improved through a process known as broadbanding, whereby a number of [civil service] titles are combined into a single title, thus enlarging the pool from which key promotions and transfers may be made. Civil [service] regulations were changed so as to allow me the authority to appoint my top 50 career civil servant managers from a broad pool of about 130 candidates. . . . The resulting influx of young energetic officers . . . had a tremendous effect on the vitality of the headquarters operation. . . .
>
> A second broadbanding change was the consolidation of the field supervisory positions of assistant foreman and foreman. This move eliminated existing redundancy through job consolidation and resulted in some budget savings. Perhaps more important, it was an early exercise in cooperative productivity negotiations with one of the two major unions in the department, whereby in return for slightly higher salaries, obsolete civil service job differentiations were eliminated and the total number of officer positions reduced (Steisel, 1984, pp. 107-108).

Recruitment and Selection

Some people are more competent and dedicated than others. By attracting and enlisting promising people, good recruitment and selection procedures can potentiate productivity. The technique of utility analysis throws light upon the difference a selection decision can make:

> An organization hires two typists. . . . Typist A types 75 words per minute, and typist B types 50 words per minute. On the job, typist A completes an average of 30 typed reports per day, while typist B completes 25. . . . If both typists earn the same salary, say $15,000, typist B is "worth" only $12,000 compared to typist A, and typist A is "worth" $18,000 compared to typist B (Carr, 1988, p. 133). (See also Ammons, 1991, pp. 134-141.)

The recruitment net should be cast widely to attract a large pool of candidates who already possess or have the aptitude to master the requisite knowledge, skills, and attitudes. Job requirements should be relevant and accurately described.

Advertisements and notices that emphasize the mission of the agency and the opportunities for career development will attract people interested in more than "just a job."

Selection should be done as expeditiously as possible. When the process drags on, it is the better candidates who are lost to other employers. Selection criteria and procedures should be job-focused:

> The second major role stressor is role inadequacy. The first and foremost reason this occurs is that a person is not psychologically qualified to be a correctional officer. Not everyone is qualified to serve as a correctional officer, supervisor, or administrator. At times, because of the economic situation and job opportunities, certain people who do not belong in the profession are allowed in (Lorinskas, 1984, p. 147).

Orientation

Orientation should be thorough. It should include an understanding of the mission, clientele, and philosophy. It should describe the entire organization and the unit's place in it. Orientation should be realistic:

> A consistent finding has been higher job survival rates for those receiving realistic job previews. . . .
>
> A realistic job preview might function as a 'screening device' for certain types of individuals, namely, those who would be most likely to quit as a result of a poor 'match' with the organization. . . .
>
> A second way in which job preview realism may lead to higher job survival is by reducing the chances for subsequent (i.e., on-the-job) 'disillusionment' or 'disenchantment.' . . .
>
> The results [of the experiment] indicate that the job previews had virtually no effect on job acceptance (Wanous, 1973, pp. 328-329).

Probation

The probation period should be taken seriously as the opportunity to assess performance and potential. Permanent status should not be granted by inertia and disinclination for confrontation, but rather as the result of a positive assessment that the candidate is right for the job. Probationers should be given every opportunity to correct behavior and performance, but if improvement does not take place, letting the employee go makes it possible to recruit a more appropriate person. It is also a message to everyone about expectations and standards.

Promotions and Reductions in Force

The decisions on who gets promoted or who is let go during a budget-mandated cutback in personnel are often based only on seniority. Taking performance into consideration alongside longevity provides the opportunity to retain and reward productive workers and to inculcate the perception that performance counts. This was the rationale behind the new personnel plan of the U.S. Department of the Navy:

> Performance will also be used as a primary retention factor during reduction-in-force procedures.
> Under the existing system four criteria are used to judge which employees will be retained in case of staff cutbacks: (1) whether they are career or career conditional employees (based on a three-year tenure period); (2) veterans' preference; (3) length of service; and (4) performance.
> The new system has moved performance to first place with the rest following consecutively (Anders-Michalski, 1981, p. 4).

Training the Worker

"Except for the military and a few civilian agencies . . . there is no tradition in the United States for training public servants. The merit system assumed that the best (that is, pretrained) job candidates would be placed in appropriate positions" (Vocino & Rabin, 1981, p. 304). The 1930s saw a few "trail-blazing in-service training programs" (Stahl, 1983, p. 278), but "the federal government was not even authorized to spend any significant sums on training" (Shafritz, Hyde, & Rosenbloom, 1986, p. 419) until passage of the Government Employees Training Act of 1958. Since then, the role of training in public agencies has become firmly established for a variety of reasons:

1. As had always been true for some public sector fields, such as the military, diplomatic, police, corrections, and fire-fighting services, there is no private sector source of preparation. Employees must be hired on

the basis of aptitude, not experience, and training must take place after hiring.

2. Governments have generally been unable to compete with the private sector in attracting managerial talent. By training their own promising employees, public agencies could obtain the needed managers and, in the process, offer ambitious recruits the possibility of a career, not just a job.

3. In this era of "future shock" (Toffler, 1970), retraining is often essential. Fields of practice undergo increasingly rapid and radical change: New problems arise and new technologies are developed. Even the best-prepared professionals need to update skills and knowledge periodically, simply to continue effectively in the same job.

4. The effort to afford opportunity for public service to nontraditional recruits (women, ethnic minorities, the handicapped, part-time workers) sometimes involves preparatory training.

5. Productivity improvement programs, increasingly important because of fiscal constraints, produce changes in organizational routine. People may be doing different tasks, using new technology, or participating in new decision-making modes. Preparation for these new situations is essential if the innovations are to be successful.

Formal Training

Needs Assessment

In general, training is important for helping workers to understand the organizational mission (the history of the field, legislative intent, court interpretations, or client attitudes and needs), gain familiarity with innovations (new rules, techniques, forms, guidelines, or equipment), upgrade present skills (such as ability to write, prepare an audit report, or conduct an investigation), add new skills (such as group dynamics, problem analysis, or conflict management), and prepare for career advancement.

The immediate purpose of training is to change behavior. Training is indicated when corrections officers behave unprofessionally, supervisors produce unclear and incomplete reports, clients complain about discourteous service, or new promotees evince difficulty in perceiving themselves as managers. New changes may call for unaccustomed behaviors. Cohen-Rosenthal and Burton have identified six different "audiences" to receive training in preparation for a joint labor-management program (1987, p. 181).

A needs assessment should be the first step in the training process. The need should dictate the nature of the training. All too often, training content is chosen for the wrong reasons: tradition, imitation, trainee interests, trainer interests, schedule convenience, and so on.

Delivering the Training

Training is usually done on agency time. Sessions may range in length from one or two briefings to a series of intensive, multiday workshops or retreats. Training may take place on the agency premises, which is convenient, although it has the drawback that trainees may be distracted or interrupted by work problems; or training may be done off-site, at a conference center or university, for example. In larger agencies, curriculum development and teaching may be performed by in-house experts, often from the human resources unit. Alternatively, outside trainers may be utilized, coming from consulting firms, university faculties, or on loan from other agencies.

Formal course work may be encouraged. An agency may contract with a college for dedicated courses, offered at hours compatible with the work schedule and open only to agency personnel. Or it may underwrite tuition for individuals to attend regular graduate or undergraduate courses on specific subjects. Finally, by specifying such formal study as a requirement for advancement, an agency may encourage employees to take courses or even complete a baccalaureate or master's degree program.

Evaluating the Training

Training should be undertaken for specific purposes, to meet defined organizational needs. In order to determine the impact of the training and to assess the cost-effectiveness of alternative training delivery modes, it is important to conduct evaluations of the training. Preferably, this should be done both formatively, during the training process, for the purpose of correcting whatever does not seem to be working, and summatively, after the process, to find out what did and did not pay off. "Happiness scores," reflecting trainee satisfaction with the trainer, the setting, the curriculum, and so forth, are not adequate measures of the value of a course of training. Evaluators should also seek to ascertain what before-and-after changes have occurred in trainee knowledge or understanding. To ensure the objectivity of this process, it is not uncommon to employ an independent, third-party evaluator.

Other Types of Training

Formal training of the kind discussed thus far is not the only training workers receive. Any "education" that affects the worker's goals, values, skills, and behaviors is a kind of training.

Orientation

Most recruits to public service receive their first experience as agency employees in some kind of orientation process. As we have seen, it is important that orientation be realistic. This is the golden opportunity for management to educate an impressionable newcomer as to the agency mission, environment, structure, operations, and expectations of its employees.

Some orientations are elaborate, including films, lectures, and tours. At the other extreme, the new worker may just be shown a desk, told where coats are hung, and given a key to the washroom. The implication of these differences for employee attitudes and future behavior should be obvious.

On-the-Job Training

This refers to the usual process of having the new employee work at first under supervision, receiving guidance and correction by a supervisor or co-worker. What is learned in the beginning becomes imprinted and resistant to future modification. Care should be taken, therefore, that the supervisor possesses the appropriate attitudes, understanding, and skills; it may be necessary to train the trainer.

Learning the Ropes

Everyone needs to learn the "informal" rules, procedures, cliques, and power relationships in the work unit. Whose word carries weight? Which rules are really operant, and which generally disregarded? Is there an accepted shortcut for circumventing an awkward procedure? What can one generally get away with? What do we really owe the clients? The wise manager will exercise some control over what version of the "facts of life" are learned by placing the recruit alongside a responsible member of the social group and not with the resident cynic, goldbrick, or "operator."

Retraining

To deal with displacements resulting from job cutbacks, new technology, reorganizations, or other changes in the work unit, workers may need to be taught new methods, new skills, and even new jobs.

[A] 1968 federal housing program . . . provided insurance for homes purchased by low-income families who had been renting. Numerous homes turned out to be 'substandard.' . . .

Detroit suggested to HUD [Department of Housing and Urban Development] that the problem might be alleviated if the maximum feasible number of inspections were made on such houses. . . . The four-in-one inspection seemed to offer the best way to shorten inspection time. . . .

Most of the trainees were young persons who had been city health inspectors. . . . Had the opportunity to retrain not existed, all these inspectors would have been permanently laid off. . . . A course of in-house and field instruction had to be developed quickly by the chief and assistant chief inspectors of the electrical, heating, plumbing, and structural divisions. . . .

The 35 former health inspectors developed new skills and upgraded their earnings. . . . Productivity has risen nearly threefold; travel time has decreased; scheduling has been simplified; and several in-house evaluations show that the four-in-one inspectors have 'the highest productivity and the highest morale' of any other group (National Center for Productivity and Quality of Working Life, 1977).

Cross-Training

Cross-training involves teaching current workers how to do other jobs, as well as their own. In addition to preparing workers for possible advancement, it affords organizational flexibility. If someone is absent for a day or leaves permanently, someone else knows the job and is prepared to step in. If work piles up at one step of the work procedure, trained reserves can be redeployed temporarily to help out. The best cross-training prospects include critical jobs, high-turnover jobs, jobs held by mature employees, and high-skill jobs (Phillips, 1981, p. 35). Cross-training methods include job rotation (switching jobs) and part-time reassignment on a regular basis (perhaps one morning a week).

Motivating the Worker

Introduction

What are the forces that impel a worker to produce and to produce work of quality? There are no proven answers, but slowly, over the years, a body of theory and research has been building, providing insights and some partial understanding. Let us piece together some of what we know.

We begin with what is most obvious but seldom stated: Work seems to fulfill some basic human need. Forced idleness is a punishment. Hobbies, amateur activities, and volunteer work all testify to effort as a source of satisfaction. There is pleasure in using valued skills and abilities. This propensity is a basic asset, an ally of productivity.

Workers can be rewarded both for and through work. Rewards *for* the work have importance: Pay, benefits, security, and sociability are among the compensations enjoyed in exchange for time and effort invested in the workplace, and they affect motivation. However, much of the productivity improvement effort focuses on providing the rewards that come *through* the work itself: pleasure in the free exercise of skill, excitement from solving problems, pride in accomplishment.

There is a psychological satisfaction in "closure," in a sense of a beginning and an end. Anyone who has watched a movie on video only to find the last scene missing knows the frustration of being deprived of the sense of closure. For most of human history, working alone or in small groups enabled the individual to see a project in its entirety and to its end. This is true today for only a few workers. The artist, the operating room team, and the lawyer know how things turned out: The painting is right, the patient lived, the client lost. Free to decide what is needed and how to proceed, these workers enjoy a sense of ownership of the enterprise. For most others, the bureaucratization of modern society has changed the nature of work so that they see only a part of the process. Decisions are out of their hands; work is less varied, more boring. The psychological horizon comes to focus on procedures, not results.

What do workers say they want from their jobs? Quality of work life (or sometimes quality of working life) (QWL) has been endowed with many meanings, some very narrow and specific (Chisholm, 1983, pp. 10-13; Cohen-Rosenthal & Burton, 1987, p. 120; Accordino, 1989, p. 345). But it has also been used broadly, as a shorthand term for "the work place in which the full range of human needs are met" (Lawler & Ledford, 1981-82, p. 25).

Quality of working life states that organizations should be designed (and redesigned) to support the positive characteristics of people:
—people have the need for and take pride in achievement
—people have the need and the ability for on-going learning
—people need continual stimulation of their mind and senses
—people are naturally social and enjoy mutually supportive relations with others
—people are purposeful; for self-esteem, they need to know that they are making a contribution of value to society
—people need freedom and autonomy and are capable of responsible self-regulation. . . .
QWL means that all organization structures and processes, including jobs, should be designed to ensure that:
—decisions are made at the lowest level possible. Self-regulation for individuals and groups is a primary goal.
—individuals or integrated groups of workers are responsible for a 'whole job.' People do not work on fragmented, meaningless tasks.
—the potential (technical and social) of individuals, of groups and of the overall organization is developed to the full (Mansell & Rankin, 1983, pp. 9-10).

The list goes on. As we will see, a motivating job characteristically offers autonomy (personal responsibility and "ownership" of outcomes), task identity (closure and a chance to use valued abilities), sufficient variety, and feedback (from the task itself and from co-workers) (Miner, 1980, pp. 233-234).

Perhaps QWL can best be appreciated from the negative perspective. As a result of his study of the phenomenon of burnout, Robert Golembiewski has proposed a "fifth freedom" to add to Franklin D. Roosevelt's four freedoms: "freedom from noxious and stultifying worksites" (1988, p. 225). Consider the following:

In Indianapolis last January, management at the central [U.S. Postal Service] mail facility installed a glass cage in the middle of the mail room. Postal workers injured on the job were required to spend the day in the cage, rather than at home, and were not allowed even to read (Judis, 1988, p. 50).

The topsy-turvy shift schedules maintained by a majority of the nation's police departments are a detriment to the physical and mental health of officers, according to a prominent sleep researcher. . . . Such ill-planned shift patterns—characterized by frequent changes from day to night duties—can result in chronic fatigue, health problems, sleep disorders, a lowered quality of family life, and, even more dangerous for police officers, lapses in judgment and reduced levels of alertness ("Police Agencies," 1989, p. 1).

How do human needs relate to performance? Specifically, what can be done in the course of day-to-day operations that will cause workers to want to do a good job? In productivity terms, how can that unit of input, a day of labor, be managed so as to bring forth more and better output of service for the clientele?

Needs and desires function as motivators to action. Here is the creative tension: A worker must perceive that productivity offers a path to a personal goal (Miner, 1980, p. 135), to a reward contingent upon behavior. Two conditions inhere in this statement. First, a "reward" *is* a "reward" only if it is something the worker desires and values; beauty, here, is truly in the eye of the beholder. Second, the person being motivated must see the link between behavior and reward; the expectation must exist that the reward is achievable.

There is a powerful implication here. Improving worker productivity is contingent upon making the work more rewarding. Productivity improvement and human satisfaction are directly related. They are not antithetical, myths to the contrary.

Motivators and Rewards

What, specifically, motivates people? Sixty years of study and a mountain of literature have shed some light on the process of motivation and the nature of motivators. The following discussion draws from a few basic and influential ideas.

A motivator is an inducement. Abraham Maslow is famous for having suggested (1970) that all human motivators can be grouped into five classes and that these classes fall into a natural hierarchy, a ladder of needs, so that each rung becomes operational as long as the more basic needs are fulfilled. The most basic motivator is physiological satisfaction—food, water, bodily needs. Without these, nothing else matters. Once these are satisfied, a second type of motivator comes into play—the desire for security, for safety. Next in the hierarchy come the social desire to belong, then a desire for esteem, and, highest of all, the desire to actualize oneself —to grow, to influence, to exercise autonomy.

In contemporary terms, the linkage between QWL and improved quality of services hinges on this highest motivator. Only with some power to make decisions—as a function of an enriched job or as part of a participative management system, such as a task force or labor-management committee —can workers bring to bear their insights and ideas on the nature of the service.

Maslow's classification of motivators provides a convenient framework for examining workplace reward systems.

Money as Motivator

The most basic, physiological needs, such as the need for food, clothing, and shelter, are satisfied through money. We capture this linguistically when we say that we "earn our living." The earliest priority of organized labor was "a living wage."

The regular paycheck, coming in constant size and frequency, regardless of performance, does not motivate productivity. Monetary rewards are effective only if they are contingent upon performance.

Merit Increases. Automatic annual increases in pay may reward longevity, but they do not motivate performance. Quite the opposite: The highly productive junior worker may be demoralized by the inequity of being paid no more than an incompetent but senior worker.

Tying pay to performance is a straightforward and obvious step in encouraging productive performance and in introducing equity into the system. In point of fact, however, "pay for performance has been shown to be very problematic in the federal sector. . . . Inadequate or ineffective performance appraisal can be a real barrier to having a pay for performance system" (Cohen-Rosenthal & Burton, 1987, p. 225).

Aside from the practical problem of how to appraise performance fairly, there is another disadvantage to systems of pay for individual performance. Individual rewards undermine teamwork and the development of productivity as a group norm. Group rewards encourage the sharing of know-how, mutual help, and the transfer of competitiveness from the individual to the group level.

Piecework. The scientific management system relied on payment for each unit of work produced to motivate higher worker output. That principle underlies the introduction of public sector piecework incentive programs such as the one in the Electronic Data Processing Unit of Pennsylvania's Bureau of Employment Security:

The piecework plan was originally installed to counter the effects of a shrinking supply of job applicants and a high turnover of personnel. . . . A quota of 115,000 wage records per quarter per employee was established. . . . For production in excess of this standard, a bonus at the rate of 32 cents per 10 wage records is awarded. Quality is controlled through a penalty for errors. . . .

The plan is reported to have: substantially increased production; permitted deadlines to be met on or before schedule; reduced turnover to a bare minimum; rendered absenteeism practically nonexistent; reduced needed training; led to the hiring of more highly qualified trainees; provided a capability to absorb more work (Sweeny, 1978, pp. 30-32).

However, because piecework plans "can only be used in cases where work can be defined and measured in unit terms" (Morley, 1986, p. 120), they are of limited applicability to the public sector.

Bonuses. Monetary rewards may take the form of bonuses for superior group or individual performance. Generally, some source of special funding is necessary. The states of North Carolina and Kansas have pioneered in the use of public sector employee bonus systems (Jarrett, 1981). Local governments use them as well:

In addition to Pay for Performance, Scottsdale [Arizona] offers cash bonuses to employees at all ranks for outstanding performance. The city recently paid a $200 bonus to an alert secretary, who realized the city was being deliberately double-billed; and another $200 to each of two detectives who performed a brilliant apprehension of criminals. And the city is now preparing to institute Gain Sharing . . . whereby up to 4% of a department's cash savings from productivity improvements is rebated to employees as salary (Hayes, 1989, p. 260).

To be effective, bonus systems do not have to be large or very formal:

The purpose of the staff incentive program is twofold: to express appreciation to Building 27's direct-care staff for the superb and sensitive care they presently provide the children, and to gently prompt everyone to strive for even higher standards of excellence in their everyday job performance.

As an integral part of the program, many parents of Building 27's children have generously contributed tickets to sporting events, theaters, free restaurant meals, and prizes . . . to be awarded to either individual staff members or the entire direct-care staff on a specific ward for outstanding job performance. To determine the victor, several criteria will be evaluated by means of a comprehensive checklist: care and appearance of the children, cleanliness and aesthetic enrichment of the environment, and completion of required paperwork ("Staff Incentive," 1981).

Bonus systems can be used toward other ends, such as containing organizational health plan costs ("The Human Factor," 1982) or reducing absenteeism.

Gain Sharing. Under this arrangement, workers receive a share of the dollar savings achieved by a productivity improvement to which they have contributed. It provides an answer to the question, "What's in it for me?"

The workers' contribution may be limited to a specific function, as when the city of Lake Charles, Louisiana, "agreed to share with the employees any savings generated by the workman's compensation insurance refunds which would result from reduced accident rates" (Sweeny, 1978, p. 36). Or the contribution may be general:

> A shared savings plan, in which everyone at one [Forest Service] forest shared in the financial savings resulting from efficiencies achieved through the pilot. The decision was to share 2 percent of such savings with the employees; all employees received an equal amount. At this forest, a total of $177,000 was saved in the first year (Linden, 1990, p. 60).

The contribution may have been worker suggestions for improvement:

> Phoenix, Arizona, lets employees keep 10 percent of any earnings or savings their suggestions generate, up to a maximum of $2,500 per employee (Osborne, 1992).

Or it may have come in the form of a labor contract concession:

> The need for productivity improvement had been acknowledged by the union and its advisors in the 1975 collective bargaining agreement signed at the height of the fiscal crisis. They agreed to jointly work with the department towards productivity enhancing techniques with the understanding that there would be some sharing of the resultant savings. . . .
>
> Under the terms of the agreement, each crew member of a two-man truck received an $11 payment for each truck shift worked, as long as one-for-one replacement for rear loaders was maintained. . . . With all 450 trucks in use with two-man crews, annual savings were approximately $13.6 million, of

which $2.4 million were returned to the crew members (Steisel, 1984, pp. 122-124).

As these examples show, the reward may come in the form of fixed bonuses or cash percentages of the savings. Managers may be rewarded with discretion over some portion of unexpended funds. Gain sharing is by its nature inapplicable to those productivity improvements that achieve more or better outputs without a reduction in costs. But wherever the innovation results in dollars saved and a share of that savings returns to the contributor in some form, gain sharing is taking place.

Special Awards. Exemplary individual, group, or agency performance can be encouraged and publicized by the awarding of special prizes. These may be funded from various sources, including governments, private individuals, civic groups, schools, centers, and foundations. They range in magnitude from modest cash prizes to individual employees to the "most prestigious" program under which ten $100,000 Innovations Awards are given annually by the Ford Foundation and Harvard University's Kennedy School of Government (Shanahan, 1991, p. 36).

The Exemplary State and Local Awards Program (EXSL), sponsored by the National Center for Public Productivity (NCPP) and the William C. Norris Institute, is specifically designed to reward productivity improvement. It "recognizes outstanding public sector projects and programs that have produced significant cost savings, measurable increases in productivity, and improvements in the quality and effectiveness of government services" (National Center for Public Productivity, 1991).

New York City provides an example of a municipal awards program to recognize individual excellence:

> For the 18th successive year, New York's municipal establishment assembles to pay homage to six public servants who light up the city they so unstintingly serve. That payment, made manifest by a day and evening of public acclaim and an award to each star of $5,000, is by now a firmly rooted civic rite. . . .
>
> The guidelines that mold the Sloan Public Service Awards competition and inform the Selection Panel are:
>   —Extraordinary work delivered with energy, ingenuity and compassion. . . .
>   —Willingness to put reputation and chances of promotion on the line, if necessary, to improve services or correct abuses and inequities;

—Responsiveness to public needs by cutting through red tape and developing more effective methods of service delivery; and
—Outstanding and reliable performance, both in situations of crisis and under the formidable pressures of daily routine ("Six Bright Stars," 1990, pp. 1-2).

Security as Motivator

In the workplace, workers may be prey to fears of job loss, helplessness in the face of exploitation, physical injury, and vulnerability to illness or old age. Most fundamentally, workers fear that productivity improvement means firings. Before anything else can be done by way of productivity improvement, therefore, this fear must be allayed. Credible reassurances must be made that, while people will be involved in changes—including possible reassignment, retraining, or both—no one will be fired as part of a productivity improvement plan. For this reason, attrition is often used to achieve necessary cutbacks.

Dorothy Riddle (1988) has pointed out that an employee's concern for security can undercut good service. "Since human circumstances seldom conform neatly to outlined procedures, there are bound to be many times when 'fair treatment' or basic survival of the client necessitates a bending, or creative reinterpretation, of the rules [. . . . But] while fair treatment of clients may help ensure job retention, the best insurance is an absolute conformity to procedures" (p. 196). Giving the worker greater autonomy can provide some relief from this bind.

In addition to job security, other security benefits can serve as inducements. Workers may agree to a new work schedule, for example, in exchange for additional medical coverage, funded from part of the savings. Improved benefits may not mean greater coverage, but they may mean different coverage: individualized "cafeteria" plans, for example, permitting each employee to tailor a personally preferred set of benefits from a "menu."

For some areas of the public service, physical safety is a significant security concern. Cooperation in a productivity improvement effort may be inspired by the desire for things such as bulletproof glass for token booths, new safety clothing for fire fighters, or better security for night workers.

Belonging as Motivator

People want to belong, to feel accepted and valued. For people with strong social needs, this is a prime motivator; whom they work with is more important than precisely what they do. For everyone, personal interactions and group identity help bind them to the large, abstract organization. To appreciate the importance of belonging, consider the severity of punishment inflicted by hostility, harassment, or the "silent treatment."

Workgroup. The workgroup is more than the sum of its parts. The group affords sympathy, a safe place to vent feelings, a sounding board for ideas, and a general feeling that one is not alone. It is a way of sharing risk and experiencing some power. In considering productivity improvements, the function of the group should not be overlooked, whether in dealing with existing groups or creating new ones.

One misgiving that underlies resistance to change is the fear that a congenial workgroup will be broken up. Like the fear of firings, this should be dealt with. If groups will remain intact, that reassurance is needed. If people are to be reshuffled, an effort should be made to ensure that individuals with strong social needs will be placed with congenial co-workers. The promise that one will be able to work with a friend may sustain a conservative individual through substantial changes.

New groups can be created to activate these social forces and this source of motivation:

> Bloomington, Minnesota, divided its 36-man police force into six teams, each consisting of five patrolmen and one supervisor. Each team works as a unit, with the same schedules and shifts, duties, and days off. Team policing is reported to have increased morale and enthusiasm. Patrolmen now feel part of a unit (Sweeny, 1978, pp. 38- 39).

Social Interaction. The right to interact and opportunities to do so are social rewards. Work is a sociotechnical phenomenon. Part of the inhumanity of the assembly line as an organizational form is that it inhibits or precludes social interaction. A change that produces efficiencies will be more likely to succeed if workers perceive in it the chance to obtain opportunities for eating, exercising, or relaxing together. For example, a concession will probably get more support if workers hope for a lounge or bowling alley from a piece of the savings.

Quality circles, task forces, and similar vehicles motivate at more than one level. Their chief virtue is that they provide some autonomy, but they also satisfy social needs by providing a legitimate forum for exchange and interaction among workers. Any delegation of decision making to a group becomes a reward of social needs because group decisions require discussion, debate, and sometimes the excitement of high political drama.

Employee Assistance Programs. At the individual level, troubled workers need support if they are to overcome personal problems and uncertainties that undercut their performance and undermine productivity. The State of Florida once estimated that of its 30,000 employees, at least 3,000 formed an "at risk" population, "people with medical or behavioral problems sufficiently severe to hamper their effectiveness" (U.S. Office of Personnel Management, 1981, p. 4). Employee assistance programs are often used to help such workers in coping with substance abuse and financial, legal, marital, psychological, and other problems. These programs operate confidentially, providing either in-house counseling or, more often, referrals to outside agencies.

> Wagner has worked closely with Project Concern, the City of Phoenix EAP, since 1974. He claims that in 1980 alone 1,130 of the city's 8,700 employees received some form of counseling through the program and that approximately half of these (565) "returned to full productivity." . . . The $2.4 million saved represents a handsome return on an annual investment of $58,200 to operate Project Concern (Zemke, 1983, p. 46).

The savings come from lowered accidents, errors, unproductive time, quarrels, and grievances. "Based on a formula developed by the U.S. Postal Service and United Technologies, a successful treatment [for alcoholism] can produce up to one-fourth of a participant's salary" (Uranek, 1981, p. 81).

EAPs offer another benefit that springs from an analysis of patterns: "[I]nformation about recurring 'personal' issues in the workplace may provide important clues for needed organizational change, health hazards, or other ways the structure exacerbates personal difficulties" (Cohen-Rosenthal & Burton, 1987, p. 101).

Family Responsibilities. The incidence of one-parent families and the entry of increasing numbers of women into the work force has made child care an important issue. Day care for children, provided at the worksite, offers parents conveniently located, reliable, professional child care, relieving those working parents of anxiety and reducing the need to stay home from work because child care arrangements have broken down.

On a voluntary basis or as a legal requirement, employers are also moving toward permitting workers to take some weeks of unpaid leave when a child is born or when a member of the family suffers a serious health problem and needs attending.

Mentoring. An employee's sense of "belonging" is reinforced by the perception that he or she is valued by the organization and has help and guidance at hand.

A managerial practice in Japan suggests a simple but potentially important innovation. It costs nothing and can be institutionalized at a slow or fast pace as desired. The Japanese assign every new employee to an "Uncle," a senior, usually higher-ranking, member of the organization, to whom the employee can go personally for advice and counsel, much as a college student goes to a faculty advisor. This mentor does not intervene directly to advance the career of the employee but does help the individual in solving problems and setting career goals.

The significance of mentoring is indicated by a study finding that "the public executive who had had a mentor attained an executive position at a younger age and made an average of over 11 percent more than the executive who had never had a mentor" (Henderson, 1985, p. 861).

Status as Motivator

First, people want to be accepted; then they want to "rate." Recognition is a reward; knowing that nothing you do will be acknowledged discourages effort.

Esteem takes two forms: external recognition and self-regard. Marks of respect convey external recognition. Symbols are important: Everyone knows what it means to have a top-floor, corner office with a view, large desk, and carpeting on the floor. The wrist watch awarded for 25 years of service, the stripe on the sleeve, the new title, the picture in the agency newspaper—all bestow recognition symbolically. It is common to dismiss these verbally, but, as the case at the end of Chapter 10 shows, they *are* valued as rewards.

The cash bonus awards discussed earlier also provide the reward of recognition—in the form of an award ceremony, receptions, and coverage in general and in-house media. The recognition alone is a reward:

> Missouri initiated an Employee-of-the-Month program in which employees are nominated by their peers and selected by a central committee for their "extra efforts." No financial awards are provided, but the selected employees receive substantial recognition and publicity including a meeting with the governor. Massachusetts also recently began a similar recognition program, but again with rewards limited to a small percentage (1 percent) of employees (Poister, Hatry, Fisk, & Greiner, 1985, p. 15).

Money, security, social ties, and recognition are important needs that can be fulfilled as rewards for individual or group performance in the many ways we have just seen. But far and away the most important motivator in terms of direct consequences for service quality, as well as efficiency, is worker empowerment. In the next chapter we will examine some ways of satisfying the desire for self-actualization—autonomy, discretion, and a role in decision making—as a means toward energizing the worker and reaping the benefits of worker perceptions and ideas.

References

Accordino, J. J. (1989). Quality-of-working-life systems in large cities: An assessment. *Public Productivity Review, 12*, 345-360.

Ammons, D. N. (1991). *Administrative analysis for local government: Practical application of selected techniques.* Athens: Carl Vinson Institute of Government, University of Georgia.

Anders-Michalski, J. (1981, January 15). Navy links performance to pay in trial project. *PA Times*, pp. 1, 4.

Balfour, D. L., & Wechsler, B. (1991). Commitment, performance, and productivity in public organizations. *Public Productivity & Management Review, 14*, 355-367.

Burns, T., & Stalker, G. M. (1978). Mechanistic and organic systems. In J. M. Shafritz & P. H. Whitbeck (Eds.), *Classics of organization theory* (pp. 207-211). Oak Park, IL: Moore.

Campbell, J. (1984). Japanese public bureaucracy: Lessons? *Public Productivity Review, 8*, 135-138.

Carr, A. F. (1988). Utility analysis and human resources management. *Public Productivity Review, 12*, 131-147.

Chisholm, R. F. (1983). Quality of working life: Critical issues for the 1980s. *Public Productivity Review, 7*, 10-25.

Cohen-Rosenthal, E., & Burton, C. E. (1987). *Mutual gains: A guide to union-management cooperation.* New York: Praeger.

Federal employee quality has declined, survey says. (1991, July 1). *PA Times*, p. 6.

Golembiewski, R. T. (1988). Policy initiatives in worksite research: Implications from research on a phase model of burnout. In R. M. Kelly (Ed.), *Promoting productivity in the public sector: Problems, strategies and prospects* (pp. 209-227). New York: St. Martin's.

Hayes, E. C. (Ed.). (1989). *The hidden wealth of cities: Policy and productivity methods for American local governments.* Greenwich, CT: JAI.

Henderson, D. (1985). Enlightened mentoring: A characteristic of public management professionalism. *Public Administration Review, 45*, 857-863.

The human factor: Caging the health-cost beast. (1982). *Productivity, 3*, 7.

Jarrett, J. E. (1981). *Improving productivity through monetary incentives: North Carolina's bonus experiment.* Lexington, KY: Council of State Governments.

Judis, J. B. (1988, September 25). U.S. mail: Mission impossible. *New York Times Magazine*, pp. 30-33, 50-51, 54.

Kanter, R. M. (1981). Forces for work improvement in the public sector. *QWL Review, 1*, 3-8.

Lawler, E. E., III, & Ledford, G. E., Jr. (1981-82). Productivity and the quality of work life. *National Productivity Review*, *1*, 23-36.

Linden, R. M. (1990). *From vision to reality: Strategies of successful innovators in government*. Charlottesville, VA: LEL Enterprises.

Lorinskas, R. (1984). Dealing with organizational stress. In D. B. Kalinich & T. Pitcher (Eds.), *Surviving in corrections: A guide for corrections professionals* (pp. 146-158). Springfield, IL: Charles C Thomas.

Mansell, J., & Rankin, T. (1983). *Changing organizations: The quality of working life process*. Toronto, Canada: Ontario Quality of Working Life Centre.

Maslow, A. (1970). *Motivation and personality* (2nd ed.). New York: Harper & Row.

McLeod, D. (1991, November). Mixed signals stymie enrollees: New benefit hits bump. *AARP Bulletin*, pp. 6-7.

Miner, J. (1980). *Theories of organizational behavior*. Hinsdale, IL: Dryden.

Morley, E. (1986). *A practitioner's guide to public sector productivity improvement*. Malabar, FL: Krieger.

National Center for Productivity and Quality of Working Life. (1977). Productivity and job security: Retraining to adapt to technological change. In M. Holzer, E. D. Rosen, & C. Zalk, *Local Government Productivity* (pp. 131-139). Washington, DC: Academy in the Public Service, Georgetown University Graduate School.

National Center for Public Productivity. (1991, August). National Center for Public Productivity seeks nominations for the 1991 Exemplary State and Local Awards. Advertisement in *Governing*, p. 87.

The control room that didn't control [New York Times editorial]. (1981). In M. Holzer & E. D. Rosen (Eds.), *Current cases in public administration* (pp. 88-89). New York: Harper & Row.

Osborne, D. (1992, May). How to turn a bureaucracy into a profit center. *Governing*, p. 63.

Phillips, J. J. (1981, July). How cross-training leads to effective on-the-job development. *Training/HRD*, pp. 35-37.

Poister, T. H., Hatry, H. P., Fisk, D. M., & Greiner, J. M. (1985). Centralized productivity improvement efforts in state government. *Public Productivity Review*, *9*, 5-24.

Police agencies said to be asleep at the wheel in designing shifts. (1989, October 15). *Law Enforcement News*, pp. 1, 21.

Riddle, D. I. (1988). Public sector productivity and role conflicts. In R. M. Kelly (Ed.), *Promoting productivity in the public sector: Problems, strategies and prospects* (pp. 191-208). New York: St. Martin's.

Roll, J. L., & Roll, D. L. (1983). The potential for application of quality circles in the American public sector. *Public Productivity Review*, *7*, 122-142.

Schwartz, J. (1991, September 30). Facing the human factor: High tech isn't AT&T's biggest problem. *Newsweek*, p. 48.

Shafritz, J. M., Hyde, A. C., & Rosenbloom, D. H. (1986). *Personnel management in government* (3rd ed.). New York: Marcel Dekker.

Shanahan, E. (1991, October). The mysteries of innovative government. *Governing*, pp. 35-47.

Six bright stars: Another lustrous year in the public service. (1990). *Public Papers of the Fund for the City of New York*, *9*, 1-8.

Staff incentive program underway. (1981, July). *Thursday's Child* (Suffolk Developmental Center, Melville, NY), p. 8.

Stahl, O. G. (1983). *Public Personnel Administration* (8th ed.). New York: Harper & Row.

Steisel, N. (1984). Productivity in the New York City Department of Sanitation: The role of the public sector manager. *Public Productivity Review*, *8*, 103-126.

Study links conviction to arrest technique. (1981, April 1). *PA Times*, p. 3.

Sweeny, M. (1978, July). *Development of incentive systems for worker productivity*. Unpublished memorandum, New Jersey Department of Civil Service.

Taylor, F. W. (1978). The principles of scientific management. In J. M. Shafritz & P. H. Whitbeck (Eds.), *Classics of organization theory* (pp. 9-23). Oak Park, IL: Moore.

Toffler, A. (1970). *Future shock*. New York: Bantam.

Uranek, W. (1981). Providing assistance to state employees. *Public Productivity Review, 5*, 80-82.

U.S. Office of Personnel Management. (1981). *People and productivity*. (IPP 152-107). Washington, DC: Government Printing Office.

Vocino, T., & Rabin, J. (1981). *Contemporary public administration*. Orlando, FL: Harcourt Brace Jovanovich.

Wanous, J. P. (1973). Effects of a realistic job preview on job acceptance, job attitudes, and job survival. *Journal of Applied Psychology, 58*, 327-332.

Weber, M. (1987). Bureaucracy. In J. M. Shafritz & A. C. Hyde (Eds.), *Classics of public administration* (2nd ed.) (pp. 50-55). Homewood, IL: Dorsey.

Zemke, R. (1983, March). Should supervisors be counselors? *Training/HRD*, pp. 44-46, 48, 50, 53.

8

Empowering the Worker

It is paradoxical that what is probably the most effective motivator of worker productivity is also the most difficult to document. It is easy to demonstrate in dollar terms the profit from rewarding workers for suggestions or concessions with a share of the savings. The benefit of an employee assistance program or child care program can be shown through the dollar value of reduced absenteeism, accidents, and turnover. These programs are relatively clear-cut, installed relatively quickly, and produce their effects within a relatively short time.

But the highest motivator—the self-actualization of the individual worker—requires a psychological turnaround for workers and management alike. It takes time and consistency of purpose to overcome skepticism, evoke and then reinforce new behaviors, and create new mechanisms and a new culture in which the worker is free to participate as a legitimate element in managing operations and making decisions. Worker morale takes time to build. The impact of worker participation—on the quality of decisions, the quality of services, and client satisfaction—is not immediately evident.

Empowerment of the worker is impelled, then, not so much by objectively demonstrable payoffs as by its promise as a solution to more immediate problems of public dissatisfaction with public services and the demoralization of the public sector work force. It proceeds on the basis of some hard evidence that there is, indeed, a work ethic and a desire to serve, that team building and a sense of ownership raise morale and improve performance, and that workers have a valuable contribution to make, if only allowed the authority to do so.

"Participative management is based on studies such as those completed at the University of Michigan's Survey Research Center in 1969 which showed that *all* of a sample of 1,533 workers interviewed ranked interesting work and personal authority far ahead of good pay and job security" (Chandler & Plano, 1982, p. 136). Research over the years consistently demonstrates that public sector employees differ from private sector employees, *not* in being stereotypically "lazy, indolent, security-conscious and 'bureaucratic' " but in terms of "work-related values, reward preferences, needs, and personality types" (Wittmer, 1991, p. 369). Public workers place a high value on service:

> [Research] . . . generally supports the view that public managers value financial rewards less and social or public service more than their private sector counterparts. . . .
> Such findings lend empirical support to the hypothesis that there is indeed a service ethic among government employees and managers, whether such differences result from the personal characteristics of those selecting public service or from socialization and organization culture (Wittmer, 1991, pp. 371-372).

But public workers also feel relatively ineffective:

> The results raise some particular concerns about public managers, who were lower on job satisfaction, on the questions about impact on important activities and about making a difference. . . . The results suggest somewhat greater problems with discouragement (Falcone, 1991, p. 395).

Like managers, workers have long been frustrated. They feel undervalued and underutilized:

Public servants take a beating from the press and are held in contempt by their neighbors. To their neighbors and the public, the idea of working for government has a negative association—as though employees are cheating them either in taking too much of their tax money, or giving too little effort, or both. . . .

No one is really concerned about the worker and his input. . . . Productivity is co-determination with labor and management really working together on a job and moving together. We don't have that and we aren't even touching that yet (Gotbaum & Handman, 1978, p. 19).

Workers yearn for, and benefit from, more autonomy:

One often hears about the "autonomy" teachers have in their classroom, but most teachers realize that it is a limited autonomy, that all of the decisions and policies outside of their control eventually find their way into the classroom, impinge upon that autonomy, and profoundly limit or expand a teacher's ability to do a good job. . . . As a result, in my opinion, not only have teachers been robbed of a full expression of their professional abilities, but the schools and our students have been denied the full benefits of their expertise. . . .

[Since the introduction of participative management], there has been a tremendous release of energy and creativity. It's true what they say about this sense of ownership, it's very powerful. When people really believe that what they think, what they say, what they do will make a difference, they take hold, they make things happen, they look for what needs changing and they change it, be it in the system or in themselves ("Shared Decision Making," 1987, p. 46).

Individual Self-Actualization

It is useful to think of worker autonomy in two senses, both of them capable of being bestowed by the power of the organization. The first sense focuses on making each individual's role more autonomous through job enrichment and by provision of opportunities for career advancement. The second sense of increasing worker autonomy concerns workers as a class through provision of mechanisms that allow members of the work force to participate in management and decision making. We start with consideration of the individual worker's role.

Job Redesign

We have already studied how jobs may be redesigned from the standpoint of the work to make the production process more rational. Now let us consider the subject from the standpoint of the worker.

First, it is important to realize that some jobs should not be enriched, because they already demand too much of the worker—too much stimulus, interaction, frustration. Burnout is real, and we know some things about it (Golembiewski, 1988, pp. 210-224, passim): It is measurable, progressive, and prevalent. It affects "people-helpers" and goes through phases, starting with the depersonalization of others, to a low sense of personal accomplishment, and on to emotional exhaustion. Demographics such as gender, age, and rank account for little variance. Golembiewski has cautioned against applying to such workers the kinds of job enrichment and organizational changes that we will be discussing (1988, pp. 221-222); their first need is a low-stimulus job design, perhaps one permitting periodic escape from stress by rotating "from high-contact to low-contact aspects of service provision" (Riddle, 1988, p. 204).

The phenomenon of burnout provides some lessons on the relationship between employee satisfaction and the quality of service. Caught between concern for the client's needs and a work structure that cannot be made responsive to those needs, the increasingly frustrated worker, as a matter of self-protection, becomes turned off. The client receives uncaring, pedestrian attention. The worker who feels unavailing sees no hope of organizational improvement. These workers are the walking wounded, and improvements will have to be done without them, at least until they recover.

For many public employees, however, the job offers too little scope, opportunity, and autonomy. To counter this, the job enrichment approach makes a presumption in favor of reversing tradition and leaving as much power as possible in the hands of those at the bottom of the hierarchy. Jobs may be enriched by introducing self-management, by giving the individual worker or small work team responsibility for seeing an entire piece of work through and deciding how the work is to proceed. Control is achieved not through adherence to procedure but through performance. For example, custodial work performed at night is difficult to supervise: A task system ensures that a standard night's work is done to specification by rewarding the worker with permission to go home when it passes inspection (Ammons, 1991, p. 63).

Xenia, Ohio's experience illustrates the use of measured work standards in designing a task system for sanitation workers. This approach is finding increasing use in local government. . . .

Under the task system collection crews are paid for eight hours work, even if their routes are completed in less time. The quality of collection is monitored by two inspectors and supervisory personnel. Both management and labor appear satisfied with the plan (Sweeny, 1978, p. 42).

The opportunity to select an alternative work schedule and the right to take unpaid leave in time of family emergency also afford the worker increased discretion and autonomy.

Career Development

The traditional attitude toward hiring has been that someone is needed to fill a job—period. The worker is seen as a job occupant, and the job is seen as an end in itself. There are many dead-end jobs in the public sector. Kanter and Stein have identified seven ways that people get stuck (1981, pp. 46-47):

- They may be on a very short ladder (as secretary or scientist, for example);
- they arrived through an unorthodox career path (parachuted from another unit or advanced in one specialty; there is no way to cross to another ladder);
- they have been squeezed by the organizational pyramid shape (which affects older employees not chosen for upper positions);
- they are caught in promotion freezes because of the economy;
- they are getting discouraging messages from managers;
- they see no role models; and
- they act stuck (dreaming, gossiping, or griping).

The organization is more likely to attract and retain people with initiative and drive if the worker is seen as more than filling one role and is seen instead as a recruit who—for his or her own sake and that of the organization—should be developed and helped to advance to new positions. There should be clear built-in opportunities for advancement:

The ideal relationship between people and productivity is one where there is a primary effort toward creating productive opportunities, appropriately recognizing those who grasp these opportunities, and building career pathways that are open to the extent they foster job enrichment and enlargement (Beckman, 1979, p. 1).

Providing Career Paths

Some of the causes of being stuck can be eliminated by developing career paths.

> If an organization wants to establish new career ladders where there are dead ends, it may *restructure* the work so that the dead-ended positions include new duties and responsibilities that will prepare the employees to move into higher level[s] and more rewarding jobs. In some situations, the result may be a new kind of position that contains elements of both the old and new jobs. In effect, it is a bridge from one to the other (U.S. Civil Service Commission, 1976, p. 15).

The rules may be changed so that, for example, the only way to a job with the parks department is through several years' service with the sanitation department. Clerks may be offered the opportunity to learn secretarial or computer skills with particular jobs in mind. Through cross-training or job rotation, other workers may learn new skills, making them good candidates for specific openings when senior employees retire.

> Inglewood, California, has a career development program for sanitation employees. The city hires only high school graduates and helps them find appropriate slots for in-house training or college courses. The city pays tuition costs. The program has produced a cadre of young, ambitious refuse collectors who work efficiently and move up the career ladder to skilled jobs in other city departments. Benefits are high morale by the sanitation department, excellent service given to the citizens, and a favorable image of the city because of the impressions created by some of its most visible employees (Sweeny, 1978, pp. 44-45).

Another option is available for those caught in the realities of remaining in rank because there are not as many higher-level opportunities as lower-level people or because promotions have been frozen. A dual career ladder system affords two kinds of opportunity to advance: (1) traditional upward promotion and (2) advancement in grade—to better rewards and distinguishing titles in recognition of continuing progress *within rank*. At the end of this chapter, one such system for police officers will be described, chosen because it illustrates the use of many motivators for improving worker satisfaction and enhancing organizational productivity.

Reshaping Attitudes

Some of the barriers to upward progress are attitudinal and can be removed by education, career counseling, and guidance. Workers need to be shown how to prepare for possible advancement through retraining, transitional positions, and other avenues. They may need encouragement, the opportunity to speak with models—people who are like them and who have achieved such positions. They need to be told when they are behaving like losers. Supervisors need to know that their success in developing and advancing the people under them is regarded as an indication of good performance.

Finally, if opportunities for advancement are few, the organization can reduce the demotivating sense of relative lack of status by downplaying symbols of advanced rank and reminding workers that "up is not the only way to grow" (Kanter & Stein, 1981, p. 48). Workers can be advised, for example, that service on a task force or other participative management committee not only provides a way to exert influence, but also can be used as an opportunity to be seen by new people and in a new light. Older workers trapped in the pyramid may find this a satisfying activity and probably have a lot to contribute.

Participative Management

Autonomy comes in several shapes. It may take the form of job enrichment, with greater personal freedom to perform duties in accordance with internalized preferences as to methods and priorities: a sort of "freedom from" being micromanaged.

A different form of autonomy comes as "freedom to"—the power to participate in making decisions over the work and working life. Unionization and the collective bargaining process gave U.S. workers some leverage as a class in protecting their common interests but did not extend to industrial democracy and worker roles on governing boards (as it did in Europe). In recent years, however, participative management programs have begun to expand the decision process in various ways, opening it up to include workers in what had once been management's exclusive domain.

Participative management has several mechanisms, including suggestion systems, task forces, joint labor-management committees, and quality circles. These vehicles may be temporary or permanent, localized or organization-wide. What they have in common is a formal procedure for worker input to decisions about the work and the "product."

Benefits for the Workplace

The point has already been made that there exists evidence, if not proof, of the organizational benefits to be derived from participative management. Greater worker satisfaction should result in lower absenteeism, less turnover, and fewer grievances. To the extent that workers are in touch with production problems that become addressable when a worker participation program provides the leverage for bringing them forward, participation results in greater organizational efficiency through cutting waste, spotting roadblocks and bottlenecks, correcting poor procedures, and avoiding problems attributable to lack of understanding or training on the part of workers. The quality of services is improved by a strengthened sense of purpose and esprit de corps.

Better decisions result from better knowledge of client needs and a better grasp of organizational capacities:

> The labor team becomes an extension of the chief operating officer, because now their eyes and ears are his eyes and ears. He is not a captive of his bureaucracy, because he knows exactly what is going on. The information isn't manipulated on the way up or on the way down (Benton, Contino, Grace, Sullivan, & White, 1989, pp. 109-110).

A New Organizational Culture

The advent of participative management represents a step into a new organizational culture. It is not the "bureaucratic" culture that emphasizes structure and process; it is not simply the "supportive" culture that befriends the worker; it is an "innovative" culture. "Innovativeness refers to a creative, results-oriented, challenging work environment" (Odom, Boxx, & Dunn, 1990, p. 158). As we will see in Chapter 10, this culture is important in times of change. In the words of Enid Beaumont, president of the American Society for Public Administration: "The more change in the environment, the more important it is for organizations to innovate. The code words now include responsiveness, creativity, diversity, adaptation and change" (1991).

An innovative culture emphasizes communication based on who has the expertise and who needs to know. Hierarchical position becomes less important than the situational context. The locus of expertise shifts according to the type of information needed: one moment the expert is the computer person, the next it may be the training expert or the fieldworker. The neat vertical and lateral communication patterns of the bureaucratic organization give way to an untidy network.

In an innovative culture, results are central, and performance is measured. Feedback is important, the source often being the workers in direct contact with the client. Measurement is important, and everyone needs to learn to use solid information in making judgments.

An innovative culture is participative, and that participation must be both real and mainstream (Accordino, 1989, p. 355).

> People will accept change more readily if they are involved in the decision-making process where the change is created. This involvement enables employees to increase their awareness of the problem, their understanding of the new procedure, and their commitment to its successful implementation.
>
> Still another reason for using group [decision making] is the need for creative solutions for complex new problems. It is a fact that groups are significantly more creative in [problem solving] than individuals working alone (Burton, 1986, p. 133).

For this to work, managers need to learn to listen to workers and be ready to approve actions they would not have undertaken toward goals they might not have given priority. Workers need to gain the skills to work in creative groups and analyze problems; they need to gain the confidence to talk to power. Everyone needs to learn to use solid information in making judgments, and workers are included in the development of measurement systems. "The key factor is to involve those who are controlled by a norm to change the norm itself" (Blake & Mouton, 1981, p. 75).

An innovative culture is one in which everyone wins something. Savings are shared. Individuals and groups are coached and nurtured.

We have suggested that such radical change in culture does not happen overnight. Grafting a quality circle or other participative management system onto an incompatible cultural rootstock will not produce fruit. It is better, perhaps, to move incrementally, building changed attitudes and habits along with perceptible achievements. For that reason, stress will be placed here on the task force as an opening strategy: Much of the public work force may be moving beyond satisfaction with a suggestion system but not yet be ready for the formal quality circle or joint labor-management committee program.

Suggestion Systems

In the simplest terms, a suggestion system provides a formal way for employees to offer ideas to management—a way other than going through the chain of command. The limitations of the chain of command are obvious. Uninvited suggestions may be unwelcome, and superiors may construe suggestions as criticism or take credit themselves for good ideas. The existence of a suggestion system legitimizes the suggestion, puts it before a wider audience, and credits the author.

For the individual making the suggestion, the system provides the satisfaction of being able to express concerns and influence decisions. Because most systems provide awards for approved suggestions, money and recognition are added to the rewards for participation. For the organization, it conveys an assurance that it values the worker's opinions while evoking new ideas for ways to save money and improve operations:

> The first employee to win a $10,000 cash award for a suggestion, Lt. Tom Black, helped to improve the safety of officers in the city [Mesa, Arizona]. In 1988, Black suggested using a video arraignment system between the city court and city jail which would eliminate the need of police and detention officers to work the off-duty court detail. These officers transported prisoners back and forth between the city court and the jail, and were often paid overtime. Black's suggestion saved the Mesa Police department $74,334 (Desky, 1992, p. 3).

Suggestion systems originated more than 100 years ago in the private sector. In 1912, "legislation . . . authorized the secretary of war to pay cash awards to army ordinance shop workers who provided useful innovations" (Downey & Balk, 1976, p. 3). Federal use of suggestions grew so that "the Federal Incentives Awards Program showed tangible benefits for suggestions in 1972 . . . in excess of $200 million at the amazingly low cost of about $4.5 million in awards to suggesters" (Downey & Balk, 1976, p. 1). By 1985, 17 states had reported employee suggestion award systems (Poister, Hatry, Fisk, & Greiner, 1985, p. 14). Today, the majority of the members of the National Association of Suggestion Systems come from the public sector (Desky, 1992, p. 16).

The operation of a typical traditional suggestion system has been described by Downey and Balk (1976, Chapter 2). An employee submits a suggestion, usually on a special form and placed in a designated suggestion box. In different variations, the employee may or may not be identified by name. An administrator screens all suggestions for eligibility, and a committee then evaluates the suggestion and decides on acceptance and award. For cash savings, a percentage is commonly awarded. For example, New Jersey has awarded 10% of the first year's savings up to $5,000 (Sweeny, 1978, p. 4). In North Carolina, employees have also received as much as $5,000 as a percentage of first-year savings *or* taken their reward in the form of additional days off (Poister, Hatry, Fisk, & Greiner, 1985, p. 14). Suggestions yielding intangible benefits (those without monetary value) usually receive some fixed award.

Suggestion systems need not be limited to the suggestion box. The Crawford slip method has been developed for use in addressing particular problems. A relevant group is assembled; everyone writes one idea at a time on a single slip of paper. The papers are then collected, classified, and analyzed. The advantage of this system is that it creates focus and speed while preserving anonymity.

> A police sergeant and a professor teamed up to use CSM to improve police operations in a major city:
> They got slips from police on what they needed to be taught HOW TO DO in police work. Examples were: (a) How to broadcast for help while chasing a fleeing car. (b) How to check pickpockets in a crowd. Soon 4,000 police personnel were getting the fifteen-minute "lessons of the day" when they reported for work (Ballard & Trent, 1989, p. 382).

Hotlines constitute a kind of suggestion system that is open to the public. Employees have made particular use of these channels:

> [Texas Comptroller] Sharp had a toll-free hotline installed to allow Texans to call in with suggestions for saving money.
> To everyone's surprise, the calls poured in—more than 4,000 in the first 20 days. While callers could remain anonymous, Sharp says the suggestions were so detailed that it was obvious that most calls were coming from inside government. They were mainly from mid- and lower-level employees. . . . These people, [says Sharp], "know more than anyone about what would help them do their jobs better, but they had never before been asked. We asked" (Sylvester, 1992).

The Coral Springs, Florida, Personnel Department provides a special telephone hotline for employees who want to make anonymous suggestions (International City Management Association, 1990, PRM-23).

Suggestion systems are an excellent channel for eliciting individual perspectives and ideas. What they lack is the satisfaction of social interaction and the benefit of shaping ideas through multiple perspectives and group discussion. These are provided by task forces, quality circles, and joint labor-management committees.

Task Forces

A task force is a temporary group convened for a particular purpose, such as solving one problem or developing one system, and then disbanded after the task has been accomplished. When the task force comprises volunteer workers in whole or in part, it becomes a vehicle for participative management, for empowering workers by giving them a role and a voice in making decisions that affect them.

In general, the need for a task force is initiated by a management announcement that sets forth the situation and calls for volunteers. A leader is chosen by the membership or may be designated from above. The group investigates its task and proceeds, in relative independence, to identify a solution. A task force may be used to plan a new system (such as new technology or a productivity measurement system) or to solve an old problem (such as turnover). When the task calls for it, the task force may represent more than one agency:

A new project, the Fire House Renovation Task Force, attracted the fire fighters to the Quality of Work Life program.

We brought the fire fighters union together with the people from our Department of General Services, who really are the ones responsible for the relationship with the contractors. Then we added people from the Mayor's Office with construction and design responsibilities. We brought these people together to look at the conditions of the fire houses, which are often more than a hundred years old. . . .

Through this effort of bringing these people together, they have identified a new contracting procedure. The new procedure has reduced the time to three months. It is now being used for a whole variety of repair work in the firehouses. I understand that it will be extended to other city buildings. . . . We found a better, faster way by bringing together fire fighters, the people who know the process of getting a contract through the city's bureaucracy, and the people who know construction and design. That project is actually going to lead to a process of completely renovating a firehouse in less time, for less money, by internal staff (Susan Grace in Benton, Contino, Grace, Sullivan, & White, 1989, p. 115).

For an organization that is just starting to experiment with participative management, the task force is an ideal way to begin. The stakes are low. The task force can be seen as a pilot project, a small-scale, limited-scope adventure. Management is committing itself only in one well-defined instance; workers will be able to back off gracefully from the next invitation to join if they find themselves unhappy with the process. Each project provides an occasion to test the waters, to see what went well and what did not, and to find newer and better ways of locating members, assembling a group, organizing the project, and presenting results.

The task force provides focus: The group is task-specific, assembled only for one purpose, a task with a beginning and an end. The task force system provides flexibility: Groups will vary in makeup, according to nature of the task and the interests and expertise of the participants. Differing memberships provide information on how member characteristics, group size, and group mix may relate to task force success. Involving new members in each task force permits many people from various parts of the organization to experience the collaborative process and to spread the word of their experience throughout the agency.

Satisfaction with the task force experiment may lead to the establishment of more permanent participative groups, to quality circles, or to labor-management committees. The lessons learned and the experiences gained will enhance the likelihood of successful implementation. Some evidence of this progression comes from a survey of motivational programs used by police departments for the period 1981-84: Task forces and special problem-solving teams were the most common medium and were used by 62% of the respondent departments, labor-management committees were used by 37%, and quality circles by 16% (Hatry & Greiner, 1986, p. 6).

The existence of permanent groups does not obviate the continued use of task forces. Specific problems or needs may be best met by specially constituted, short-term, ad hoc groups.

Joint Labor-Management Committees

The Rationale

As we have seen, workers are motivated by more than money. One powerful motivator is the ability to exert some influence and control, to make the workplace one's own, at least in part. Labor-management cooperation provides such an opportunity for self-esteem and autonomy. The experience of the New York City Department of Sanitation is the most famous case, because it was so successful and because it has been so well documented and disseminated. The sureness with which the turnaround was engineered is evidence of the importance of a solid grounding in the productivity field: "Contino brought to his new job a background in industrial management that included an MBA, 17 years in the aerospace industry, and an 18-month stint at the now defunct National Center for Productivity and the Quality of Work Life in Washington, DC" ("Miracle," 1982, p. 9).

From A to Z

> Mobilizing the work force was accomplished by transforming BME [Bureau of Motor Equipment] from the traditional "Type A" organization, with a majority of decision-making authority emanating from one person, to what Ouchi has labeled a "Theory Z" organization, where most decisions are based upon quantitative and qualitative input from the entire spectrum of its members, both labor and management. Most effectively applied to an organization with problems of labor mistrust, poor productivity, poor quality of work, and high turnover (the same problems afflicting BME in late 1978), Theory Z seeks to tap a previously unused resource within the organization—the skill and experience of all its employees. This was an abundant resource in BME because the bureau was manned by an extremely talented pool of tradesmen with thousands of years of collective experience at the repair and maintenance tasks in question. Accordingly, a Labor-Management Committee was formed and activated within one month of the establishment of the new management team (Contino & Lorusso, 1982, p. 69).

Manager Contino's report illustrates the basic, sensible input that workers can supply to the management of an organization:

> I sent the labor team to find out why we had so many out-of-service vehicles. They found what you might expect: the workers said, "First of all, how can you even have the gall to talk to us about getting work done when you have us working in these terrible conditions? The lights are poor, the heat does not work, and when it rains, we get wet. . . . Second, you must not have a system for production, because we run out of two-cent parts, and it takes us weeks and weeks to get a small part to fix something that would take us an hour to do." . . . Ninety-nine percent of the time the labor team was right and the managers were wrong (Contino & Giuliano, 1991, p. 188).

Union shop steward John Giuliano added:

Prior to Ron Contino, it was "them versus us." Management did not care about us, and we worked like pigs in pigsties. Morale was low. There were hundreds of grievances. The union was fighting management every day. . . . We were not telling management about problems repairing their trucks until Ron Contino came along with the concept of involving the work force (Contino & Giuliano, 1991, p. 189).

This was the result of this labor-management participative program:

The bureau . . . has been transformed from an organization deep in the red and unable to complete its assigned job to one [that] is operating so efficiently that it is actually beginning to generate an income. . . .

In spite of the managers' restricted ability to award bonuses and other monetary incentives, much of the work force, now aware of a new method of management in the bureau, has contributed an immeasurable amount of constructive and positive thinking to the overall effort (Contino & Lorusso, 1982, p. 71).

The Technique

The distinguishing characteristic of the joint labor-management committee arrangement is that worker participation comes through the official union. In fact, the joint labor-management committee is by far the most common mechanism for union-management cooperation (Cohen-Rosenthal & Burton, 1987, p. 93). Its chief virtue as a participative management vehicle is that it provides an arena for union-management interaction that is different and distinct from the confrontational tug-of-war of contract negotiations.

Labor management committee organizers and participants should remember that committees do not replace the bargaining process, but act as a complement to it. The topics considered in committee meetings should be kept separate from those of the bargaining sessions. The latter consider wages and benefits, along with working conditions, while a committee's work often [concerns] work-related problems of low motivation, productivity, morale, and poor communications (U.S. Office of Personnel Management, 1981, p. 4).

The labor-management committee form is particularly suited to a jurisdiction that is highly unionized. It is not surprising, therefore, that New York City and New York state provide leading examples. The New York City

Labor-Management Committee Program, begun in 1981 with the endorse-
ment of the city's Productivity Council, had expanded by 1983 to cover
50,000 employees in eight of the city's larger agencies; in addition to the
central steering committees, more than 60 subcommittees were in operation (Powell, 1983, p. 139). New York state's Committee on Work Environment and Productivity (CWEP) Program began in 1979 as the result of
contract agreements between the New York state governor's Office of
Employee Relations (OER) and the Civil Service Employees' Association
(CSEA).

> From 1979 through 1982, . . . CWEP-funded programs accomplished the
> following: retrained direct patient care workers for new jobs in commu-
> nity-based residences; helped displaced workers through a referral program
> in the Civil Service Department; provided a career ladder for operators of
> sophisticated power plants; provided start-up money for a network of on-site
> day-care centers for children of state workers (Lemmon, 1983, p. 132).

Unlike the task force, this is a stable, long-term arrangement with an
open agenda. Each joint labor-management committee typically comprises an equal number of chosen representatives from management and
the union; there may also be a neutral person from the outside, especially
during the formative period or if a particularly controversial topic is to be
discussed (U.S. Office of Personnel Management, 1981, p. 5). Help may
be needed:

> As in many social situations, breaking the ice can be a tough initial hurdle.
> Barriers to effective interaction between labor and management relate to
> unequal distributions of power, different social and educational back-
> grounds, and varying expectations and experiences. CWEP learned that it
> is unrealistic to expect traditional labor-management adversaries to under-
> take collaborative problem-solving without training and assistance. . . .
> [Focusing] on the "process" issues at an initial workshop . . . not only
> provides participants with the basic tools they need to begin their work, it
> also gives them something to divert their attention away from their old
> wounds and grudges.
>   The assistance of a skilled facilitator is also helpful (Lemmon, 1983,
> pp. 132-133).

An important part of the preparation for labor-management committees
and for quality circle members is training in group decision making. The

content of such a training program might include the advantages of using groups (quality decisions, acceptance and commitment, and the discovery of group standards), the disadvantages of using groups (time, cost, hidden agendas, the risky shift, and groupthink), and techniques (preplanning, brainstorming, mediating arguments, and assuming group roles) (National Center for Public Productivity, n.d., pp. 3-27). A 1987 assessment points up the importance of careful preparation and training.

> To be honest, labor-management committees have a mixed record of accomplishment. They can be excellent and provide a real forum for common analysis and [decision making]. In practice, many of these committees never meet their potential. . . . They often wither away when the person most interested in the topic leaves or becomes concerned with other issues. Members of labor-management committees rarely receive training on how to manage a committee or how to engage in joint problem-solving, and sometimes the results show this lack of skill base (Cohen-Rosenthal & Burton, p. 94).

Quality Circles

Like the joint labor-management committee system, the quality circle is a relatively formal and stable framework for worker participation. However, the mechanisms differ in that the operation of quality circles takes place independently of any union, although there may be union representation on the central steering committee in jointly sponsored programs (Cohen-Rosenthal & Burton, 1987, p. 109). Membership in a quality circle is individual and voluntary. Also, while a labor-management committee may function at any and all levels of the organization, quality circles tend to be located at the lower echelons. Quality circles are made up of people who are in the same work unit, and they usually focus on identifying and solving problems immediately affecting the production process and output quality.

The quality circle concept originated in the United States but found little reception here. It was developed in Japan under its originator, W. Edward Deming, and reintroduced into the United States in 1974. Quality circles were almost unknown in government in 1976, but 32% of those jurisdictions responding to a 1987-88 survey of municipal managers had adopted their use (Poister & Streib, 1989, p. 6). In 1985 there were more than 1,200 active quality circles in the Department of Defense alone (Mento & Steel, 1985, p. 35).

While the Japanese version emphasizes the prevention of defects, the American version of the quality circle concept has tended to stress the participative nature of the process. As a participative management mechanism, the quality circle offers those who are closest to the work the opportunity to identify problems and the skills with which to develop solutions. The quality circle is a relatively sophisticated procedure, requiring meticulous groundwork if it is to succeed.

The system works as follows. A central steering committee plans and develops the overall quality circle program: It decides such matters as "where in the organization quality circles should be introduced and what types of problems are appropriate for the quality circles to work on" (Blair, Cohen, & Hurwitz, 1982, p. 9). In establishing the steering committee, management has to be aware that it is undertaking to support and accept, as much as it can, the proposals that will be initiated by the various quality circles.

> Unlike some programs, quality circles do not offer employees direct financial benefit. . . . Since one of the program's most alluring features is the personal satisfaction and boosted morale it can provide employees, management must be careful to ensure it is prepared to deal with the creativity the program unleashes in employees. . . . Disregarding or dismissing employee ideas and solutions without explanation can create frustration and negate the benefits of the program ("Quality Circles," 1981, p. 3).

This management commitment is a radical leap from traditional management and toward the sharing of real power with the lowest-level workers and represents the first key decision. Quality circle systems are sometimes initiated—and fail, flawed from the beginning—because management wants the appearance but not the reality of worker empowerment.

The steering committee selects one or more facilitators, often, but not always, from the ranks of middle management.

> At present, each facilitator at NNSY [Norfolk Naval Station Shipyard] is responsible for 10 to 15 circles. Theirs are full-time jobs. Facilitators are shipyard employees who volunteer for one-year assignments to work with the QC program. Once the year is up, they return to their original duties ("Quality Circles," 1981, p. 2).

Selecting the facilitator is the most significant choice for the success or failure of the program. The facilitator must be carefully trained in preparation for his or her crucial role. The facilitator trains the quality circle leaders, oversees the constituting of the committees, ascertains that meetings proceed properly, assists circles in obtaining necessary resources (such as expertise in a particular area) and, most importantly, acts as intermediary between the quality circle and management. The facilitator must understand the organization and be skilled in dealing with people.

Every circle has a leader, usually the work supervisor, although elected leaders are also used; the leader chairs the circle sessions. Each circle has 3 to 15 members, all volunteers. Having been trained in leadership skills as well as group dynamics, the leader in turn trains the members in group participation and analytical techniques. The circle meets for one hour each week—on organization time in the United States, but on personal time in Japan. Meeting time must be held "sacred" if the system is to work ("Florida Launches QCs," 1981, p. 2).

The first order of business is the circle's choice of a name:

> After completing the eight hours of training session, each circle began to function. The initial problem for each circle was to name the circle. Many imaginative names such as "Sparkers," "Rectifiers," and "Dry Dock Club" were selected, giving the circles unique identities. This process enabled the circles to use the training concepts, and produce results quickly. At this point, the circles began to serve as problem-solving units ("The Quality Circle Program," 1981, p. 7).

In the course of the meetings, workers raise issues they see as problems with the work, then prioritize the problems and select one for immediate attention. They analyze that problem and ultimately arrive at a solution, which they present as a group to management. In preparation for this kind of participation, members have a great deal to learn. They need to understand group dynamics: They need to learn how to generate ideas freely and constructively, using brainstorming techniques. They need to learn methods of problem analysis, such as Pareto analysis for pinpointing the major sources of trouble and cause-and-effect diagramming to distinguish the "machinery, materials, methods, and people" sources of production problems (Morley, 1986, p. 168).

> After setting up a successful QC [quality circle] program, the Norfolk Naval Shipyard made its own observations as to what promotes a good program:
> * A well-organized steering committee is useful. At NNSY, representatives from many areas of the shipyard as well as members from the employees' union sit on the committee. . . .

- The role of the facilitator is the most important aspect of a QC program. Whoever fills the function must be able to work with people at all levels of the organization, be creative and flexible, and be aware of the political atmosphere of the organization.
- Management must support the quality circle program. If a union is involved, it also should support the program and its support and views should be solicited.
- The program is voluntary for employees, but management should encourage the establishment of circles.
- Within established limits, circle members must feel free to work on problems of their choosing.
- Facilitators must keep management informed of what the circles are working on and on their progress.
- Quality, not quantity, should be the first consideration. The program will spread as word-of-mouth spreads success stories.
- A successful program must adhere to the concept and principles of the program. One of the facilitator's most crucial tasks is to see that circles follow correct procedures ("Quality Circles," 1981, p. 4).

A well-run quality circle provides the social satisfaction of group interaction and cooperative problem solving. It gives workers at the lowest levels of the organization new skills and the opportunity to speak to management.

The management presentation represents a positive interaction between labor and management which seldom occurs outside of the Quality Circle model. "Line" workers may have never seen a top management person, much less enjoyed his or her rapt attention while describing a potential solution to a work problem (Roll & Roll, 1983, p. 137).

Workers set the agenda; they originate the ideas and identify the problems. Supervisors gain leadership skills, build a cohesive work group, profit from worker insights, and benefit from heading a group that is productive. The work is smoother and of better quality. The client is better served.

However, in order for a quality circle system to run well, many elements have to be in place: real management willingness to share power; skillful facilitators; well-trained facilitators, leaders, and members; and the sacredness of the meeting time. This represents a considerable physical and psychological investment. The undertaking should be carefully considered and well thought through.

Quality circles are clearly a valuable addition to the repertoire of improvement strategies that can be used by federal managers, but only when they are used with realistic expectations and introduced into appropriate organizational settings (Blair, Cohen, & Hurwitz, 1982, p. 18).

Participation and the Public Sector

The public sector stands to gain more than the private sector from the idea of worker participation. There is more turnover at the top of public agencies. The middle and lower ranks are the more permanent, experienced, and knowledgeable about the work and the clientele.

> The high degree of job security, which has traditionally been seen by management as a detriment to productivity, is considered a benefit within the Quality Circle model due to the stability it lends to circle and organizational membership. A major contributor to low morale in civil service may be the sense of powerlessness that is experienced, particularly at the lower ranks (Roll & Roll, 1983, p. 141).

Public agencies tend to be large, and it is in the larger organizations that the distance from the top to the client is greatest. "Washington is not the real world. It is Paper City, where paper problems are confronted, ultimately being provided with paper solutions" (Bethell, 1981, p. 58). The boundary-spanning, service-delivering, bottom-of-the-line workers are familiar with the shortcomings of the work process and the service, which makes their input valuable.

A Case of Motivation

A productivity project, started in 1979 in the police department of Palatine, Illinois, provides a stellar example of how the worker, the organization, and the public can all benefit from one program to improve the workers' knowledge and morale through the provision of motivators of every kind. The project was the establishment of a dual career ladder (DCL) to overcome the problem of a dead end job:

> The DCL program addresses the problems of the lack of promotional opportunities in a police organization, the lack of incentives at police officer rank, the lack of career alternatives for officers who desire to remain "on the streets," and the need for a mechanism to identify and reward superior performance. . . .

> The program combined the traditional career ladder with a new path of
> lateral advancement below the rank of sergeant. . . . Each position includes
> an attendant pay bonus, identifiable insignia, departmental recognition, and
> increased job responsibilities. Movement along these positions is predi-
> cated on the officer's performance and contributions, demonstrated profi-
> ciency in job-related knowledge and skill areas, educational attainment,
> and tenure (Bratcher & Gasior, 1982, p. 130).

What Palatine did was to construct an alternative to the "ladder" from
police officer to sergeant to lieutenant and on up to police chief. The
second ladder is climbed within rank. It motivates self-improvement and
high performance because, unlike a promotion, the higher step on the
ladder has to be earned anew each year.

The Requirements

To be eligible for advancement, the officer has to meet five criteria
(Bratcher & Gasior, 1981, p. 50):

1. *Tenure.* At least one year must be spent at the top position in the pay
classification system for the first advancement. Then, at least one year
must be spent in the previous position.

2. *Basic knowledge and skills.* Officers must show proficiency in 25
knowledge and skill areas that are considered to be fundamental.

3. *Advanced knowledge and skills.* Officers must be proficient in areas
such as firearms instruction or technical accident investigation. These are
job-related skills gained through specialized training.

4. *Educational requirements.* Varying amounts of college work are
required, more for recent hires, less for those hired before the introduction
of educational requirements.

5. *Performance requirements.* These requirements are measured against
a set of standards developed specially for the DCL program.

The Rewards

Title. A range of titles are conferred following satisfaction of the DCL
requirements: Advanced Officer, Police Office I, Police Officer II, and
Police Officer III.

Money. Bonuses are offered that range from $1,000 for Advanced Officer to $3,500 for Police Officer III.

> These pay bonuses are distributed in two equal amounts—one prior to Christmas holidays and the other prior to summer vacations. Rather than include a portion of the bonus in each paycheck, it was felt that the impact of the pay bonus would be greater on the officer and the officer's family if it was given in a large amount (Bratcher & Gasior, 1981, p. 54).

Insignia. Each position has an identifiable insignia: a shirt pocket button or sleeve stripes. "What that button says to that officer, to his family, to the people in the community, and to other officers in our organization and in other departments is that this guy's something special" (Gasior, 1984, p. 66).

The Process

The dual career ladder was developed participatively:

> After conducting a series of presentations in which the dual career ladder concept and program ideas were explained to department personnel, a task force, consisting of representatives from all ranks within the department, was established. The mission of the task force was to transform the dual career ladder concept into a fair and equitable program by involving as many department personnel as possible.
>
> Five subcommittees were established. . . . Task force members chaired each subcommittee and any officers who expressed interest in the particular topic served as members. The meetings were open to all officers, with the task force and subcommittee members participating on their own time (Bratcher & Gasior, 1981, pp. 52-53).

The program is administered supportively:

> When an officer doesn't make it, it's the organization's responsibility to help the officer. We want to get away from the "gotcha" game, where at the end of the year you tell the guy that his performance wasn't up to standard, we gotcha (Gasior, 1984, p. 68).

Note how many of the motivators discussed in this and the preceding chapter are demonstrated at work in Palatine: money, status symbols, self-development, and participative management. The results? The program "has worked beyond our wildest expectations" (Gasior, 1984, p. 68):

We've been in this program almost three years now, and in that period we've been able to increase department overall activity by 50 percent, with the same people. . . .

Crime rates are down by about 20 percent over the last three years. Our supposition, and we want to keep testing it, is that the officers are out there with a much greater visible presence; they're not hiding somewhere from their supervisor. . . . We are writing 500 percent more drunk-driving arrests, and . . . [we] have been able to reduce accidents about 35 percent since the program started (Gasior, 1984, pp. 68-69).

References

Accordino, J. J. (1989). Quality-of-working-life systems in large cities: An assessment. *Public Productivity Review*, *12*, 345-360.

Ammons, D. N. (1991). *Administrative analysis for local government: Practical application of selected techniques*. Athens: Carl Vinson Institute of Government, University of Georgia.

Ballard, J. A., & Trent, D. M. (1989). Idea generation and productivity: The promise of CSM. *Public Productivity Review*, *12*, 373-386.

Beaumont, E. (1991, July 1). President's column. *PA Times*, p. 5.

Beckman, N. (1979). Foreword. In R. G. Pajer, *Employee performance evaluation—A practical guide to development and implementation for state, county, and municipal governments* (pp. 1-2). (OIPP 152-114). Washington, DC: Government Printing Office.

Benton, F. W., Contino, R., Grace, S., Sullivan, W., & White, B. (1989). Human resources and labor-management cooperation (panel discussion at the Third National Public-Sector Productivity Conference, New York). *Public Productivity & Management Review*, *13*, 107-116.

Bethell, T. (1981). The wealth of Washington. In M. Holzer & E. D. Rosen (Eds.), *Current cases in public administration* (pp. 49-58). New York: Harper & Row.

Blair, J. D., Cohen, S. L., & Hurwitz, J. V. (1982). Quality circles: Practical considerations for public managers. *Public Productivity Review*, *6*, 9-18.

Blake, R. R., & Mouton, J. S. (1981). *Productivity: The human side*. New York: AMACOM.

Bratcher, J., & Gasior, W. D. (1981, October). The dual career ladder. *The Police Chief*, pp. 50-55.

Bratcher, J., & Gasior, W. D. (1982). The dual career ladder program for police. *Public Productivity Review*, *6*, 130-132.

Burton, G. E. (1986). The group process: Key to more productive management. In J. Matzer, Jr. (Ed.), *Productivity improvement techniques: Creative approaches for local government* (pp. 132-142). Washington, DC: International City Management Association.

Chandler, R. C., & Plano, J. C. (1982). *The public administration dictionary*. New York: John Wiley.

Cohen-Rosenthal, E., & Burton, C. E. (1987). *Mutual gains: A guide to union-management cooperation*. New York: Praeger.

Contino, R. A., & Giuliano, J. (1991). Productivity gains through employee participation at the New York City Department of Sanitation. *Public Productivity & Management Review*, *15*, 185-190.

Contino, R., & Lorusso, R. M. (1982). The Theory Z turnaround of a public agency. *Public Administration Review*, *42*, 66-72.

Desky, J. (1992, March 1). City saves money with employee suggestions. *PA Times*, pp. 3, 16.

Downey, E. H., & Balk, W. L. (1976). *Employee innovation and government productivity: A study of suggestion systems in the public sector*. Chicago: International Personnel Management Association.

Falcone, S. (1991). Self-assessments and job satisfaction in public and private organizations. *Public Productivity & Management Review*, *14*, 385-396.

Florida launches QCs. (1981, August/September). *Florida Productivity Reporter*, *2*, 1-2.

Gasior, W. (1984). The dual career ladder program. *Public Productivity Review*, *8*, 63-69.

Golembiewski, R. T. (1988). Policy initiatives in worksite research: Implications from research on a phase model of burnout. In R. M. Kelly (Ed.), *Promoting productivity in the public sector: Problems, strategies and prospects* (pp. 209-227). New York: St. Martin's.

Gotbaum, V., & Handman, E. (1978). A conversation with Victor Gotbaum. *Public Administration Review*, *38*, 19-21.

Hatry, H. P., & Greiner, J. M. (1986). Improving the use of quality circles in police departments. Washington, DC: Urban Institute.

International City Management Association. (1990). *The guide to management improvement projects in local government*. Washington, DC: Author.

Kanter, R. M., & Stein, B. A. (1981, July). Ungluing the stuck: Motivating performance and productivity through expanding opportunity. *Management Review*, pp. 45-49.

Lemmon, C. S. (1983). New York State: Moving on to worker involvement issues. In N. Q. Herrick (Ed.), *Improving government: Experiments with quality of working life systems* (pp. 130-135). New York: Praeger.

Mento, A. J., & Steel, R. P. (1985). Conducting quality circles research: Toward a comprehensive perspective. *Public Productivity Review*, *9*, 35-48.

Miracle on Worth Street. (1982). *Productivity*, *3*, 1, 9-11.

Morley, E. (1986). *A practitioner's guide to public sector productivity improvement*. Malabar, FL: Krieger.

National Center for Public Productivity. (n.d.). *JLMC group decision-making techniques and issues*. Unpublished module for trainee workbook-manual, National Center for Public Productivity, New York.

Odom, R. Y., Boxx, W. R., & Dunn, M. G. (1990). Organizational cultures, commitment, satisfaction, and cohesion. *Public Productivity & Management Review*, *14*, 157-169.

Poister, T. H., Hatry, H. P., Fisk, D. M., & Greiner, J. M. (1985). Centralized productivity improvement efforts in state government. *Public Productivity Review*, *9*, 5-24.

Poister, T. H., & Streib, G. (1989). Municipal managers' concerns for productivity improvement. *Public Productivity & Management Review*, *13*, 3-11.

Powell, M. (1983). New York City: From the top down. In N. Q. Herrick (Ed.), *Improving government: Experiments with quality of working life systems* (pp. 136-140). New York: Praeger.

The quality circle program of the Norfolk Naval Shipyard. (1981, April). (WPR-17). Washington, DC: Government Printing Office.

Quality circles on the rise. (1981). *Performance*, *2*, 1-4.

Riddle, D. I. (1988). Public sector productivity and role conflicts. In R. M. Kelly (Ed.), *Promoting productivity in the public sector: Problems, strategies and prospects* (pp. 191-208). New York: St. Martin's.

Roll, J. L., & Roll, D. L. (1983). The potential for application of quality circles in the American public sector. *Public Productivity Review, 7,* 122-142.

Shared decision making at the school site: Moving toward a professional model. (1987, Spring). *American Educator,* pp. 10-17, 46.

Sweeny, M. (1978, July). *Development of incentive systems for worker productivity.* Unpublished memorandum, New Jersey Department of Civil Service.

Sylvester, K. (1992, May). The $2.4 billion suggestion box. *Governing,* p. 24.

U.S. Civil Service Commission. (1976). *Fair and effective employee advancement: A guide for state and local government managers.* (BIPP 152-65). Washington, DC: Government Printing Office.

U.S. Office of Personnel Management. (1981, February). *Productivity 6: Labor-management committees.* (OIPP 152-151). Washington, DC: Government Printing Office.

Wittmer, D. (1991). Serving the people or serving for pay: Reward preferences among government, hybrid sector, and business managers. *Public Productivity & Management Review, 14,* 369-383.

9

Management Options for Obtaining Resources

In this chapter we begin to consider how an agency can improve its efficiency and the quality of its service by opening its eyes to its environment—to how it is perceived and what the environment has to offer. This is an open systems perspective, one concerned with the management of organizational well-being in its environment.

The most recent approaches to improving public sector productivity focus on the management process. They deal with new and open modes for making decisions, alternative ways of acquiring resources, and alternative modes of delivering services. They give high priority to service quality as it is perceived by the public. To that end, managerial openness is the hallmark of this era—openness of style and openness to the organizational environment. Communicativeness and broad participation take on increasing importance.

Earlier approaches to public productivity improvement kept the focus inward, concerned first with streamlining the work process and then with energizing the work force. Attention was paid to external models and standards: businesslike efficiency, new technology, employee motivation, and staff development. But, despite their external origin, these ideas were essentially seen as grist for the internal mill.

Under conditions of relative stability and certainty, that focus is not inappropriate. If mission, funding, clientele, operating conditions, supply sources, and competition remain constant, a closed system frame of reference is natural. But those premises are now challenged. Adequate budgetary funding is uncertain; public antipathy has brought home to public employees and managers the importance of public relations; privatization looms as a formidable source of competition. The "closed" model will no longer do. Uncertainty, scarcity, and disfavor have combined to awaken a new concern for reputation and spur the search for additional resources with which to create "customer" satisfaction.

This chapter will describe many nontraditional ways of obtaining resources. Some, such as volunteer labor, are free. This raises a question: If you do more by obtaining more resources, is this really a productivity improvement? Has the ratio of input to output changed?

Yes. Productivity in the public sector is generally predicated only on *officially allocated* resources: It expresses the ratio of outputs per budget dollar or per unit of (official position) labor, (budgeted) equipment, and so on. Volunteers, donated equipment, and cash gifts that can be brought to bear on the agency mission are, in a sense, "silent resources," distinct from the official ones: They are not counted officially when calculating productivity. Within this framework, the manager who can find additional (uncounted) resources and use them to improve (counted) service is, indeed, making the agency more productive.

Let us consider nontraditional options for acquiring and managing resources of money, labor, equipment, and space.

Monetary Resources

Personal financial resources can be augmented in two ways: (1) make better use of current income and (2) find additional sources. It is the same for public sector agencies.

Recycling Internal Funds

It is a rare organization that does not have some monies that could be put to better use. Managers know about them or could find out with little effort, but the rules and the reward system give them little opportunity or incentive to try. Budget categories create impermeable walls; unspent funds engender future budget cuts. With due retention of accountability, some simple, cost-free changes in the ground rules can reshape this situation. Managers may be held to account by results and audits. The micromanagement of managers through detailed regulation is discouraging for the individual and for the process.

Budgetary Discretion

Commonly, central approval is required for transferring even trivial amounts from one budget category to another. This is not the only way to structure things. Budget rules can be, and often are, written to permit shifting a given percentage of the funds in one budget category to another, without the need for approval.

Every budget year brings unpredicted savings: An unusual number of long-time employees leave and are replaced at lower cost; the need for snow removal turns out to be lower than anticipated. Given discretion and latitude, managers can take advantage of unexpected economies in one aspect of the operation to finance improvement in others.

Gain-Sharing for the Manager

The budget system is a motivator. Managers with budget discretion should not punish economical subunits. If every unspent budget dollar reverts back to the system at the end of the budget year, managers have nothing to gain and everything to lose by efforts to spend less. On the other hand, if they know that some portion of every unspent dollar will remain with the agency, to use as it sees fit, then managers have something to gain. This gain sharing is particularly relevant to the productivity effort, not just because it rewards the productive manager, but also because it is a way of getting seed money for new improvements.

Cash Management

Some agencies collect cash payments: user fees, fines, and license charges, for example. Every day that the cash or checks sit on someone's desk is a day's interest lost. In these agencies it is particularly important that mail be opened promptly and checks processed immediately. Receipts should be deposited daily, at least. Some jurisdictions, not content with bank interest rates, invest receipts in short-term U.S. Treasury bills.

Inventory Maintenance

The allegedly true story is told that in 1975 a board of education had in its warehouse enough wooden beads for kindergarten use until the year 2000. Reserves are important as buffers against potential disruptions to operations, but excessive stockpiling not only ties up monies, but also adds costs of storage space, inventory maintenance, and damage resulting from the ravages of time. The work force is condemned to make do with outmoded equipment and materials until they are used up and newer versions can be ordered. Funds that are not sunk in inventory can be kept maneuverable, preferably earning interest until needed.

The Brooklyn Academy of Music alleviated two problems by a fresh look at inventory. Short of space and short of money, the managers decided to auction off old stage sets and costumes and gained on both fronts (S. Levy, personal communication, October 4, 1991).

External Sources of Funds

Donations

The philanthropic civic culture that generates personal volunteerism, pro bono work, and the loan of corporate executives to public service also leads individual citizens and private organizations to make gifts to public agencies. Some jurisdictions are developing sophisticated devices to encourage giving and to direct funds toward specific needs. Columbus, Ohio, is among the cities that distribute a gift catalog, listing items that city departments need (International City Management Association, 1990, CCR-17). Another example:

> In our budget for next year, we've proposed a challenge appropriation for the purchase of library books: The city will put in up to $100,000 on the basis of $1 for every $1 the private sector contributes. We think we'll wind up with the whole $200,000, or maybe even more. Everybody knows we need new books for our library system (Briseno, 1991).

User Fees

Charging for the use of certain public services is an established practice: municipal parking permits, state toll roads, and entrance fees for national parks are just a few examples. Beyond the obvious effect of stretching the public dollar, fees can be used to limit the use of or to control access to services. For example, user fees for the municipal tennis court can level demand by setting cheaper rates for less popular days and hours. Arizona applies user fees to combat an expensive problem:

> In Arizona, nearly 2 million waste tires a year accumulate in landfills or become litter that spoils the desert. . . . In 1990, the state legislature . . . [imposed] a 2 percent fee on the purchase price of all tires sold . . . with [the Arizona Department of Environmental Quality] keeping just 5 percent of the fees for administering the program. The remaining 95% [goes] . . . for developing solutions to the waste tire problem, . . . an example of the use of user fees to implement a program that benefits all the citizens of the state (Aerni & Burgess, 1991).

Productivity Investment Funds

Productivity improvement costs money. It takes funds to acquire new equipment, conduct training, and hire consultants. The rationale for investing is that it will produce greater efficiencies in the long run; the money will come back multiplied. Although the emphasis in productivity improvement has shifted toward improving output quality, opportunities for improving efficiency have by no means been exhausted. Even in times of severe constraint—*especially* in times of severe constraint—money must flow into such productivity improvement undertakings.

In the 1970s and early 1980s, special funds were arranged at the federal, state, and local levels for the purpose of endowing productivity improvement projects. They have generally fallen into decline or disuse for a variety of reasons, including changing administrations, tight budgets, and short time horizons. But those programs should not be overlooked. They merit new attention as models for today. Even modest investments can still produce significant impacts on productivity if they are carefully allocated and monitored.

The Federal Level. The Department of Defense followed up its 1975 fast payback Productivity-Enhancing Capital Investment (PECI) Program with a Productivity Investment Fund (PIF):

Under this fund projects compete for approval on the basis of their individual merit. . . . The Secretary of Defense establishes . . . a fixed level of productivity investment funds. . . . Each service and agency is asked to submit candidate projects. . . .

During the last six years, DOD has invested a total of $380 million in the various types of investments. . . . We expect to produce savings of $1 billion from this program within the next five years. . . .

In summary, we believe the program has proven, at the very least, its essential premise—that is, that if managers are given the opportunity and the concurrent financial support, they can and will take aggressive action to improve "status quo" (Ackard, 1985, pp. 86-89, passim).

The State Level. In 1978, New Jersey's treasury department established a Productivity Improvement Investment Account. Among the projects funded in the first years were word processing systems, alarm systems to replace patrol on a state college campus, and food systems for state hospitals and prisons (State Government Productivity Research Center, 1980, pp. 10, 11). The assistant director of the state's Office of Management Services described the program as he saw it in 1983:

So we have this productivity investment account, put into effect about 1978 or so. We are running it more or less along the following lines. You want money? All you have to do is ask for it. We are like a friendly banker. All you have to do is: identify your operating costs "before," and what you will have "after." Just tell us that. Two, lay out a curt description of how you are going to get there that will stand the test of reasonable, man-in-the-street logic. Nothing fancy, half a page will do, just as long as you can stand behind it. The next thing we say is, at a minimum, whatever money we are going to give you, we want you to be able to identify clearly that you are going to get tangible savings over a period of three years. . . . Simple? The last thing is that you have got to commit your cabinet officer, so that we can embarrass him if you do not deliver. Get his signature. . . .

[W]e are getting $6.3 million back out of the $1 million we have put out. As of 1982 we had already got our hands on half of that. . . .

Now just stop for a second. Listen to what I am saying. I am trying to describe at the moment a technique that I suggest is transferable (Gaissert, 1985, pp. 100- 101).

The Local Level. Dayton, Ohio, provides an example of productivity investment funding at the local level, as described by an official of the city's Office of Management and Budget:

Each year, Dayton sets aside about one-half of one percent of its budget, earmarked for technology improvements [about $600,000 per year]. . . . The Technology Improvement Fund is a separate pot of money that the departments compete for. It does not come out of their normal operating budgets. We wanted to make it as much of an incentive as possible for departments to stick their necks out, to take some risk. . . .

A submission . . . had to have at least a four-year payback, in terms of either productivity increases or reduced operating costs, and it had to have some kind of enhancement of our service capability. . . .

[One example] . . . is a brush chipper. That sounds like a silly thing. . . . But what the crews used to do was trim the branches, dump all the trimmings on the truck, haul it back to where we had a brush chipper, chip it, put the chips back on the truck, take the truck back to the park, and spread the chips around the trees. What we did was provide brush chippers that they could carry with them at all times—to trim the trees, make the chips, and dump them around the trees right there.

As you can see, a lot of the things that we have funded have not been high-technology kinds of things; they have been common-sense kinds of things where somebody low in the organization has said, "Hey!, if I had money to do this I would be able to bring about some productivity." What we have done is set aside a pile of money to allow for that to happen (Gillespie, 1985, pp. 91-94, passim).

Labor Resources

The traditional source of labor for public sector agencies is the full-time civil service appointee, or the full-time political appointee, whose salary is paid by budgetary allocation. But fiscal problems have inspired a new search for every means of stretching, facilitating, and augmenting the present labor force.

A report recently released by the U.S. Merit Systems Protection Board surveyed 22 of the largest departments and federal agencies on alternative work programs and family-oriented services. The report found that the federal government "now finds itself lagging behind both what many other employers provide and what many employees need." According to the report, there are 65 federally operated child-care centers with 45 scheduled to open by 1993 and about 19 percent of the federal work force [using] flexitime ("Report Finds," 1991).

Enhancing Present Labor Resources

It is almost always possible to make better use of existing budgeted "positions." Here are some of the options.

Inside Consultant Groups

Agencies have traditionally turned to paid outside consultants for special expertise in solving problems and instituting innovations, such as computerization, work measurement systems, and training programs. However, "[a]ny multiservice municipality, of medium to large size, is likely to have more skills, knowledge, and abilities available to it in its many city agencies than most private consulting firms" (Gianakis & Friedel, 1989, p. 70).

As early as 1976, the state of Michigan had created an in-house consulting group within its Department of Management and Budget. In its first three years, the group had worked on 31 projects and saved the state an estimated $1.2 million in outside consulting costs ("Michigan—In-House Consulting," 1981).

Inside consulting "firms" are now used in many cities, among them St. Petersburg (Gianakis & Friedel, 1989), San Diego (Epstein & Fass, 1989, p. 123), and Glendale, Arizona:

> Like most local governments, the city of Glendale, Arizona (113,000) relies on outside consultants in areas that require special expertise. However, the city realized that there was an exceptional amount of expertise in its budget and research office . . . in areas ranging from statistics to program analysis. In order to take advantage of these resources, an internal consulting firm, BR Associates, was created. Using letterhead and marketing efforts similar to private-sector consultants, staff members now provide [no-charge] consulting assistance to other departments during the off-season in the budget year. . . . By using BR Associates the city has saved more than $10,000. At the same time, the budget staff members are gaining experience in organization and management issues (International City Management Association, 1990, MGT-4).

Civilianization and Use of Paraprofessionals

Talent and money are wasted when highly trained professionals spend time on tasks that do not require full use of their professional skills. New positions, such as paralegal aide, nurse's aide, and teacher's aide, have been developed to make optimal use of professional personnel. Civilianization represents the same principle as applied to uniformed officers. Despite some union opposition, the practice has spread because of its advantages:

> We've also improved productivity in our police department by adding civilian positions, which has increased . . . to 28 percent the proportion of an officer's time that he or she is engaged in preventive patrol, as opposed to writing reports or responding to nonemergency calls. We expect to increase patrol availability again next year, to nearly 35 percent, by adding $700,000 worth of civilian positions. That is the equivalent of 23 full-time police officers, fully equipped with cars, weapons and everything else they need, which would cost $1.3 million (Briseno, 1991).

Reducing Absenteeism

Absenteeism imposes high costs. It burdens managers, who have to make rearrangements, and delays co-workers who depend on the absentee's output. Clients may have to wait or return for service. If a substitute is provided, it costs a day's pay; in remotely located, round-the-clock agencies, such as prisons, the substitute is often a worker on overtime, in which case the cost to the agency is one and one-half days' pay.

Absenteeism can be addressed by eliminating some of the causes and by rewarding attendance.

Attendance Programs. If there is a team spirit in the workplace, a simple reminder of the costs of frequent absences to agency, co-workers, and clients may touch a sense of social responsibility in the worker and thus improve attendance. In most U.S. public sector workplaces, however, workers are more likely to respond to personal profit as an inducement.

The citation is lost to history, but an object lesson in how motivation to attend can be provided simply, inexpensively, and imaginatively comes from one of the least rewarding fields of employment—custodial work. Upon reporting for work each day, each worker is dealt a playing card. By the end of the week everyone holds a poker hand. High hand wins a prize. Absence for a day means inability to compete that week. The ambivalent worker is drawn toward coming to work by the drama of the game and the hope of winning.

"Personal days" and "sick days," originally provisions against emergency, have come to be regarded as entitlements, squandered if not used. Some fair exchange, some reward, is expected for nonuse. As long as the outlay costs less than the savings, it is profitable to institute a reward system.

The poker hand is an unconventional scheme. The state of Iowa uses an exchange program, permitting employees who have not used sick leave for a full calendar month to trade one and one-half days of sick leave for one-half day of additional vacation leave ("Iowa, Ohio—Sick Leave," 1981). Some jurisdictions use a "buy-back" approach:

> The town of Hindmarsh, South Australia (14,500) has hit upon an incentive scheme that has reduced employee absenteeism. Absenteeism had been growing alarmingly, and the town . . . reasoned it was possible to pay staff for sick leave not taken, and still gain in productivity and lower administrative costs. The following scale was formulated: an employee taking no sick leave receives 10 days' pay, . . . an employee taking one sick day receives 90% of 9 days' pay, and so on down to no bonus at all for an employee using all [10] days of leave. . . . After the first year . . . the average time lost per employee dropped from 8.33 days to 4.53 days (International City Management Association, 1981, pp. 14, 15).

Wellness Programs. It is not just benevolent to make an effort to keep employees healthy; it is good economics. The prevention or early treatment of problems not only reduces absenteeism but also helps to control the cost of medical benefit plans.

> Employees of the state of New York may be able to prove that "an ounce of prevention is worth a pound of cure." . . .
> The pilot project, "Stay Healthy—It Pays," is a comprehensive health education and risk reduction program that begins with a health risk appraisal [and follow-up]. . . . A bi-monthly employee bulletin will discuss self-care, weight control, smoking, alcohol abuse, nutrition, and stress management. Special risk reduction programs on quitting smoking, exercise and hypertension screening and monitoring will also be made available. . . .
> [The Governor's Office of Employee Relations] has budgeted $40,000 for the program. The office said the cost savings comes in when employees are healthier, and thus use less health insurance and take fewer sick days ("Wellness Program Set," 1983).

Reassignment of Injured Workers. Where work-related injuries are common, labor resources can be conserved by assigning injured employees to work on other duties until they recover.

> According to Police Chief Ralph Pampena, the [Pittsburgh, Pennsylvania] Police Bureau has two types of programs aimed at getting injured officers

back to work. The light-duty or alternative duty program involves employees who have been injured and who are "in the process of coming back." "We assign them to a desk job . . . until such time that they are 100 percent recovered and then they come back to work."

The second type of program is modified duty, in which an officer who is not expected to return to full-time sworn duties is assigned to administrative tasks "thereby releasing someone who is capable for full duty out onto the streets." . . . Modified duty can involve . . . telephone interviews, taking crime reports from victims, performing desk duties, . . . handling radios and incoming calls or instructing at the police academy ("Injured Pittsburgh Cops," 1990, p. 6).

This was accomplished despite problems. The union filed grievances, claiming that officers were being given duties above their rank, and officers said they lost money by coming to work because workmen's compensation gives them full pay *tax-free* when they are out ("Injured Pittsburgh Cops," 1990, pp. 5, 6).

Child Care. The traditional family—working father, mother at home, and extended family as backup—is no longer the American norm. For today's working couples and single-parent households, child care has become a significant employment issue. Child care is costly, chancy, and often makeshift. Breakdowns in child care arrangements occasion parental absence from work. For some organizations, the investment in a day care center pays off in easy minds and less absence—and a recruiting attraction.

Alternative Schedules

The 9 a.m. to 5 p.m., Monday through Friday workweek at the office may be the conventional work arrangement, but it is not the only one possible. Alternative schedules may make more economical use of resources, accommodate employees, and enhance service to the client. They come in a rich variety.

Flexitime

Under this arrangement, which also is called "flextime," some workers elect to begin and end the workday early; others begin and end late. Everyone works during a "core period." For example, some staff members might work from 7 a.m. to 3 p.m., others from 9 a.m. to 5 p.m., and still others from 10 a.m. to 6 p.m., leaving everyone available for meetings and communication between 10 a.m. and 3 p.m. In some plans, each worker's schedule, once chosen, remains fixed; in others it may vary from week to week, depending on needs. The "gliding hours" version of flexitime permits each worker to choose his or her own time each day.

The advantages for the worker are obvious: A working parent can be home when school ends, early risers and night people can work according to their own rhythms, and travel is less problematic for everyone. At another level, the worker's right to choose validates his or her autonomy and offers some control over work life. For the agency, flexitime can raise employee morale, make more efficient use of facilities by extending hours of use, and cut overtime costs. For the clientele, having the office open longer means more convenient service. Flexitime makes it possible, for example, for a social service agency to make counseling, group sessions, and home visits available in the evenings, just by using staff members who want the mornings free.

The Social Security Administration began an experiment with flexitime in 1974:

> Flextime was adopted to help the large proportion of working mothers employed in the mainly clerical jobs . . . at the Baltimore office. In that work force, 80 percent are black people from the inner city; a majority have dependent children; and a high proportion are heads of households. Many depend on public transportation. To meet both work and home responsibilities, most were using about 12 of their 13 allowable sick leave days each year and took leave without pay (the equivalent of 284 person-years in 1974). . . .
>
> [Says management,] "We realized immediate productivity increases, and these have been sustained. We eliminated tardiness. People get down to their work sooner in the mornings and get up from it later in the afternoons. We seem to have made some inroads on the problem of short-term leave usage." . . .
>
> [Says the union,] Problems proved not to be significant. . . . Flextime is an innovation [that] is comparatively easy to introduce—it is not necessary to revise wage rates, work routines, or general personnel policies. . . . A good atmosphere is created by this kind of innovation (Committee on Alternative Work Patterns & National Center for Productivity and Quality of Working Life, 1976, pp. 2, 3).

The disadvantages of flexitime include the administrative burden of tracking hours, monitoring promptness, deciding from among conflicting preferences, providing supervision, and ensuring that all hours have coverage. Flexitime also limits the period during which meetings and training can take place.

Compressed Workweek

A compressed workweek means working fewer but longer days each week. A typical arrangement would involve four 9- or 10-hour days per week. It offers many of the advantages of flexitime: worker autonomy (if workers are free to choose), more efficient use of facilities, and extended hours for clients. In addition, a compressed workweek cuts each employee's travel time and expenses by 20%; provides a day off when schools, banks, and other businesses are open; and permits extended weekends. For the agency, it permits an extended day without the administrative and communications difficulties inherent in flexitime.

In remotely located prisons or mental hospitals, employees may prefer a highly compressed workweek. A few very long workdays, with sleeping taking place at the facility or nearby, are alternated with several sequential days off. For the worker, this means traveling only once a week to and from work. For the agency, it means having substitutes near at hand if needed.

The chief disadvantage of the compressed workweek is that people become tired, and presumably less productive, at the end of the day. This may be stressful for the older or infirm employee. Atlanta, Georgia, experimented with a four-day week in 1971, abandoning the experiment after six months because workers objected to the long day and "conflicts with an eight-hour, five day working world" (Sweeny, 1978, p. 43).

Alternative Workweek

Some public sector fields such as law enforcement, fire fighting, corrections, and hospital service regularly use alternative, sometimes rotating, duty calendars. The principle has potential in other fields:

In 1980 the City of Milaca's [Minnesota] four-man public works department was faced with the prospect of two of its employees retiring. At that time, the work schedule was such that each man worked forty hours Monday through Friday. In addition, the workload demanded that at least one man had to work Saturday and Sunday for three hours or more each day. This schedule meant approximately ten hours overtime per week. In many organizations, the retirement of half of the work force would be disruptive to a department's operation. Our city used this condition as an advantage. . . .

The job offers were promoted as modified workweek shifts: one position working Sunday through Thursday, the other Tuesday through Saturday. Under these conditions, the overtime burden could be reduced substantially. . . . An employee would now be available seven days a week.

This would better serve the city's working people, who may have problems but cannot deal with them until the weekend (Von Drak, 1982).

Flexiplace

The computer age has opened up possibilities for employees to work at home and yet interact with co-workers in "real time." This responds to staff needs and opens the door to a new set of recruits:

> The advent of information technology in general and telecommunications in particular offers new ways to accommodate employees with special needs, including those with impairments to hearing, sight, speech, mobility, or manual dexterity as well as those on maternity or extended leave.
>
> The new technology allows the workplace to be transplanted into the home, so that meaningful employment is preserved. This flexibility by itself can make a difference to the mental health, self-respect, recovery, and general functioning of the individuals involved (Halachmi, 1991, pp. 333-334).

Flexiplace arrangements can offer advantages to society as a whole, as in this state experiment to control air pollution:

> Arizona agreed to give it a shot with employees from four departments. . . . After identifying employees with job responsibilities that would permit them to telecommute, Arizona managers asked them if they would like to participate in the pilot program. . . .
>
> At the end of the first six months, a survey of both telecommuting and non-telecommuting employees and supervisors was taken. The 134 tele-commuters who responded drove 97,078 fewer miles during that six-month period, endured 3,705 fewer hours of stressful driving time and avoided emitting 1.9 tons of air pollutants. They also saved an estimated $10,372 in travel expenses. . . .
>
> Eight out of 10 telecommuters said the experience enabled them to meet work objectives, work at "personal peak times" and manage their time more effectively. They added that tasks requiring focused attention—planning, evaluations, reviews, analyses, audits and research—were done better at home (Richter, 1991).

Flexiplace arrangements make regular employment a possibility for people who can function full-time but not at a regular worksite. There is another labor pool: people who are available at the worksite but not on a full-time basis—retirees, parents, homemakers, and students among them.

Alternative scheduling can also bring these people into the public service. Here are common arrangements.

Permanent Part-Time

Under this arrangement, an employee works permanently and regularly, although for less than the regular number of hours per week. A 20-hour week is common. Part-time employees solve the problem of having available a skill that is not needed full-time. They tend to make good use of their time because it is limited, and they may prefer working the evening or weekend hours that regular employees disfavor.

> Higher productivity is cited as one of numerous advantages provided by permanent part-time employees in state governments. Other advantages to state government operations provided by these employees are greater flexibility in shifting personnel to meet fluctuating work loads, expanded service hours to the public, retention of experienced employees who cannot or do not wish to continue working full-time, and recruitment of individuals from a different labor pool. . . . Presently, [in Massachusetts] there are 4,582 permanent part-time employees representing the equivalent of 2,030 full-time positions ("Massachusetts," 1981).

Job Sharing

A job-sharing arrangement makes it possible to retain or hire for a full-time job people who want to work only part-time. One worker may want to ease into retirement; another to continue his or her education. Together, they can fill one position. They may divide the time, working different days of the week or mornings or afternoons, or they may divide the responsibilities. Job sharing also makes it possible to recruit people of superior skill who are unavailable full-time, and it brings the benefit of two sets of talent and two perspectives to bear on a job. On the other hand, it creates double work for personnel and payroll officers, and communication between the two employees must be carefully maintained, if the left hand is to know what the right is doing.

Temporary Employment

People who do not want permanent jobs but welcome the opportunity to work on a temporary basis can provide coverage when regular employees are absent or reinforce the permanent staff in times of seasonal or sporadic burdens: lifeguards for the summer season, laborers for snow removal, typists when a big report is due. A useful model is provided by the substitute-teacher system, which maintains prepared rosters of people whose credentials have been verified and times of availability listed.

Alternative Recruits

Young and Old

While the core of the public service remains the professional, full-time, civil service worker, the boundaries of the traditional bureaucracy are becoming softened and permeable, allowing new classes of recruits to enter, serve, and influence the agency. It provides entrée to those who are younger and older than the traditional work force:

> San Antonio has a summertime problem with rapidly growing weeds clogging our drainage ditches, and in today's tough budgetary situation, we've had to cut back on the crew we usually hire to clean the ditches. For next year, we've proposed to the council that we hire our own teenagers to do the job. . . . We'd be providing the kids with a work experience, some money and a positive alternative to getting into gangs and crime during the long, idle vacation days. And we'd get the ditches cleaned (Briseno, 1991).

> Clearwater, Florida's (97,000) internal audit department uses senior citizens to increase productivity in the department. The workers, provided through an AARP (American Association of Retired Persons) program, spend 20 hours a week assisting the city auditor. . . . All senior workers have previous experience as accountant or auditor, thereby reducing training time. . . . The department has employed up to three workers at a time. Other departments in the city are also taking advantage of the program (International City Management Association, 1990, MGT-13).

Students

Public sector agencies can aggressively seek out and engage college students, especially those who have an interest in fields that are needed for the public service. This is the time when career choices are made. Among the vehicles are cadet programs and scholarships:

> Dunedin, Florida (38,500), has implemented a police cadet program to free full-time police officers and department employees from minor adminis-

trative duties. Participants in the program must be . . . enrolled in criminal justice-related courses full-time at a local junior college or university. . . . Cadets assist the department in fingerprinting and booking; microfilming; communications; property, evidence and supply duties; and records filing. They are paid $5 an hour and work 20 hours a week (International City Management Association, 1990, PS-18).

Kentucky's Department of Environmental Protection has found a way to increase the number of qualified workers in some of its critical job classifications. The agency is offering full scholarships to a number of college students studying at Kentucky state universities for careers in such fields as groundwater hydrology, biology and chemical engineering. In return for each year of the scholarship, students must work a year and a half for the state. The program is currently funding nine juniors and seniors ("Keeping the Bluegrass Green," 1991).

Contracted Labor

Special personnel recruitment difficulties can sometimes be solved by contracting. A typical example comes from Madera County, California, which found a satisfactory solution to its problems with civil service public defenders by contracting for the services of private attorneys (International City Management Association, 1990, MGT-19). A less typical example comes from Virginia:

> The City of Manassas . . . is involved in an innovative public-private agreement that not only provides a city service, but also provides employment for the handicapped. . . . The city had found it difficult to recruit and employ persons in this kind of low-paying labor position [picking up trash from containers]. Through this contract, which provides training and employment for handicapped persons, the city did not have to recruit for part-time positions to perform this trash service (International City Management Association, 1990, MGT-22).

Unpaid Labor

People on Loan From the Private Sector

It is in the interest of private sector organizations to have a viable, smooth-running public system. Private, for-profit companies have traditionally contributed "dollar-a-year men" to the federal bureaucracy in wartime and to cities in need. One contemporary example:

**Freebie Prosecutors are Cutting
the Drug Caseload**

Drug cases are doubling the caseload in many courts around the country. Pro bono prosecutors are providing one solution.

In Massachusetts, for example, a large law firm and the Suffolk County district attorney's office have signed an agreement that gives the county a lawyer for eight months. . . . The county turned to the law firm after losing 35 out of about 130 prosecutors due to budget cuts over the last two years. A huge backlog of cases resulted. "The economic crunch put us in a position where we had to reach out," says Suffolk County District Attorney Newman A. Flanagan.

While the district attorney's office gets a free prosecutor for eight months, the lawyer gets some much-needed jury trial experience. And . . . the backload is shrinking (Platt, 1991).

Interns

Graduate and undergraduate programs in public administration, criminal justice, and allied fields commonly offer fieldwork courses that are designed to expose students to the realities and practicalities of agency life. An intern usually works without pay one day per week for a 15-week semester. Interns often possess special expertise (computers, statistics, or budgeting, for example) and should not be overlooked as a resource for collecting data, performing analyses, or drafting reports. An internship permits the student to try out the field and the agency to look the student over without obligation.

To be successful, internships require careful matching, a clear contractual understanding of what is expected of student and agency, and close attention from the agency supervisor.

Volunteers

Writing in 1833, Alexis de Tocqueville was struck by the uniquely American propensity for forming voluntary associations (1945, p. 115). Voluntary service still constitutes a rich resource to augment the public work force: Students, retirees, and even the fully employed willingly contribute.

When volunteers are doing such things as aiding stranded motorists, providing victim assistance and teaching a sexual-assault survival course, they can see the results of their efforts. The same is true of volunteers who groom horses for a mounted patrol unit [and] schedule citizen ride-alongs. . . .

With a professional coordinator and meaningful work assignments, the Tempe (Arizona) Police Department has seen its Volunteers in Policing (VIP) participants increase from 3 to 120 in a little over two years. The result, says Police Chief Dave Brown, is that the department "can provide services that we couldn't provide otherwise." At the same time, Brown says, the 12,000 volunteer hours per year have had a significant impact on the officers' workload ("No Mere Paper-Pushers," 1991, p. 9).

The AARP is quick to point out that the ranks of the retired offer a rich source of free talent.

A volunteer sleuth in Takoma Park, Md., Hugh Irey proves what more police departments are finding out: You don't have to be paid to be good. . . . A retired police commissioner from Los Angeles, he spends seven hours each week analyzing local crime reports and other information to develop profiles of suspects. . . . "It's my line of work—and I love it," says Irey, . . . who will turn 90 in May.

Best of all, Irey gets results. For instance, after a recent string of house burglaries, Irey's discovery of a pattern led to the apprehension of two suspects.

Although he may be unique, Irey is by no means alone. He's one of Takoma Park's eight volunteer gumshoes. . . .

Carrie Spicer logs in tickets from out-of-town offenders, while Frank Neri pursues out-of-state scofflaws. Last year, the department collected an additional $10,000 in fines, thanks to Neri's efforts ("Spare-Time Gumshoes," 1987).

In Florida, Operation GRAMPA (Getting Retirees Actively Motivated to Policing Again) has helped the Fort Myers Police Department "continue lecturing and counseling about drug and alcohol abuse in the city's schools at less than half the cost of using full-time, sworn police officers" ("Retirees Are Back," 1990).

Like everything else, the use of volunteer labor has its costs. Able volunteers must be recruited, given appropriate work, encouraged, and held accountable. There may be opposition from paid staff or from unions. The chief of the 24-member auxiliary police in Quincy, Massachusetts, moved the entire force to the town of Braintree, charging they were "pushed out . . . by pressure from the local police union" ("Auxiliary Cops," 1987, p. 3).

Equipment and Space

Labor is the predominant public sector resource, but the management of equipment and space should not be overlooked in the search for better productivity. Alternatives to the traditional sources and purchasing arrangements can help make these resources more affordable.

Alternative Sources

Changing equipment and space involves some special problems. The cost of labor flows fairly constantly as an operating expense; changes in job design or incumbency cause only minor effects on the spending pattern. But the situation is different when it comes to replacing or acquiring major equipment. Capital investments often require special budget allocations. Up-front costs, even those with fine potential for savings in the long run, are visible and easy to cut or postpone in the effort to stretch a slim budget. Not surprisingly, therefore, much of the search for creative alternatives in the management of equipment and space has to do with acquiring them.

Needed materials or facilities may lie right at hand and yet be unnoticed. Managers who keep alert to the world around them and who exercise some imagination are often rewarded in large and small ways for their vigilance. Other public sector agencies may be a source:

> Across the country, states are eyeing Resolution Trust Corporation property for housing for families who can't afford today's real estate market. But a few states are looking at some of the property once owned by failed savings and loans for a different kind of affordable housing: for their own agencies and departments.
>
> Florida seems to be leading the way. . . . The Department of Professional Regulation . . . was planning to purchase the Freedom Savings and Loan Operation Center in Orlando for $1.85 million for use as a testing center. . . .
>
> Several other state agencies, including the Department of Transportation and the Department of Health and Rehabilitative Services, as well as some school systems, have inquired about possible property acquisition from the RTC. The major attraction is the price—no more than 80 percent of market value (Lichtenstein, 1991).

Private companies can be approached. They might already have a program for providing just what is needed:

The Iowa Park, Texas (6,000), police department needed a crime scene vehicle. . . . So, the department took advantage of a program offered by Southwestern Bell Telephone Company that donates used telephone company vans to public agencies and applied for a van. . . . With private donations of labor and materials and participation by local businesses, the van was air-conditioned and remodeled (International City Management Association, 1990, PS-3).

Sometimes, it is possible to catch two fish with one hook, as with the following description of "other waste management options":

Various municipal departments may be able to safely use up citizens' unwanted products. . . .
  • Parks departments accept usable, unbanned pesticides, . . . swimming pool chemicals for public pools, paints for graffiti eradication projects and building maintenance, and wood preservatives for their picnic shelters and other outdoor structures.
  • Fire departments collect flammable products from citizens to use in training demonstrations and drills (Dewey & Steinwachs, 1991, p. 11).

Leasing

In general, leasing is a costly alternative to ownership. But, where appropriate, leasing is a way to acquire the use of new equipment in a political environment that makes major capital allocations unlikely. It avoids the need for up-front funding and the troublesome "budget lump." Rental fees run smoothly from one month to the next; they become operating costs. Leasing permits flexibility and is a way to test equipment and judge its practical utility in the field before a purchasing decision is made. It eliminates not only start-up costs but also the delays created by detailed purchasing procedures. And the agency need not be stranded with obsolete equipment. The use of a leasing arrangement may also be more economical, particularly if equipment is not needed for full-time or year-round use. Finally, leasing relieves the agency of the cost of equipment maintenance, an important consideration for smaller jurisdictions:

The city of Toppenish, Washington (6,100), police department is leasing its vehicles and making out like a bandit. Before vehicle leasing took hold, the department had city-owned vehicles that were ill-equipped and not uniform, and it had no facilities or personnel to handle maintenance and repair. . . . The city now has patrol vehicles in better mechanical condition for a lower cost, and funds are spent over a 12-month period, rather than in a single, lump sum (International City Management Association, 1981, p. 24).

"Lease-purchase" arrangements permit part of each payment to go toward eventual purchase. At the end of the contract period, ownership of the item passes to the agency. Capital acquisitions from computers to entire buildings can be managed this way. The chief disadvantage of lease-purchase is that the cost of rental is inflated by the cost of financing the purchase.

Summary

The above options represent some of the many ways that agencies can and do improve productivity when management takes advantage of new or different opportunities to strengthen and enrich their resources. These options constitute natural targets of opportunity, identified by managers' alertness to factors and models in the agency's environment.

In the following chapter we turn to management options that are, by contrast, more centrally initiated, organization-wide, and revolutionary departures from the traditional mode of the independent bureaucracy, staffed by a public workforce and pursuing its routines within the boundaries of its jurisdiction.

References

Ackard, R. W. (1985). The DOD Productivity Enhancing Capital Investment Program. In E. D. Rosen (Ed.), Financing productivity. Proceedings of the Second National Public Sector Productivity Conference. *Public Productivity Review*, *9*, 83-107.

Aerni, W., & Burgess, L. (1991, July 1). Solving the waste tire problem in Arizona. *PA Times*, p. 8.

Auxiliary cops get bumped, are welcomed in next town. (1987, November 24). *Law Enforcement News*, pp. 3, 15.

Briseno, A. E. (1991, October). Managing local government with your back to the wall. *Governing*, p. 11.

Committee on Alternative Work Patterns & National Center for Productivity and Quality of Working Life. (1976). *Alternatives in the world of work* (GPO 913-166). Washington, DC: Government Printing Office.

de Tocqueville, A. (1945). *Democracy in America* (Vol. 2). New York: Random House.

Dewey, S., & Steinwachs, M. (1991, July 1). Household waste: Not just for landfills anymore. *PA Times*, pp. 11, 17.

Epstein, P. D., & Fass, S. (1989). Comprehensive productivity programs: A leveraged investment. In E. C. Hayes (Ed.), *The hidden wealth of cities: Policy and productivity methods for American local governments* (pp. 111-131). Greenwich, CT: JAI.

Gaissert, A. B. (1985). Financing productivity improvements in New Jersey. In E. D. Rosen (Ed.), Financing productivity. Proceedings of the Second National Public Sector Productivity Conference. *Public Productivity Review*, 9, 83-107.

Gianakis, G. A., & Friedel, G. K. (1989). The utility of internal consultant groups. *Public Productivity Review*, 13, 61-75.

Gillespie, W. (1985). The Technology Improvement Fund and its impact on productivity in Dayton, Ohio. In E. D. Rosen (Ed.), Financing productivity. Proceedings of the Second National Public Sector Productivity Conference. *Public Productivity Review*, 9, 83-107.

Halachmi, A. (1991). Productivity and information technology: Emerging issues and considerations. *Public Productivity & Management Review*, 14, 327-350.

Injured Pittsburgh cops get the call to cut overtime and boost productivity. (1990, September 15). *Law Enforcement News*, pp. 5, 6.

International City Management Association. (1981). *The guide to management improvement projects in local government.* Washington, DC: Author.

International City Management Association. (1990). *The guide to management improvement projects in local government.* Washington, DC: Author.

Iowa, Ohio—sick leave. (1981, May). *Productivity Probe*, p. 2.

Keeping the bluegrass green. (1991, November). *Governing*, p. 17.

Lichtenstein, D. H. (1991, October). Good deals for states in S&L woes? *Governing*, pp. 18-19.

Massachusetts—Permanent part-time employment. (1981, May). *Productivity Probe*, p. 2.

Michigan—In-house consulting. (1981, May). *Productivity Probe*, p. 1.

No mere paper-pushers, Tempe police volunteers are making a difference. (1991, November 30). *Law Enforcement News*, pp. 9, 15.

Platt, J. R. (1991, July). Freebie prosecutors are cutting the drug caseload. *Governing*, pp. 16-17.

Report finds feds lag behind in flexible work place. (1991, December 1). *PA Times*, p. 3.

Retirees are back in the saddle again. (1990, January 15). *Law Enforcement News*, p. 1.

Richter, M. J. (1991, July). Telecommuting in Arizona: Compounded benefits. *Governing*, p. 67.

Spare-time gumshoes get their men. (1987, March). *AARP News Bulletin*, pp. 1, 7.

State Government Productivity Research Center. (1980, October). *New Jersey's Productivity Improvement Investment Account* (Report No. RM: 690). Lexington, KY: Council of State Governments.

Sweeny, M. (1978, July). *Development of incentive systems for worker productivity.* Unpublished memorandum, New Jersey Department of Civil Service.

Von Drak, P. C. (1982). A modified workweek for a small city agency. *Public Productivity Review*, 6, 121-122.

Wellness program set for New York State employees. (1983, October 1). *Public Administration Times*, p. 7.

10

Managing for Productivity

This chapter looks at new managerial perspectives on the two basic productivity improvement questions: Are there ways of achieving greater efficiency? Can better services be produced? The contemporary perspective on these key questions turns to nontraditional, extra-organizational options and a radically new view of how public sector organizations should operate. What has impelled the new thinking?

The Challenge to Tradition

Let us start by looking at classical, orthodox public administration. It produces public services by using budgeted funds, the bureaucratic form of organization, and public employees as workforce. The system has important virtues: Relatively speaking, it has provided stability, reliability, predictability, efficiency, accountability, and professionalism.

216

Bureaucracy has survived and thrived because of its strengths. The development of the classic bureaucratic model not only represented real administrative and managerial progress in most instances, but [also] embodied and advanced several significant democratic ideals. . . .

As a protection against corruption and the willful misuse of power, the impersonal and "inflexible" rules and regulations of bureaucracy have been a relief and an advance (Wriston, 1980, pp. 179-180).

But the structure and rules that make it stable also make the bureaucratic organization clumsy in accommodating to a world of constant and rapid change. It relies on process—planned from on high and controlled by rules and a reward system that values adherence to procedure. It is not built to take in feedback. All older organizations tend to fatten up, grow more conservative and top-heavy; "bureaucracy . . . is especially prey to this tendency" (Wriston, 1980, p. 183). Finally, the old management system assumes that workers are hands, not heads.

Much of the productivity movement to date has been devoted to effecting incremental changes in the traditional system. For parts of the public service, that evolutionary advance will do. The march of events will overtake others, however. Driven by impatience with the old system— "reinventing government" is one theme (Osborne & Gaebler, 1992b)—the newer approaches to improving efficiency and service quality start from a radically different premise. They are grounded in the open systems concept of equifinality, which is just another way of saying, "There is more than one way to get there from here." In this view, the important thing is the end product. The traditional bureaucratic agency is reduced to only one among several alternative instruments, and there is a readiness to abandon or transform it.

Two Lines of Current Thought

The two basic current lines of thought on how to produce better public services are (1) let someone else do it and (2) fundamentally change how we do it. As it turns out, arguments for the first rest chiefly on improved efficiency, while arguments for the second turn on enhanced quality.

Letting Someone Else Do It

Some theorists suggest coproduction: Have the clients themselves do part of the work. Some writers show how interlocal cooperative agreements to share resources or form new, interjurisdictional agencies achieve economies of scale and make more services affordable. Some urge opening up the production of many public services to the private sector.

Changing How We Do It

The "managing for quality" movement would transform the rationale of public agencies by making service quality the prime objective and keeping process and structure subservient to "customer satisfaction." Agencies would be changed in fundamental ways, including the adoption of an open management style, the use of hard data to inform decision making, and the empowerment of workers and clients.

These two major lines of thought share a preoccupation with the end product but differ in pursuing the use of alternative delivery modes or the transformation of public agencies.

Alternative Service Delivery Options

Sometimes there is a creative, better way:

City Hall to Be in Feature Film

The City of Orlando helped to offset the cost of destroying its old city hall by attracting Warner Brothers to film the destruction and use the tape in the production of *Lethal Weapon III*. The implosion of city hall, just five feet away from the new $36 million new city hall, will open the movie ("City Hall," 1992).

Let us examine alternatives for producing and delivering public services.

Intergovernmental Cooperation

Cooperation across jurisdictional lines can improve efficiency and service quality, especially for small governmental units. The chief spurs to seeking cooperation include the desire to achieve economies of scale, a lack of facilities or qualified personnel, and a desire for flexibility (Talley, 1980, pp. 449-450). Through cooperative arrangement it is possible to compensate selectively for the limitations posed by small jurisdiction size or other thriftless conditions created by the fragmented nature of the political system.

The discussion that follows is heavily indebted to the *Intergovernmental Cooperation Handbook*, an excellent publication of the Pennsylvania Department of Community Affairs (1990).

Forms of Agreement

Mutually beneficial arrangements can be transacted by informal, "handshake" agreements or by formal compact.

> Handshake agreement is the generic name for all those unwritten working arrangements between municipalities. . . . A borough plows a township street and vice versa because it results in better snowplow routes for both. A township buys copier paper and sells some of it to another municipality at cost. A city lends a street sweeper to a township for a few weeks and obtains use of a paver for several weeks in return (Pennsylvania Department of Community Affairs, 1990, p. 6).

Informal arrangements evolve naturally and easily but leave a lot undefined, which can lead to misunderstandings and conflict. More formal, written agreements are needed for contract programs, joint ownership, or the establishment of joint service units. The items to be spelled out in advance include conditions of joining and dropping out of the arrangement; how costs will be shared; location, maintenance, scheduling, operation, and order of use of jointly owned resources; rental conditions; and dispute resolution. Sample intergovernmental agreements may be found in Leonard Ruchelman, *A Workbook in Redesigning Public Services* (1989, pp. 68-72).

Forms of Cooperation

Consortia. A consortium is a cooperative arrangement between agencies for the sharing of resources. It achieves economies of scale, making it possible to acquire and use items that would otherwise be too costly or entirely unaffordable.

> A joint library project sponsored by the city of Scottsdale, Arizona, . . . and the local school district was initiated in 1988, after the district formulated plans for a new middle school/high school complex. . . . Plans for a joint use library were formulated to allow students and citizens to share the same resources and books; to save dollars by building one, rather than two facilities;

to expand operational hours, allowing residents and students to use the library at night and on weekends; and to provide students access after school to research materials not ordinarily found in a school library (International City Management Association, 1990, LHS-12).

In the same cooperative mode, whole jurisdictions are increasingly joining together to achieve administrative ends:

> The most common, and the most rapidly growing, form of regionalism . . . consists of simple agreements to consolidate specific services, cooperate in their provision, or shift their provision from one government to another. . . .
>
> Public safety agencies lead the parade in service sharing. Police departments and sheriffs' offices keep joint records, operate joint radio bands and 911 emergency numbers, share crime laboratories, do joint investigations, establish regional automated fingerprint identification systems, . . . and, in a variety of ways, share the costs of training law enforcement personnel (Shanahan, 1991, pp. 70, 72).

Joint Purchasing. Joint purchasing can be undertaken either as a joint program or by contract. In the first case, writing specifications, locating vendors, and executing purchase orders is done on behalf of all members. In the second case, one "lead" jurisdiction purchases for another.

Often inadequate in the public sector, the skill of writing good specifications is basic to contracting out and to joint ventures. There is a natural inclination to overkill: to leave out no detail, no potential application, no extreme of conditions. By this logic, the Department of Defense has specified that coffee machines for the Air Force's C-5A jet transport planes "produce fifty-six ounces of coffee, tea, or hot soup every four minutes, even if the plane were to lose all cabin pressure or were to be subjected to 40 g's, enough gravitational force to kill everyone on board" (Kettl, 1988, p. 1). Every specification adds (often, exponentially) to the cost; those coffee machines cost $7,400!

Specifications may be unnecessary: A ready-made, off-the-shelf product may be modifiable or even usable as is. Necessary specifications should be written with an eye to limiting the number of different items, each of which must be acquired, warehoused, inventoried, and distributed. More parts might be made interchangeable; fewer, more generic items (such as cleaning compounds) might be substituted for many specialized ones.

Equipment Sharing. A sharing arrangement is particularly useful for infrequently used resources. Sharing mechanisms may take the form of joint ownership, rental arrangements, or equipment trades. The list of equipment particularly suitable for sharing includes animal transport cage, grader, line painting truck, survey equipment, and truck scales (Pennsylvania Department of Community Affairs, 1990, p. 20).

Cooperative Construction. Small jurisdictions can cooperate in building and operating recreation centers, libraries, parks, and theaters. "In each case, whether large or small, combining municipal resources enables communities to consider facilities not within their reach as separate entities" (Pennsylvania Department of Community Affairs, 1990, p. 28).

Joint Services. In contrast to the consortium arrangement, wherein service units retain their independence, units may merge to create one regional service that is jointly paid for and overseen.

> Eight government units in Muskegon County, Michigan, implemented a centralized police-dispatching service that has improved effectiveness and reduced costs. . . . Key provisions of this agreement are:
> 1. Membership [is] open to any incorporated city with [a] full-time, paid law enforcement department.
> 2. Each participating agency appoints a senior elective or administrative official to the Board of Directors. . . .
> 3. Each participating government agency appoints a senior law-enforcement official to the Board of Administration. . . .
> 4. Central Police Dispatch shall be financed by contributions from each of the participating agencies (Barbour, 1980, p. 963).

In addition to police service, other fertile areas for joint services agreements include legal services, landfill sites, insurance, vehicle maintenance, computer services, and ambulance service. In 1982, one third of cities and counties were using intergovernmental agencies for bus systems, sanitary inspections, and the operation of mental health and retardation programs and facilities (Honadle, 1984, p. 306).

Contract Services. Jurisdictions may contract out to other jurisdictions. Contracts are more flexible than joint services: They are more easily established and can be readily terminated or transferred to another supplier.

However, the municipality that provides the service retains control. A wide range of services—including vehicle maintenance, snow removal, fire fighting, and, as we have seen, purchasing—are amenable to inter-jurisdictional contracting.

Other Programs. Costs can be shared to the benefit of all for a variety of miscellaneous operations. For example, a cooperative auction of surplus equipment splits the cost of advertisement, site, storage facilities, and auctioneer. Jurisdictions using compatible personal computers or a common centralized computer can share costs of maintenance, training, and expertise. Employee health insurance becomes more affordable with a larger pool. Cooperative recycling programs can generate a large enough flow of materials to make recycling worthwhile.

Improving Productivity Through Cooperation

Cooperation is a source of efficiency: It is a way to benefit from economies of scale. Joint purchasing can make orders large enough to take advantage of "threshold points" at which bulk prices begin. Overhead costs must be entailed for even small operations; sharing produces a better return on the investment in basic facilities, equipment, specialists, and administrators.

Cooperation can enhance the quality of service. It can make possible the provision of facilities not otherwise affordable: recreational centers, parks, adult education, transportation for senior citizens, and so on. Offices are covered and can remain open when one employee is ill or on vacation. Cooperation is a way of affording specially skilled workers (e.g., purchasing agents, code-enforcement officers, health officers, and police investigators). Compacts can integrate natural systems: "Clogged storm sewers may be a problem in your municipality but the source of the silt-laden runoff is a subdivision in another municipality" (Pennsylvania Department of Community Affairs, 1990, p. 4).

Problems

Like everything else in life, cooperation has its problems. The legality of extrajurisdictional cooperation may be in question. Pennsylvania smoothed the way by a law that essentially provided that "if a municipality has the power to take an action or deliver a service under the provisions of its code or charter, it has the power to cooperate in doing so" (Pennsylvania Department of Community Affairs, 1990, p. 7).

The allocation of costs and the schedule for usage of shared resources may be a cause of friction. A jurisdiction may consider itself overcharged or underserved unless carefully detailed provisions have been agreed on in advance. Citizens may have problems: Centrally located joint service centers may impose travel difficulties, and clients accustomed to local officials may feel abandoned when a new agency takes charge (Honadle, 1984, p. 307).

Centralized purchasing requires standardization: Custom-ordered items must be foregone in favor of more generic, mutually acceptable ones.

Contracting In

A piece of equipment may be highly desirable but not worth investing in because it will not receive enough use to justify its cost. Such equipment can be made affordable if economies of scale can be created: Other public agencies or private organizations may be willing to pay for use of the public asset under an arrangement called "contracting in." For example, the owners of a shopping mall may be glad to pay the highway department for marking out traffic lanes and parking spaces. Public agencies have even been known to "take in washing":

> Since 1964, the Faribault Regional Treatment Center has taken in laundry to help cover the cost of its laundry service. In 1978, several non-state agencies asked Faribault if it would handle their laundry. . . . Faribault took the accounts. "In volume there was efficiency," said Dick Stowe, laundry manager. . . .
>
> New equipment installed in November 1988 cost Faribault $485,000. This cost will be paid back in three years. Stowe estimates that the state will save $1 million on the purchase price of the equipment in the next 10 years (Jimenez, 1989).

Citizen Coproduction

We have seen that agencies may turn to one another. They can also turn to the clients themselves. Clients can collaborate in the production of services, a process called *coproduction*. This is not a dramatic departure from tradition, but "seemingly small savings from active coproduction . . . realized across different city services . . . could constitute a substantial boon to the city budget" (R. C. Rich, quoted in Percy, 1987, p. 90).

Defining Coproductivity

The definition of coproduction requires discussion. At the heart of the concept is a recognition that citizen actions affect public services. Beyond that, different people ascribe so many different meanings that the concept is robbed of its utility. Some scholars define coproduction very broadly and include almost anything citizens do that affects the outcome of services: "learning new ideas or new skills, acquiring healthier habits" (Whitaker, 1980, p. 240); "anti-litter campaigns, car pool programs and exercise programs" (Ruchelman, 1989, p. 33). Some definitions include citizen actions that parallel but do not serve agency efforts: "the installation of alarms, window bars, extra locks, and outside lighting" (Percy, 1987, p. 84).

Brudney and England's view comes closer to the usage we will adopt: "[T]he major contribution of coproduction is an appreciation of the role that citizens can and do play in the actual provision of services . . . (e.g., carrying trash cans to curbside, . . . volunteering as teacher aides)" (1983, p. 62).

From the productivity standpoint, we are concerned only with how citizen actions can affect the efficiency or the quality of public services as formulated by public agencies. For that reason we will rule out any citizen activities that do not relate to agency resources, outputs, and production process. What is left after all of these exclusions is the idea that when clients pick up part of an agency's work and contribute to its output, that is coproduction, which enables the public work force to produce more output per employee-day.

Coproduction in Action

At Eastchester High School in the state of New York, students paint school walls during winter break, saving approximately $55,000 ("Vacationing Students," 1982, p. B2). Other examples of coproduction:

> Hopewell, Virginia, . . . sets aside a city truck for citizens to use over the weekends. . . . Citizens may call the city to have a truck parked in their neighborhood so that they can throw out leaves, yard debris, and other items. . . . With citizens handling their own debris cleanups, city crews are now better able to complete their regular routes (International City Management Association, 1981, p. 27).

> Austin, Texas, is one of the most fervent new converts to tree-cycling. . . . Last January, 400 volunteers, largely Boy Scouts and Girl Scouts, helped residents drop off trees at ten city parks. . . .

To get citizens involved in the program, Austin unleashes a barrage of publicity efforts. . . . You have a choir of little kids singing, "O Christmas Tree / O Christmas Tree / In Austin we recycle thee" (Shute, 1991, p. 49).

The coproducer-client may be another agency or unit. The custodial service may require that all trash baskets be placed outside the office doors at the end of the day to facilitate pickup. The mail room may have departments pick up their mail instead of having it delivered.

Contracting Out

Introduction

Government agencies can and do contract out to a variety of providers: private industry, nonprofit agencies, other governmental units, and even citizen groups. Neighborhood groups repair streets in Portland, construct sidewalks in Louisville, maintain parks in Baltimore, and operate shelters in Boulder (Herbers, 1983, p. A1). However, the most frequently used alternative service delivery approach is purchase of service contracting to private or nonprofit organizations (International City Management Association, 1989, p. 3).

This type of contracting out, "letting private industry do more of government's work" (Main, 1985, p. 92), is a form of privatization.

Two distinct and quite different objectives are pursued under the name of privatization: the improvement of the delivery of goods or services by taking advantage of marketplace efficiencies, and, alternatively, the reduction or termination of public support for particular goods or services altogether. . . . In the first case, privatization does not eliminate government accountability. . . . In the second case, government withdraws or reduces its role as a buyer, regulator, standard setter, or decision maker in particular service areas (Barnekov & Raffel, 1990, p. 136).

If a city divests itself of its airport or golf course, that is privatization in the second sense, which is outside the scope of our discussion; "such abandonment of . . . responsibility to private enterprise" has been called "false privatization" (Kettl, 1988, p. 12). In any case, "contracting out" means "privatization" only in the sense first mentioned above.

The Growth of Contracting Out

While contracting out (for military hardware) goes back to the time of George Washington (Sharkansky, 1980, p. 118), use of the private sector to deliver public services has, in Harry Hatry's word, "exploded" in recent years (Hatry, 1989, p. 1). Privatization has been called "the single most influential concept of the [1980s]" (Moe, 1987, p. 453). The popularity of privatization has many roots. The public service has been under fire (Holzer, 1990, pp. 163-165). Public agencies are visible budget items in a time of budget crises. Rightly or wrongly, the public work force is seen as costly and public agencies as rule-bound, politicized, and tied to old methods. This is reinforced by philosophical concerns about "less government," "public choice," and the need for competitive market forces to keep public agencies fit and trim (Fixler & Hayes, 1989, p. 75; Naff, 1991, p. 24). The catch phrase is that government should "steer rather than row" ("Taking the Town," 1991, p. 52). The private sector organization is increasingly perceived not only as model, but also as healthy competition for the public sector administrative agency (see, especially, Savas, 1987, 1992; Osborne & Gaebler, 1992b). Finally, although "union opposition to contracting is quite rational, for contracting often spells the elimination of the union in the contracted workplace" (Chandler & Feuille, 1991, p. 20), public unions have declined in bargaining power.

The pattern of growth is significant. As Fixler and Hayes (1989) point out, contracting started with tangible, nonclient services: refuse collection, street repair, utilities, and vehicle towing at the local level; custodial, engineering, highway maintenance at the state level; custodial, buildings and grounds, food service, and security at the federal level (pp. 79-82). It then moved to include "soft" social services: child care, drug and alcohol treatment, mental health and retardation services mostly, but not exclusively, to nonprofit organizations (Honadle, 1984, p. 311). Next, "of prime significance was the fact of the shift to contracting of services which hitherto had been considered strictly the preserve of government" (Fixler & Hayes, 1989, p. 79): some police functions, jails, prisons, and fire services.

California, Kansas, Louisiana, New Mexico, Tennessee, and Texas have turned over some state prisons to private companies, as have the U.S. Immigration and Naturalization Service and Bureau of Prisons. Robert Britton, vice president of the Corrections Corporation of America, is fond of saying that his company has more prisoners in its jails than the corrections departments of 25 states (Chase, 1992, p. 55).

This transfer of the coercive power of the state into private hands raises serious concern among those who see in it a threat to the constitutional rights of the incarcerated (Sullivan, 1987). On the other hand, the Council of State Governments and the Urban Institute have recommended that states "facing considerable overcrowding, often resulting in court orders to remedy the situation, should consider contracting. . . . Contracts should provide adequate protection of the inmates' rights and protect the state from unjust liability claims" (Allen, 1989, p. 35). This issue and other questions, such as possible threats to national security, public safety, and authority over funds, are far from resolved (Moe, 1987, p. 457).

Almost every governmental entity contracts out for something. The federal government relies heavily on private producers for defense equipment.

> In fiscal year 1985 . . . the federal government signed more than 21.5 million contracts, totaling nearly $200 billion or 21 percent of all federal spending, according to a report distributed by the U.S. General Services Administration (a report prepared, of course, by a contractor) (Kettl, 1988, p. 24).

Local governments use purchase-of-service contracting chiefly for public works, transportation, public utilities, health and human services, and support functions such as heavy equipment maintenance (International City Management Association, 1989, pp. 6-8).

> In La Mirada, California, . . . the city government consists of only sixty regular employees. They supervise contractors who take care of everything from fire and police needs to human services and public works (Kettl, 1988, p. 24).

Advantages of Contracting

How can contracting out to the private sector improve productivity? What are the advantages?

Economy. "A 1981 General Accounting Office report said it cost 50% more to use federal employees to clean government buildings than to use contractors" (Main, 1985, p. 96). "Two similar cities only 22 miles apart in the New York metropolitan area are compared, one with municipal [solid waste collection] service and the other with contract service. In the latter case, each worker collects almost three times as much waste per day" (Savas, 1992, p. 89). Why is this so?

> After extensive studies of municipal services, Savas concludes that the following factors do *not* account for the observed cost differences: salaries, fringe benefits, or service quality. . . .
>   The observed cost difference *is* accounted for by the fact that contractors (1) provide less paid time off for their employees . . . ; (2) use part-time and lower-skilled workers where possible; (3) are more likely to hold their managers responsible for equipment maintenance as well as worker activities; (4) are more likely to give their first-line managers the authority to hire and fire workers; (5) are more likely to use incentive systems; (6) are less labor intensive; (7) have younger work forces, with less seniority; and (8) have more workers per supervisor (Savas, 1992, pp. 89-90).

Economies of Scale. The scale of a public sector operation is defined by the size of the political unit. For processes that require a large investment in equipment, facilities, training, or expertise, only a large enough scale of operation to make full use of these resources can bring the unit costs down.

> Seattle, one of the leaders in the recycling movement, contracts with private business for recycling service. That arrangement has given Seattle access to the economies of scale offered by a large recycler. One contractor, Waste Management of Seattle, built a $2.5 million recycling facility. . . . The city estimates that it saves $10 a ton by recycling these materials (Chase, 1992, p. 53).

Competition. Opening up the opportunity to the private sector creates competition among private providers and with the public work force. It brings costs down and stimulates the public work force, giving it a stake in performing well.

> Newark, New Jersey, uses both municipal crews and a private contractor for refuse collection. Savings resulting from the first three-year contract were estimated at between $900,000 and $1,800,000. . . . In addition, evaluation of contractor activities helped the city focus on management, manpower, equipment, vehicle maintenance, and routing issues and the result was that city crews have increased their productivity so that the price gap between city crew and the contractor has narrowed (International City Management Association, 1989, p. 4).

For several years, Phoenix, Ariz., has posed the ultimate challenge, forcing its own workers to bid against private firms for the privilege of collecting residential trash. City workers initially lost every district, but after streamlining costs they have now won them all back ("Taking the Town," 1991, p. 53).

Expertise. A public agency may not be able to recruit, assemble, and support the expertise that is needed for some of its operations. Contracting provides a way of getting that expertise when and as needed.

Four years ago, the town of West Frankfurt, Illinois, burdened by a balky water system plagued by low pressure, leaks and labor problems, contracted to pay $400,000 a year to Environmental Management Corporation of St. Louis to manage the town water system. EMC hired the employees of the town water department and took over maintenance and billing. . . .

Not least of the benefits from Mayor Simmons' point of view is that EMC deals with the U.S. Environmental Protection Agency. "I'm in the grocery business," he says. "The only thing I know about the water is, you go to the faucet and turn it on. When the EPA people come in, the only thing I can say is 'Okay' " (Chase, 1992, p. 53).

Flexibility. Contracting is a way to experiment without big start-up costs. Seasonal or temporary needs can be met without investing in year-round salaries or full-time ownership of equipment. The dead hand of the past can be lifted:

Private corrections is not burdened with vestigial positions remaining from old, outdated programs, or featherbedding that dates back to specific, once-in-a-lifetime incidents, or particular management preferences from a long-gone administrator. Roster systems, job descriptions, hiring criteria and procedures, training standards, and other personnel management subsystems in the private sector are not laden with the history of the agency, the politics of the state, or the acrimonious labor-management atmosphere that sometimes permeates government agencies (Henderson, 1988, pp. 98, 100).

Less Red Tape. Public agencies must work within budgetary and procedural constraints that are designed to ensure accountability.

Thanks to Boss Tweed and his contemporaries . . . American society embarked on a gigantic effort to *control* what went on inside government . . . but . . . in making it difficult to steal the public's money, we made it

230 IMPROVING PUBLIC SECTOR PRODUCTIVITY

virtually impossible to *manage* the public's money. In adopting written tests scored to the third decimal point . . . we built mediocrity into our work force. In making it impossible to fire people who did not perform, we turned mediocrity into deadwood.

The product was government with a distinct ethos: slow, inefficient, impersonal (Osborne & Gaebler, 1992a, p. 49).

A case in point:

Over a period of six years and at a cost of $12.9 million dollars, New York City had made a number of attempts to rebuild the [Wollman Memorial] ice skating rink. . . .

On the morning of May 22, 1986, developer Donald J. Trump read in the newspaper that New York City would try to rebuild the rink once again. . . . Mr. Trump felt that his firm could complete the job in four months and offered to so do. . . . By the second week in November . . . the first group of skaters were happily gliding over the ice. . . .

The city sought to diagnose why it had failed while a private developer had succeeded in high style. . . . The city was confronted with serious information gathering constraints. Any discussions with outside experts before a project goes out to bid is considered collusion. . . . The city [needed] to provide . . . specifications . . . before it could solicit bids. . . . Some fifteen to twenty people would have to agree before a contract could be approved. . . . To save time, Trump asked the architects and contractors to design the project in outline, without the many details (Ruchelman, 1989, pp. 57-59).

Improved Management. Managing contracts improves the manager. In preparing requests for bidding, managers are required to think through their objectives and standards: what, precisely, constitutes a good service? Putting dollar costs on a service raises new questions about priorities, about whether the service is worth the cost. Contractors expose managers to new technology, alternative methods, and different perspectives.

As Ira Sharkansky (1980) has pointed out, contracting can also serve other, latent agendas, among them enlarging programs while abiding by freeze requirements, weakening government employee unions, and evading civil service regulations (p. 117).

Problems With Contracting Out

Donald Kettl (1988, pp. 11-13) has provided a useful "handle" to problems with privatization by reducing them to three basic areas: What should be privatized? Should the privatization be in the public interest or self-interest? How should privatization be administered? The problems are, respectively: political, behavioral, and managerial.

Political Problems. Sovereignty gives government great power over the individual. It can take property, draft individuals for service, and imprison, even execute. Protection against abuse of this great power lies in the U.S. Constitution, the laws, and the policies that constrain government and keep it accountable.

Contracting out some government functions raises concern about these constitutional, legal, and procedural protections. What happens to an inmate's constitutional protections when the prison goes into private hands? "Court decisions make it clear that government responsibility and supervision is not enough to subject a private provider to the same constitutional restrictions the state would have" (Sullivan, 1987, p. 486).

The General Accounting Office (GAO), Office of Management and Budget (OMB), and Department of Energy have been struggling to pin down a definition of those "inherently governmental functions" that should not be contracted out. GAO's review found the concept still difficult to define ("Are We Contracting," 1992).

The director of one department of corrections suggests avoiding such dubious areas by limiting contracting to partial and subordinate functions:

[Regarding prisons], there are four major ways in which the private sector has become increasingly involved in what traditionally has been a public sector responsibility. The first is operation or management of prison industries by private enterprise. . . . A second option is private financing of correctional construction, including lease-purchase arrangements. A third option is total private sector operation of correctional facilities—this is the most controversial aspect of privatization. Finally, there is the growing practice of contract services for medical treatment, food preparation, and treatment of special offenders, such as drug abusers. . . .

Philosophically, I find totally private management of our correctional institutions inappropriate. Government, for example, does not have the moral right to delegate the power of arrest and punishment to private organizations. . . . Many legitimate aspects of jail management can be efficiently handled by private organizations. These include food service, medical treatment, counseling and training programs or services (Saxton, 1988, pp. 16-17).

There are further questions. Public agencies are bound by administrative due process: advance notice of changes, public hearings, and so on. Are citizen rights to these lost with contracting out? Is the separation of church and state compromised when a church group receives a contract to administer a social service or oversee neighborhood rehabilitation? What are the consequences for equal opportunity? Some experts maintain that, because public sector employment is the "principal engine" of upward mobility for racial minorities, privatization is harmful ("Taking the Town," 1991, p. 54).

Behavioral Problems. Contracting out demoralizes the public work force, and not just because of the loss of jobs. Most workers are hired by the contractor as a requirement of the contract; many are transferred. The public work force is demoralized because it sees a message, an insult.

> Much of the force of the public choice argument comes from its logical clarity and simplicity. . . . The power of this logic, however, rests on its basic assumption . . . that the administrator single-mindedly concentrates on what is of ultimate utility to himself or herself, and that this perspective revolves around personal power, security, and income.
>
> It is hard to argue that individuals do not look to enhance their own positions. However, it is equally difficult to accept the notion that in administering government programs bureaucrats drive so hard to maximize their own utility that other, more publicly oriented objectives slip out of sight. The number of public-spirited bureaucrats is in reality quite large, and an approach to public policy that starts with such a cynical view of public servants is dangerously flawed (Kettl, 1988, pp. 12-13).

Citizens can find contracting unsettling, fearing that services may be disrupted or deteriorate (Honadle, 1984, p. 304). Contractors may go bankrupt. Strikes are real possibilities.

> Will a contractor motivated by profit faithfully perform a public service? Or will he make a low-ball bid just to get a contract and then goose up his price—or worse, walk away from a vital function if it becomes unprofitable? (Main, 1985, p. 93)

"Creaming" (giving preference to the easy tasks) and sacrificing quality are temptations to the profit-motivated. And contracting provides incentives for abuse, fraud, corruption, and even links to organized crime (Katz, 1991, p. 41). "A high incidence of some 1,000 federal, state, and local officials convicted of felonies during the 1970-76 period dealt with contracts between government agencies and private firms" (Sharkansky, 1980, p. 119).

Fixler and Hayes (1989) recommend that "a thorough reading of the anticontracting literature, published by the American Federation of State, County, and Municipal Employees [1983], will dispel any illusions about the 'guaranteed success' of contracting, and will increase the chances of successful outcomes" (p. 88).

Management Problems. The competent management and effective control of contracting require special skills in defining needs, writing specifications (as we have seen), and preparing comprehensive contracts. It takes expensive time.

> In many ways increased reliance on entities outside government places an even heavier responsibility on the government manager—assuring that the entity selected can perform with high quality and low cost; monitoring performance; and ultimately holding it accountable for results. Managers must find ways to motivate, coordinate, and monitor organizations over which they have little direct control (Staats, 1988, p. 603).

Yet, "this is where public sector managers have fallen down. In its 1987 study, the Council of State Governments found existing monitoring mechanisms weak" (Saxton, 1988, p. 17). "In an assessment of 87 contracts worth a total of about $1.4 billion . . . GAO identified deficiencies in 59 (68 percent). The deficiencies resulted in increases in contract costs ranging from several hundred dollars to over $1 million" (Dudley, 1990, p. 489).

For example, taking advantage of competition means that competition must exist:

> Welsbach Electric Corp., which already had a monopoly in the city's other two boroughs, underbid Broadway Maintenance and won the contract for the whole city. After receiving a record 180,000 complaints in one year about lights that didn't work, New York got smart. In 1981, it divided the city into eight service areas, allowing no company to contract . . . in more than two areas. Complaints are down 57% (Main, 1985, p. 94).

Contracts must provide sanctions for inadequate performance. To ensure control over the quality of contracted work done in picking up and processing recyclable trash, the city of Seattle "retains responsibility for the recycling function with a consumer complaint [hotline] staffed by city workers and a staff of inspectors to check out complaints" (Chase, 1992, p. 54).

Contracting Reconsidered

Some interesting questions arise in the context of these political, behavioral, and managerial problems. If an agency creates the managerial capacity to administer contracts—that is, to define rationales and objectives, specify and measure standards, and monitor performance—is it not also now in a position to manage its own work and work force better? "Unions argue that if the management resources that went to contract administration went instead to improve management of government-delivered services, government would reduce costs, improve quality, and retain direct control" (Nelson, 1980, p. 433).

> Labor unions say the urge to privatize too often crops up where the urge to manage well has been missing for decades. "Before you go making these dramatic changes, look at the way work is done now and try to make it more effective with government workers," says Linda Lampkin, research director of AFSCME, a union of public employees ("Taking the Town," 1991, p. 54).

Another question that arises is, if contracting circumvents procedural, budgetary, or other constraints, why can these constraints not be eased also for the public sector operation? If detailed rules are not vital, should they bind the public agency? If, on the other hand, such rules are vital, should they be sidestepped by contracting?

The debate over the pros and cons of contracting has generated a lot of heat but not enough light as yet. Despite evidence on both sides, there is no solid conclusion about the net, long-term effects of contracting out as a productivity-improving technique. Kammerman and Kahn word the situation well: "[P]rivatization is only one policy tool, not even a new one, and it is certainly not a magic potion or an all-ailment nostrum. . . . The privatization tool should not be forbidden, discarded, underplayed: nor should it be employed indiscriminately" (quoted in Barnekov & Raffel, 1990, pp. 144-145).

Clearly, the existence of the contracting option opens up choice and feeds back to possibilities for change within the public sector.

> There is much the public manager can learn from the literature and debate over privatization. . . . The use of choice and competition (for example, within public education) and attention to measuring service quantitatively (for example, in solid waste collection) may be adopted within an environment of public provision (Barnekov & Raffel, 1990, p. 150).

Some Contracting Guidelines

For decision makers considering contracting as an option, there are no definitive rules to guide choice. There are, however, guidelines and criteria that can serve as a reminder of important considerations. The following set of questions constitutes a suggestive checklist:

- What is the reason for contracting? What benefits are expected?
- What are the comparative costs (taking into account the expense of contract management)?
- What is known about the bidder's financial stability and performance record?
- What are the opportunities for kickbacks, corruption, abuse, and conflicts of interest? Can they be detected or prevented?
- What are the possibilities of disruption of service? Can substitutes be obtained?
- Can some internal capacity be retained to provide the service in case of contract breakdown?
- Do we have (or can we obtain) expertise for preparing specifications, drawing contracts, or monitoring performance?
- Does the work lend itself to measurement? What information requirements should be written into the contract?
- Are the specifications unambiguous and not unduly restrictive?
- Does real competition exist, and will choice continue to be available?
- Is the quoted price too good to be true? (Is the bidder unrealistically optimistic about costs? Is this a baiting ploy?) Can creaming be prevented and equitable service maintained?
- What quality criteria are important? Can they be monitored? How will standards be enforced?
- Can noncompliance be detected? By what process? What penalties are available?
- Is contracting legal? Is governmental responsibility being abdicated? Will client or subject rights be jeopardized?

Managing for Quality

Introduction

Two parallel threads can be traced in the progressive movement toward better public service. One, as we have just seen, is the dramatic growth of interest in privatization and other proxies. That path would bypass the public sector agency—not entirely, but as much as possible. The other thread traces a slow but steady transformation within the public service itself: a shift of focus from the management of process to the management of results. The transformation is still incomplete, but it is bringing to the public sector agency a capacity to adapt, respond, and react—to reshape goals, shift resources, and change routines in order to meet new conditions and changing client needs. That path is the subject of this section.

The two paths are not independent: The search for alternatives springs largely from frustration with moribund bureaucracies, while private competition is hastening the reformation and liberation of the public service by disarranging the status quo and pointing up the deleterious effects of locking agencies into regulatory straitjackets.

Why "Think Quality"?

Looking to the improvement of the public sector, the idea of managing for quality is now predominant. It starts with "an attitude that 'thinks quality' at every stage of a project" and "focus[es] potential and skills on goals, not roles" (Raudsepp, 1986, p. 124). Why is this shift in focus so popular? An apocryphal story illustrates.

> A man digs a hole; after he finishes, his co-worker fills it in. They walk a few feet and start again, then again. A bewildered passerby finally asks, "What are you doing? It doesn't make any sense." The digger replies, "The guy who puts the trees in the holes is out sick" (Ames, 1992).

Farfetched? U.S. Postal Service workers who operate letter-sorting machines have been forbidden to correct even the most obvious ZIP-code error. They must key into the machine what they see on the envelope, even if it is clearly wrong. This means that the letter goes to the wrong post office, which then makes the correction and sends the letter on (Judis, 1988, p. 33). But it does not make any sense: Workers are capable of making decisions that improve production; being treated like a cog in a machine is inhumane and demoralizing; redone work is a waste of resources; slow mail displeases and frustrates the public.

The Evolution of Goal-Centered Thinking

For a long time, agency goals were taken for granted. It was assumed that a political decision created the agency's mandate, and proper administration was marked by the use of efficient procedures for producing the appropriate services. The early movement to reform budget presentations arose out of the needs of those political decision makers for better information about the purposes to which resources were being put. The program planning and budgeting system (PPB or PPBS) "represented the first major innovation in budgetary planning concepts. Where the line-item budget is concerned with inputs (items of resource allocated along jurisdictional lines), program budgets deal with program objectives and program costs—regardless of function or organizational lines" (Bennewitz, 1980, p. 118).

The management-by-objectives (MBO) concept added three important thrusts. One was to align the activities of all organizational subunits to ensure a focus on achieving the organizational goal. This was done by "contracts" negotiated between each subunit supervisor and his or her superior, guaranteeing what the subunit would produce in the coming year. The second thrust was quantification: The objectives to be achieved were expressed in solid numbers. The third thrust was a move toward a more participative management system: Unit supervisors were free to decide means and be responsible only for objectives. MBO is a direct ancestor of the total quality management (TQM) approach popular today (Rodgers & Hunter, 1992, p. 37).

Zero based budgeting (ZBB) brought stronger emphasis on program goals and quantification. It added a capacity for dealing with shifting priorities: Older programs could be placed in competition with new ones on a flat playing field, a "zero base." A system of "decision packages" permitted funders to choose levels of effort, as well as programs.

The total performance measurement system developed at the U.S. General Accounting Office integrated measures of "productivity and effectiveness . . . with information on employee and customer attitudes" (Kull, 1978, p. 7). That shift to include worker and user perceptions in assessing and shaping agency direction was applied in the total program management (TPM) system embodied by the City of San Diego in its 1980 organization effectiveness program.

> [TPM] is a management philosophy and an innovative tool to help managers struggling with the problem of providing more and better public service with dwindling dollars. . . . Overall, TPM is a process [that] gives citizens a say in what gets done, employees a say in how things get done, and management a tool to determine how well things get done (City of San Diego, 1983, pp. 1-2).

Total Quality Management

The latest in this progression toward recognizing the end product as central is total quality management, a philosophy advanced by W. Edward Deming, an American who first found acceptance for his ideas in Japan. It is based upon the ideas that "quality of product and services not only results in increased customer demand, but is cost effective—competitive. . . . [and] prevention of defects is more cost effective than inspection and defect repair" (McGovern, 1990, p. 19). To achieve quality,

> Deming teaches organizations to treat the people they serve as precious customers and to place customer satisfaction as the organization's primary goal; to base decisions on carefully gathered statistical data about all facets of the operation; and to bring labor and management together and keep them working closely together to find the best ways to get the job done (Walters, 1992, p. 38).

The federal government, under the leadership of the OMB, has advanced the adoption of total quality management and, according to Office of Personnel Management Director Constance B. Newman, "the [total quality] revolution is sweeping through [f]ederal agencies and departments, services, and bureaus" (Federal Quality Institute, 1991, p. i).

Arkansas, California, North Dakota, and Vermont are among the first states to undertake statewide quality improvement efforts (Milakovich, 1990, p. 21; Walters, 1992, p. 38). Among the local jurisdictions pursuing TQM are Austin and Dallas, Texas; Fort Collins, Colorado; New York City; and Palm Beach County, Florida (Walters, 1992, p. 38).

The most familiar part of TQM is the use of quality circles (described in Chapter 9) or similar teams:

> In the mid-1980s, Madison's trash collectors ("pickers," in trash jargon) were costing the city a quarter of a million dollars in workers' compensation each year. . . .
>
> Trash collectors blamed the injuries on new equipment that cut the number of pickers on a truck from two to one. Management, meanwhile, was blaming the problem on malingering. It was not a happy situation. . . .
>
> So the Madison streets division decided to unleash TQM. It set up a project team that . . . set about gathering data on how, why, where and when injuries occur. The project's findings were a complete surprise to both sides. The most important factors in injury were not equipment or malin-

gering. They were the age of the picker and the [high-trash-flow] time of the year. . . .

On the basis of the report, Madison decided to use recycling to reduce overall volume of trash and to recruit younger pickers. . . . In the years since this was done, workers' compensation payments have declined by 80 percent. . . . Morale is way up (Walters, 1992, pp. 38-39).

The *Federal Total Quality Management Handbook* contrasts the TQM approach with traditional ways of managing (Lewis, 1991, pp. 16-17). The TQM essentials are paraphrased below:

- flatter, more flexible, less hierarchical organization structure
- focus on continuous improvement in systems and processes
- workers see supervisors as coaches, facilitators
- supervisor-subordinate relationship of interdependency, trust, and mutual commitment
- focus of employee efforts on team effort (workers see themselves as teammates)
- management perceives labor as asset and training as investment
- organization asks customers to define quality, develops measures to determine if requirements are met
- primary basis for decisions shifts to facts and systems.

James Swiss (1992) is among those who urge caution: "TQM can indeed have a useful role to play in government, but only if it is substantially modified to fit the public sector's unique characteristics. . . . In its unmodified or orthodox form, TQM is strikingly ill suited to the government environment" (pp. 356, 358). Consider one element: The "customer" is not always easily defined in the public context. For example, is a school's "customer" the pupils and their families, the local school board, or the public at large that empowers and funds the school system? Each probably holds a different standard of satisfaction.

Most agencies have less trouble identifying their customers. But how can client perceptions and needs be ascertained? The use of citizen surveys has been suggested since the early 1970s (Webb & Hatry, 1973), and their value has been borne out in practice (Watson, Juster, & Johnson, 1991, p. 238). The Minnesota STEP program utilizes and teaches an approach that sensitizes workers to client needs:

"Walking in Your Customer's Shoes" will help state employees image what the customer hopes for and experiences. Facilitator for this STEP colloquium will be Barbara A. Beashear, a private consultant from Rochester. . . .

A series of exercises will take participants through the steps of "crawling inside" the minds and hearts of a variety of state government customers ("Walk in Customer's," 1988, p. 4).

Taken as a whole, all these programs—from PPBS to TQM—establish the importance of a focus on goals rather than process, the use of quantification, and the participation of workers and citizens. It is really a matter of managing for productivity.

Managing for Productivity

Managing for productivity means making appropriate use of the various avenues or approaches presented to this point and which are summarized below.

Measuring Productivity

Managing for productivity starts with being able to determine the organization's degree of competency. Real, useful information on efficiency and quality can come only from quantification of resources, the amount of service produced, the quality of service produced, and the effect of making changes in the production process. Not only managers, but also labor-management teams, task forces, and quality circles need quantitative and analytical skills so that they can verify sources of inefficiency and test cures. To underscore a point made earlier, even simple measures, properly used, are better than impressions.

Managing the Work

Productivity management involves applying the "engineering" approaches already discussed in some detail. It means analyzing operations to detect sources of inefficiency and being ready to apply the findings by modifying organizational structure, job design, work flow, or technology. It means analyzing demand patterns and job distributions and redeploying the work force to achieve a fit between capacity and demand.

To achieve these efficiencies, use can be made of worker- and client-oriented approaches, such as alternative schedules, part-time employees, and open communication with clientele. Economies of scale may be achieved by joining a consortium, contracting out, or contracting in.

Managing the Worker

Productivity management involves applying the "human relations" approaches already discussed in detail. It means making the effort to ascertain employee morale and any sources of demoralization. It means considering training, employee assistance programs, a child care system, alternative schedules to meet worker preferences, and specific programs aimed at reducing absenteeism and turnover. It means an effort to gain employee ideas, build esprit, and encourage teamwork by involving the workers, participatively, in the making of more decisions.

Managing the Management

Productivity management involves making good use of all resources: money, equipment, fuel resources, and facilities, as well as labor. It means seeking new modalities such as donations, inside consultants, user fees, volunteers, and consortium arrangements to stretch and augment scarce resources.

Managing for productivity means openness to the environment—to client needs and perceptions, competitors, alternative arrangements, and a constant search for better efficiency and better service quality.

The following chapter will set out strategic considerations and guidelines that will help in selecting and implementing these initiatives.

References

Allen, J. W. (1989). Use of the private sector in corrections service delivery. In J. W. Allen, K. S. Chi, K. M. Devlin, H. P. Hatry, & W. Masterman, *The private sector in state service delivery: Examples of innovative practices* (pp. 13-44). Washington, DC: Urban Institute.

American Federation of State, County, and Municipal Employees (AFSCME). (1983). *Passing the bucks: The contracting out of public services.* Washington, DC: Author.

Ames, K. (1992, March 16). Don't doubt this Thomas. *Newsweek*, p. 70.

Are we contracting out government functions? (1992, February 1). *PA Times*, p. 4.

Barbour, G. P., Jr. (1980). Law enforcement. In G. J. Washnis (Ed.), *Productivity improvement handbook for state and local government* (pp. 927-970). New York: John Wiley.

Barnekov, T. K., & Raffel, J. A. (1990). Public management of privatization. *Public Productivity & Management Review, 14*, 135-152.

Bennewitz, E. (1980). Evolution of budgeting and control systems. In G. J. Washnis (Ed.), *Productivity improvement handbook for state and local government* (pp. 115-132). New York: John Wiley.

Brudney, J. L., & England, R. E. (1983). Toward a definition of the coproduction concept. *Public Administration Review, 43*, 59-65.

Chandler, T., & Feuille, P. (1991). Municipal unions and privatization. *Public Administration Review, 51*, 15-22.

Chase, A. (1992, May). Privatization: Who, what and how. *Governing*, pp. 51-60.

City hall to be in feature film. (1992, January 1). *PA Times*, p. 3.

City of San Diego. (1973, February). *The City of San Diego organization effectiveness program*. San Diego, CA: Financial Management Department.

Dudley, L. (1990). Managing efficiency: Examples from contract administration. *Public Administration Review, 50*, 486-489.

Federal Quality Institute. (1991). *Quality improvement prototype: 1926th Communications-Computer Systems Group*. Washington, DC: Author.

Fixler, P. E., Jr., & Hayes, E. C. (1989). Contracting out for local public services. In E. C. Hayes (Ed.), *The hidden wealth of cities: Policy and productivity methods for American governments* (pp. 71-109). Greenwich, CT: JAI.

Hatry, H. P. (1989). Introduction. In J. W. Allen, K. S. Chi, K. M. Devlin, H. P. Hatry, & W. Masterman, *The private sector in state service delivery: Examples of innovative practices* (pp. 1-11). Washington, DC: Urban Institute.

Henderson, J. D. (1988, October). Private sector management: Promoting efficiency and cost-effectiveness. *Corrections Today*, pp. 98, 100, 102.

Herbers, J. (1983, May 23). Cities turn to private groups to administer local services. *New York Times*, pp. A1, A15.

Holzer, M. (1990). The productivity movement. In S. W. Hays & R. C. Kearney (Eds.), *Public personnel administration: Problems and prospects* (pp. 162-176). Englewood Cliffs, NJ: Prentice-Hall.

Honadle, B. W. (1984). Alternative service delivery strategies and improvement of local government productivity. *Public Productivity Review, 8*, 301-313.

International City Management Association. (1981). *The guide to management improvement projects in local government*. Washington, DC: Author.

International City Management Association. (1989). *Service delivery in the 90s: Alternative approaches for local governments*. Washington, DC: Author.

International City Management Association. (1990). *The guide to management improvement projects in local government*. Washington, DC: Author.

Jimenez, M. (1989, April). Productivity improvement helps Regional Treatment Center at Faribault 'come clean.' *STEP Update*, p. 2. St. Paul, MN: Department of Administration.

Judis, J. B. (1988, September 25). U.S. mail: Mission impossible. *New York Times Magazine*, pp. 30-33, 50-51, 54.

Katz, J. L. (1991, June). Privatizing without tears. *Governing*, pp. 38-42.

Kettl, D. F. (1988). *Government by proxy: (Mis)managing federal programs*. Washington, DC: Congressional Quarterly Press.

Kull, D. C. (1978). Productivity programs in the federal government. *Public Administration Review, 38*, 5-9.

Lewis, F. L. (1991, May). *Introduction to Total Quality Management in the federal government*. (OPM Publication No. TQMHB-3). Washington, DC: Government Printing Office.

Main, J. (1985, May 27). When public services go private. *Fortune*, pp. 92-96, 101.

McGovern, J. P. (1990, September-October). The evolution of Total Quality Management. *Program Manager*, pp. 16-22.

Milakovich, M. E. (1990). Total Quality Management for public sector productivity improvement. *Public Productivity & Management Review*, *14*, 19-32.

Moe, R. C. (1987). Exploring the limits of privatization. *Public Administration Review*, *47*, 453-460.

Naff, K. C. (1991). Labor-management relations and privatization: A federal perspective. *Public Administration Review*, *51*, 23-30.

Nelson, B. J. (1980). Purchase of services. In G. J. Washnis (Ed.), *Productivity improvement handbook for state and local government* (pp. 427-447). New York: John Wiley.

Osborne, D., & Gaebler, T. (1992a, February). Bringing government back to life. *Governing*, pp. 46-49.

Osborne, D., & Gaebler, T. (1992b). *Reinventing government: How the entrepreneurial spirit is transforming the public service*. Reading, MA: Addison-Wesley.

Pennsylvania Department of Community Affairs. (1990). *Intergovernmental cooperation handbook*. Harrisburg: Author.

Percy, S. L. (1987). Citizen involvement in coproducing safety and security in the community. *Public Productivity Review*, No. 42, pp. 83-93.

Raudsepp, E. (1986). 101 ways to spark your employees' creative potential. In J. Matzer, Jr. (Ed.), *Productivity improvement techniques: Creative approaches for local government* (pp. 121-131). Washington, DC: International City Management Association.

Rodgers, R., & Hunter, J. E. (1992). A foundation of good management practice in government: Management by Objectives. *Public Administration Review*, *52*, 27-37.

Ruchelman, L. (1989). *A workbook in redesigning public services*. Albany: State University of New York Press.

Savas, E. S. (1987). *Privatization: The key to better government*. Chatham, NJ: Chatham House.

Savas, E. S. (1992). Privatization and productivity. In M. Holzer (Ed.), *Public productivity handbook* (pp. 79-98). New York: Marcel Dekker.

Saxton, S. F. (1988, October). Contracting for services: Different facilities, different needs. *Corrections Today*, pp. 16-18, 133.

Shanahan, E. (1991, August). Going it jointly: Regional solutions for local problems. *Governing*, pp. 70-76.

Sharkansky, I. (1980). Policy making and service delivery on the margins of government: The case of contractors. *Public Administration Review*, *40*, 116-123.

Shute, N. (1991, December-January). 'Twas the nightmare after Christmas. *National Wildlife*, pp. 48-49.

Staats, E. B. (1988). Public service and the public interest. *Public Administration Review*, *48*, 601-605.

Sullivan, H. (1987). Privatization of public services: A growing threat to constitutional rights. *Public Administration Review*, *47*, 461-467.

Swiss, J. E. (1992). Adapting Total Quality Management (TQM) to government. *Public Adminstration Review*, *52*, 356-362.

Taking the town private. (1991, March 4). *Newsweek*, pp. 52-54.

Talley, B. B. (1980). Intergovernmental cooperation. In G. J. Washnis (Ed.), *Productivity improvement handbook for state & local government* (pp. 448-472). New York: John Wiley.

Vacationing students give Westchester County school a facelift. (1982, February 18). *New York Times*, p. B1.

"Walk in Customer's Shoes" at colloquium. (1988, January-February). *STEP Update*. St. Paul, MN: State of Minnesota Department of Administration

Walters, J. (1992, May). The cult of total quality. *Governing*, pp. 38-42.

Watson, D. J., Juster, R. J., & Johnson, G. W. (1991). Institutionalized use of citizen surveys in the budgetary and policy-making processes: A small city case study. *Public Administration Review, 51*, 232-239.

Webb, K., & Hatry, H. P. (1973). *Obtaining citizen feedback: The application of citizen surveys to local government*. Washington, DC: Urban Institute.

Whitaker, G. P. (1980). Coproduction: Citizen participation in service delivery. *Public Administration Review, 40*, 240-246.

Wriston, M. J. (1980). In defense of bureaucracy. *Public Administration Review, 40*, 179-183.

11

Strategy

Improving productivity is an art, not unlike medicine. It begins with diagnosis, for which the practitioner needs instruments for determining the patient's condition. It depends on knowing the patient, as well as common malfunctions and their symptoms. The ability to choose from among treatments depends on familiarity with all the options, including their mechanisms, time frames, risks, and side effects. The more the professional knows about the underlying anatomy and organic processes, the more likely the treatment will prove effective. But there is no absolute certainty. That is why improving productivity is an art. And that is why feedback is essential: "Call me in the morning."

Our patient is the work organization—of any size, from work crew to office to full agency. We have seen how a comparison of current productivity "readings" with what is "normal" (as defined by the "patient's" own history or by comparison with other organizations) can help determine whether and where problems exist. We have reviewed common symptoms of trouble, such as delays, poor quality, and low morale.

Much of this book deals with possible treatments, such as new technology, job redesign, training, participative management, and contracting out. Background information on things such as organizational structure, worker motivation, and the nature of systems provides some insight into the underlying dynamics of how these changes work.

In short, by now the reader has learned how to measure, spot problems, and assess techniques, setting, and players. How is all this to be applied? There is no set formula, but there is an art, illuminated by some strategic principles and options. Life, someone has said, is a stochastic walk: This chapter offers a rough map of the terrain and some guiding principles for deciding on the objectives, scale, structure, location, and instruments for public sector productivity improvement efforts.

The Big Picture

A productivity improvement effort (sometimes called a PIE) can be highly publicized or pursued without fanfare. It can emphasize enhanced efficiency, better service quality, or both. It can create dramatic, short-term change or a slower, long-term evolution. It may be centrally planned and controlled from the top or emerge out of initiatives from the grass roots. The effort can be limited to one project in one agency or extended over a network of consortia and partnerships, transcending jurisdictional lines, departmental divisions, and even the private-public boundary, as in Minnesota's "Strive Toward Excellence in Performance" (STEP) program. The productivity improvement concept is not a narrow one; it includes any action or change that enhances the quantity or quality (or both) of outputs per unit input—regardless of scale, emphasis, or structure.

The shaping of a productivity improvement effort involves basic choices about these variables.

High or Low Profile

Productivity improvement can take the form of a clearly labeled, highly visible, jurisdiction-wide crusade, a "flamboyant act of political entrepreneurship" as exemplified by the Lindsay administration's productivity program in New York City (Hayes, 1977, p. 245). On the other hand, the program may be presented as a consistent but low-profile emphasis on technological improvement and better management, as it has been in the cities of Dallas and Phoenix.

Strategically, different situations make different choices logical. Central, visible productivity programs are advantageous in focusing attention, building momentum, justifying the acquisition of technical expertise, and effecting changes in the general rules. On the other hand, they create political risk by raising high expectations, galvanizing opposition, and making any failures large-scale and highly visible.

The lessons of the past indicate that high-profile programs in general should be regarded with caution and due respect for the hazards. However, in certain situations, where waste, inefficiency, and poor service are made manifest as the result of a legislative investigation or media publicity about an agency's operations, a visible, urgent improvement program is appropriate.

Target: Efficiency or Quality Improvement

Earlier productivity improvement efforts have stressed efficiency, the search for ways to produce more service with fewer resources. That priority lingers in the perception of municipal managers, who still see the most productivity improvement potential not in incentives or delivery alternatives, but in training, equipment and facilities, and operations improvement (Poister & Streib, 1989, p. 9).

Most recently, citizen discontent and the prospect of privatization have been drawing attention to improving the quality of services (though it is often misstated as "effectiveness," which, as we suggested in Chapter 3, embodies both quantity and quality). Improving quality calls for citizen input, because quality is in the eye of the user. It also makes worker input and participation more important, because the technical core, as deliverer of the service to the clientele, spans boundaries and is a source of feedback.

Conserving resources, improving output quantity, and improving output quality, singly or together, are all appropriate objectives in productivity improvement. However, it is important to be clear on which one(s) are being pursued, so that the appropriate measurement system and improvement approach(es) are adopted.

Time Horizon

Productivity improvement can be designed as a short-term, quick-fix effort. That presents some advantages, like being able to grasp a target of opportunity when it arises and disposing of a problem successfully while it is still fresh in people's minds. Funds to support a project are more likely to be forthcoming if it will produce results within the term of elected or appointed officials, rewarding them with a demonstration of their accomplishment in time for the next election. Short-term projects avoid the danger of losing support if another incumbent takes office. On the other hand, political emphasis on fast results creates pressure on managers for short-term efficiency gains, often at the cost of infrastructure and service quality and without enough time for pilot projects or the nurturing of participative programs (Mann, 1980, p. 358). Short-term efforts can produce long-term detrimental effects.

On one hand, an impulse to short-term efforts comes from the political system: an impatience to see demonstrable results, a disinclination to invest in the future, and an inability to guarantee continuing support. On the other hand, basic improvement in public sector productivity requires time, more so than in the private sector, as Swiss has pointed out (1983, p. 26). As we have seen, productivity improvement is a matter of changing people and their routines under conditions of uncertainty. Attitudes and habits change slowly; learning (for example, how to lead or take part in a quality circle) takes time. Good programs and good solutions to problems evolve through a process of shaping and reshaping, perhaps beginning with a trial run or pilot project to test and debug the system. That takes time. A new, productive climate builds as experiences are shared; enthusiasm is a matter of contagion. That takes time.

One way of accommodating the advantages of both time frames is to find a way to break a long-term project down into a series of short-term steps that achieve individual results and yet build into an integrated new system or approach.

> Productivity improvement should not be viewed as a crash program, or as a one-time effort, or as the exclusive responsibility of a specialized office or department. Rather, it is a continuing priority responsibility of all departments to find more efficient ways to deliver services (National Commission on Productivity and Work Quality, n.d., p. 13).

Centralize or Decentralize

The question of whether to centralize or decentralize is the question of whether productivity improvement should take place top-down or bottom-up. A centralized productivity improvement effort constitutes an identifiable program, directed by a centrally located unit, and extending uniformly to various agencies (Poister, Hatry, Fisk, & Greiner, 1985, p. 8). In 1985, 10 states and 29% of cities were reported as having such centralized productivity improvement efforts (Poister et al., 1985, p. 9).

Top support is essential for initiating change. "Innovation doesn't take place at the bottom unless those at the top arrange for it to happen. . . . There must be a powerful sponsor of this process, with authority" (Shanahan, 1991, p. 36). Centralized programs have that. They also facilitate exchanges, such as the transfer of personnel among units, and they can engineer changes, such as compensation systems, that affect more than one unit (Poister et al., 1985, p. 8). They provide a central locus of expertise.

A centralized effort, however, is not close to unit operations and conditions. "By their very nature, efforts to improve productivity by changing organizational formats, service delivery mechanisms, or detailed operating procedures are usually agency or program specific. Centralized PIEs usually have little direct . . . applicability in these areas" (Poister et al., 1985, p. 16). Centralization does not take advantage of the occasional unit that is a particularly fertile area for productivity improvement, because of an innovative manager, a new hire who brings experience with a better method, and so on. Central efforts are remote from internal actors and their concerns; it is hard to make them stick: "A dominant theme that emerged [from a study of state PIEs] was the lack of stability of centralized productivity improvement efforts in state government; these programs do not appear to become 'institutionalized' " (Poister et al., 1985, p. 18).

By contrast, decentralized programs, such as the Japanese system, provide incremental, bottom-up improvement flow.

> Progress through strategic leaps requires intensive involvement by high-level management and numerous staff specialists, . . . a top-down, highly visible, and usually expensive approach that requires little or no input from the employees at lower organizational tiers. The incremental improvements approach, on the other hand, assumes progress comes through many small steps, few of which are highly visible or necessarily expensive. It is a bottom-up orientation that encourages and supports employees at the lowest levels in identifying improvements to enhance organizational effectiveness and efficiency (Ballard & Trent, 1989, p. 373).

But such ad hoc improvements may suffer from a lack of technical expertise, especially when it comes to measurement. They waste effort, because many groups in many units may be struggling to invent the same wheel. In many cases, success is not shared and others do not benefit.

It is becoming evident that the best system is a blending that takes advantage of the strengths of each alternative. The central authority becomes not the source of planning and direction, but a facilitator, providing impetus, support, expertise, and the transfer of experiences. It induces individual agencies or offices to give attention to the question of productivity improvement; it can provide in-house consultants in productivity measurement, accounting, analysis, and productivity improvement; it may provide courses or workshops or conferences on productivity improvement or offer training in specific techniques; it may undertake to negotiate with legislatures or civil service commissions for needed waivers or rule changes. The individual, decentralized offices or units are the ones who identify the problems and the opportunities for improvement and who initiate and administer changes. In this way, central know-how, analytical capacity, and support can be combined with local esprit, knowledge of the customer, and the small unit's potential for developing a "driving set" of shared values that makes for excellence (Kee & Black, 1985, p. 30).

Magnitude of the Change

Somewhere along the road, decisions will have to be taken regarding the scope of change, its depth, and whether it will be applied to one or many units. Taken together, these factors determine the magnitude or intensity of the productivity improvement effort.

The scope of a change describes its horizontal dimension: how many people it covers. If the entire staff goes onto a compressed workweek, the change has been broad in scope. If a proposed new system is well tried and reliable, and if serious opposition is not expected from any quarter, then such broad change makes sense. It has the virtue of speed and keeps everyone in synch. However, where opposition is anticipated, an effective strategy is to narrow the scope of the innovation, to "divide and conquer." That approach undercuts across-the-board resistance, permits the change to begin advantageously with a group that is relatively receptive, and facilitates the next phase—expanding the innovation—by giving everyone the chance to see that misgivings were not warranted. The pilot project represents such a narrow-scoped undertaking.

The depth of a change refers to the number of behaviors that people are being asked to change. Requiring the staff to use a modified version of an

Table 11.1 Productivity Improvement

Broad Scope	Great Depth	Many Units	Example
+	+	+	Total revamp of troubled agency
+	+	-	Computerizing one office
+	-	+	General training program
-	+	+	Developing three people in every unit into productivity experts
-	-	+	Skills upgrade for file clerks
-	+	-	Pilot project
+	-	-	Absenteeism program for one unit

accustomed form represents a shallow change. Computerizing a library represents radical change: changed skills, routines, relationships. Radical change can be made less threatening and more palatable and evoke less resistance if it is broken up into a series of small changes. There is less to adjust to at one time and after awhile the very idea of change becomes natural.

Change may be confined to one unit or shake up the entire organization. Inducing change in an organization requires time for people to adjust, although under conditions of great urgency or where one part cannot change without change in the others, many units may have to be involved at once.

The typology in Table 11.1 classifies productivity improvement undertakings according to the three factors just discussed: scope, breadth, and number of different work units covered. Note that a "+" means broad scope, radical change, and many units, respectively. Unity of purpose is facilitated by a common understanding of just which kind of enterprise is taking place.

Strategic Guidelines

The following is a set of commonly mentioned principles to apply in making decisions about productivity improvements. They reflect lessons learned in practice in the field and are grouped together and numbered for convenience. Some, if not all, are applicable to productivity improvement undertakings of any magnitude, in any substantive field, and at any level of government. They need to make sense in context, "other things being equal."

General Orientation

1. *Make haste slowly.* The road to productivity improvement is not paved. Invest in thinking things through, probing and testing each step of the way. We are dealing with uncertainty.

> The first steps are the hardest. . . . The initial segments of feasibility assessment, building involvement . . . , setting goals and objectives, making deliberate choices on whether to proceed, and clear design are often rushed through or left out entirely. Later, these omissions . . . come home to roost. Lasting change rarely occurs overnight (Cohen-Rosenthal & Burton, 1987, p. 139).

2. *Keep it simple.* Seek only relevant changes: Search for real improvement opportunities and the minimal effective treatment. Use only what you need. Measure simply. Do not oversell the project's potential, raising expectations too high.

3. *Start with an easy project.*

> An easy project exhibits consensus among the participating [entities], involves limited financial risk, and has a high potential for success. If such an opportunity exists, it is an excellent way to start off. The . . . officials can savor firsthand a successful effort and build future . . . efforts on this solid foundation (Pennsylvania Department of Community Affairs, 1990, p. 39).

4. *Be participative.* Invite the participation of managers, experts, workers, and, where appropriate, clients. Participation takes time and effort, but it creates better plans because it is an economical way to collect and incorporate many perspectives. It facilitates implementation of the program, because the participants understand it, "own" it, and sell it to their peers.

> A series of studies have found that systems engender less employee resistance (including cheating) when they are perceived as fair. This sense of fairness . . . is often increased by employee participation in the design and maintenance of the system (Swiss, 1983, p. 35).

And strive for consensus, not just a majority:

When an outcome is negotiated among only a subset of the parties who have something at stake, it is likely to be rejected by those who have been left out. The QWL [quality of working life] committee's elegant plan to accommodate both the interests of management and the majority of the workers was ultimately rejected because it failed to reconcile the dispute among the workers (Ronchi & Morgan, 1983, pp. 50-51).

5. *Consider pilot projects.* A pilot project is a small-scale, preliminary version of an innovation that will later be installed full-scale. In addition to the advantages already mentioned (limited opposition, receptive site, demonstrable feasibility), pilot projects provide a chance to detect "bugs" in the system and correct them in time. The experience of a first run makes the full-scale institutionalization faster and easier.

6. *Keep evaluating.* As the undertaking progresses, keep assessing whether techniques are working, people understand the system, costs are in line with expectations, and so on. This formative feedback makes it possible to make course corrections early and frequently.

7. *Communicate.*

Public relations is an important part of a project. Make sure to acknowledge everyone's input by saying thanks—both [orally] and in writing. Also, if it's a project with potentially large ramifications, take the time to use the appropriate vehicle to keep people informed about the progress of the project. Whether it's an in-house newsletter or a memo, it's important to keep the project before people so if concerns come up they can be dealt with immediately—not when the project is near completion (Podlich, 1987).

Communication to the public . . . is also important. If the public has a perception that something is being hidden or kept secret, the reaction is swift and negative regardless of the merits of the program (Pennsylvania Department of Community Affairs, 1990, p. 40).

Anticipate Resistance

8. *Keep the pressure on.* Change comes only as long as the forces for change exceed those against it. Project-specific, top-level support and interest is essential if the effort is to achieve and maintain momentum.

9. *Discuss.* Take the time to listen and to explain. It is important to know what each stakeholder thinks and does or does not want to see happen. Use trusted leaders as channels. Express reassurances about unjustified fears: No one will be fired; we will train you. Do not assume that everyone understands implicitly.

10. *Build rewards into the plan.* Change induces discomfort. Participants will want to change only if they receive rewards or side payments. The rewards need not cost money. They can be provided out of economies and budget savings (if the system is so structured). They can be the strong psychic rewards of ownership and the power to participate in decisions. They can come from personal pride and the respect of others. The innovation should be designed with an eye to including rewards.

For productivity improvement, reward the group, rather than the individual, whenever possible:

> Individual suggestion award systems are the natural enemies of QWL systems. QWL depends for its success on group problem solving, which requires the sharing of ideas for the common good. If people are given a choice between obtaining individual awards for their suggestions or contributing them to a problem-solving group, they are likely to behave rationally—to hoard ideas rather than share them (Herrick, 1983, p. 151).

Pick the Right Problem

11. *Choose an obvious problem.* A productivity improvement project is an undertaking to solve or alleviate a problem: a bottleneck, delays, wasted time, absenteeism, errors, complaints. [Caution: It is very common, but incorrect, to express problems in terms of presumed solutions; for instance, "our problem is that we do not have a copier on our floor." That is not the problem; the problem is that workers' time is wasted in going back and forth to the copier. The solution *might* be to acquire an additional copier; but it might be something else, such as relocating the present one, redesigning the office layout, or having one person handle all the copying. Stating the problem as "wasted time" leaves the door open to many possibilities. Posing the problem as "lack of a copier" forecloses the issue.]

Choose a problem that many people see as a problem. Improvements will be highly visible, and confidence will grow more rapidly that something can indeed be done to overcome hindrances. So many public sector workers struggle to function in dismal surroundings, using unreliable equipment, spending time on nonsensical routines, and dealing with frustrated clients they lack the discretion to help. A productivity-enhancing innovation that brings relief can release potential internal energies that have been "turned off" to avoid frustration. This enhances the organizational capacity to make further change.

12. *Seek a good payback.* Choose a problem that is well worth the effort. Look for a large ticket item, such as major equipment or the cost of training. Look for repetitive, large-scale operations, such as toll collection, where even a small saving can be important because it will be multiplied many times.

13. *Seek a quick payback.* To tackle a problem is to focus interest and raise expectations. Attention spans are short, subject to the distractions of day-to-day problems. Prefer a problem that should bring quick resolution. This keeps interest high, reinforces the connection between effort and success, and shortens the period that the risk takers have their necks out.

Pick the Right Solution

14. *Do some looking.* There has been a wealth of experience in productivity improvement, employing many approaches and techniques. One morning spent in the library, thumbing through such resources as the International City/County Management Association's (ICMA's) annual *Guide* (*The Guide to Management Improvement Projects in Local Government*), the *Public Productivity & Management Review* (formerly, *Public Productivity Review*), professional magazines, and the new magazine *Governing* will suggest ideas and the names of people to contact about their experiences. Librarians, government associations, and productivity centers can provide further leads.

15. *Do not choose a "solution" just because it is popular.* Many failed efforts to succeed with new approaches occur because the current buzzword is not really understood and is not a real solution to an important problem.

16. *Look for an approach that has worked under similar conditions.* Jurisdictions differ. A piece of parks equipment that improved operations in Florida may not work in hilly terrain; it may not be worth the capital investment in snow country, where it will sit idle half the year. Check with your counterparts in jurisdictions that have used it.

17. *Choose a solution that takes advantage of timing.* For example, when New York City introduced coterminality, the commissioner of the Department of Sanitation "saw the necessary district reorganization as an opportunity to restructure completely our collection route system using scientific methods and a team of specialists in solid waste management" (Steisel, 1984, p. 118).

18. *Choose a solution that is feasible.* Give advance consideration to questions such as: Where can funding be found? Whose support, permission,

or cooperation is needed? What are the likely effects on the work force, the clientele, and other agencies? Can the needed elements be pulled together? Can opposition be overcome?

> Equally important, says former city manager Donaldson, is knowing when to stop promoting an innovation that just doesn't have the political support to sustain itself. "You can't wed yourself to every idea, even if they're good," he says. "Your masters, the councilmen, have to get elected. You have to be sure the Red Sea is still parted when you march them across" (Shanahan, 1991, p. 37).

Define your Goal

19. *Be clear about the objective.* In qualitative terms, exactly what is the innovation expected to accomplish? For example, the new child care center may be expected to reduce employee absenteeism; the training program for workers may be expected to reduce errors or client dissatisfaction. The objective governs the choice of approach:

> It is essential to review any contemplated QWL effort in light of the outcomes desired and then choose with care the technique [that] employs the action lever most likely to lead to the objectives identified (Chisholm, 1983, p. 21).

20. *Be clear about how success will be determined.* Without falling into the pitfall of becoming unduly preoccupied with measurement as a goal in itself, as McClure has warned (1986, p. 27), it is necessary to decide on how progress and success will be gauged in quantitative terms. The measures can be simple and practical. If everyone agrees on them, they are probably valid enough. It is useful, and reassuring, to be able to check the measures out with a staff expert. But everyone has to understand just how, for example, "client dissatisfaction" will be gauged: number of complaints per month? score on a user survey? This should be decided in advance.

21. *Establish a schedule.* Open-ended undertakings tend to take longer. Even a rough timetable, modified more than once, is superior to none.

Think Systemically

22. *Be aware of linkages.* Think through how a contemplated innovation might affect and be affected by other levels of the organization, other

units from whom and to whom the work flows, and outside suppliers or consumers. They may have to be made ready for the change.

> A work organization . . . is an interconnected, complicated social system composed of many subsystems. . . . Significant change in one part or level of the system has impacts on all other parts and levels. Participants in a change process . . . need to be aware of and plan for these multiple linkages and impacts. . . . Introducing processes for bottom-level employee input into a system that did not previously allow or value such input requires prior, parallel, or resulting changes in attitudes and behaviors at other levels of the system (Brower, 1983, p. 62).

23. *Think in terms of organizational development.* An organization is an evolving entity; people, routines, the type of service produced are all changing over time. An innovation should fit into the future and can be an instrument for shaping it.

> Instead of being absolutely determined once and for all when they are designed and established, organizations and their components constantly evolve from one state or another. . . . Such a perspective requires . . . an experimental frame of mind [that] constantly seeks to determine how the system is functioning at the present time, what general organizational conditions . . . are required to enable unit to move towards the desired end state, and what specific actions are required for progress (Chisholm, 1983, p. 23).

24. *Work toward capacity building.* In choosing projects and the means for accomplishing them, factor in their long-term impact on the capacity of the organization. Successful change in itself encourages innovation and creates a positive attitude toward action. Training of workers or managers has long-term benefits. The development of participatory instrumentalities and skills gives the organization the potential to make more effective future decisions. The development and utilization of measurement and analytical skills enhances the general capacity for rationality. Productivity data add to the information system and enhance planning, budgeting, and personnel deployment decisions. Changes to remove constricting conditions written into laws, civil service regulations, or union contracts may be won for the purposes of one project, but they also afford scope for future creativity. Finally, the experience and expertise acquired in each productivity improvement enterprise builds the capacity of the organization to make productivity improvement a way of life. Like guilt, it is a gift that keeps on giving.

Doing the Project

We have deliberately used imprecise words, such as "effort" and "undertaking" to characterize productivity-improving initiatives. That is because productivity improvement should be thought of as more than just a project, with a beginning and an end. Productivity improvement takes many forms: a centralized jurisdiction-wide effort; a radical but short-lived thrust to rescue one troubled agency; and acting on a new way of thinking (a consciousness of measurement, problems, improvement possibilities, and capacity building). That having been said, it is probably fair to add that the basic building block for most productivity improvement *is* the project. The most useful handle on thinking through the elements of an improvement undertaking is to review the structure and process of a project, knowing that not all steps or considerations will pertain to everyone's unique situation.

Functional Roles

Four functions are fundamental to the conduct of a project: entrepreneurship, idea generation, measurement and analysis, and directing. More colorfully, there is need for a spark plug, a scout, a navigator, and a captain. These are roles, not people: Each function may be the full-time responsibility of one person or the part-time contribution of many individuals; one person may fulfill more than one function. The important thing is that each function be carried out.

Innovator or Entrepreneur

Somewhere, somehow, someone has to care enough about productivity improvement to rouse the agency or unit to action and then to keep the pressure on. This is the role of the innovator, who provides enthusiasm, drive, a perspective that transcends the day-to-day, and guidance through political mine fields. The occupant(s) of that role will need personal power or the support of someone else with power to move others to action.

New programs will not get adopted or become an established part of an agency's routine without entrepreneurs. The principal activities of entrepreneurs are to uncover opportunities for new programs, to become philosophical proponents for the program, to generate support and zeal for the program among those who must implement it, and to put the winning coalition of adopters, implementors, clients, and supporters needed to set the implementation process in action (Palumbo, Musheno, & Maynard-Moody, 1986, p. 79).

The National Commission on Productivity and Work Quality gave the following guidance to the mayor as entrepreneur:

> How can you keep a productivity program moving in this environment [of competing daily crises]? Insist on specific commitments. . . . Spell out and commit activities, time schedules, responsibilities. . . .
>
> And keep talking. First you'll convince yourself, and then you'll convince everyone around you, that you're really serious about productivity, and that productivity is worth being serious about (National Commission on Productivity and Work Quality, n.d., p. 15).

Idea Source

Some individual or set of individuals needs to know or find out about the kind of information that makes up much of this book: What productivity improvement means, how to locate problems and opportunities for improvement, the importance of measurement, what techniques and resources are available, what benefits and risks are to be expected, and how to proceed. This role of idea source helps frame the project by defining the possible options.

The ideas may come through people who move from one job to another, bringing experience with alternative approaches or new technology. A second source is consultants. They need not be limited to paid providers. In-house consultants may be available from staff offices or a central productivity unit. An individual with special expertise may be obtainable on loan from another agency or jurisdiction. One or more individuals might be sent to learn about productivity improvement in a formal college course. Conferences and workshops may be available:

> Dear Conference Participant:
> Why attend the Third National Court Technology Conference (CTC-III)? In short, to see and learn about technologies and applications that can help your court save money and control costs in these troubled financial times. . . .
>
> Innovative leaders from around the country will present more than 60 educational sessions in six tracks, ranging from novice to advanced levels. The sessions explore current court technology, applications used in other public- and private-sector organizations. . . .

Vendors in more than 100 exhibit booths will demonstrate exciting new products so you can see, compare, and try out innovative solutions to today's court needs (Polansky, 1992).

Measurer or Analyst

The project will need one or more individuals who think quantitatively, who can derive and interpret figures. It is astonishing how wrong intuitive impressions can be: What seems to be a problem turns out, upon careful measurement, not to be a problem, and vice versa. Numbers reveal differences, make projections of payoffs, and lend credibility to claims of accomplishment. It is an often overlooked virtue of the process of measurement that it focuses and clarifies thinking. In short, "the most successful productivity improvements usually result from assigning competent analysts to the program on a full-time basis" (National Commission on Productivity and Work Quality, n.d., p. 11).

If the work unit does not already have people with quantitative and analytical skills, expertise may be borrowed from elsewhere, possibly from a budget office, computer center, business office, auditing agency, or in-house evaluation group. Bear in mind that the analyst will need negotiating skills for gaining the confidence of the line in the give-and-take of developing measures.

One common arrangement is to pair a consultant with a member of the line unit who has quantitative aptitude but is untutored in measurement and analysis. The consultant takes responsibility for designing the measures with the in-house person's assistance. The consultant then moves on, leaving the in-house person ready to administer and modify it. A word of encouragement: There is more aptitude around than meets the eye. People tend to mistrust their own common sense and to feel that there is some occult magic in putting numbers on things. A volunteer individual or task force may, with a little training, produce a valuable, simple way of collecting and interpreting data such as the amount of service delivered, the amount of labor consumed, the number and type of complaints, and the degree to which the services meet quality criteria.

Project Director

This is the most familiar role and the easiest to fill because it requires administrative ability. However, the responsibility for day-to-day planning and direction of the improvement project must rest with someone for whom this is a prime obligation. Assigning it as an add-on to other duties is fatal: The productivity improvement project will get pushed aside whenever regular duties need urgent attention. The director should be someone who is respected and experienced in administration, someone who enjoys good rapport with the innovator.

Project Steps

There are essentially four phases in completing a productivity improvement project: preparing the ground, identifying possibilities, deciding the course of action, and implementing it.

Prepare the Ground

Prepare Yourself. Take a deep breath and think. Why is a productivity improvement project being considered? To solve an obvious problem? To conform to a vague political mandate from above? To take advantage of an attractive new idea? Or just to take a sound first step toward improvement? A clear sense of direction from the beginning will strengthen the presentation to others.

Assess the Climate. Is there general interest in productivity improvement on the part of the public, elected officials, or the media? Is funding scarce? Does competition threaten? Is morale low? Are clients discontented? Are auditing or oversight agencies urging change? Is this the time to undertake a project?

Raise the Subject. Throughout the unit, stir up discussion about the possibility of making changes. Let people know the door is open for change. Structure informal meetings to "kick the idea around." Advance notice and inclusion will minimize the feeling that something has already been decided and will be imposed.

Lay Out Ground Rules. It helps people to know the substantive and procedural norms that will prevail for the project. They might be: No one will be fired, anyone can have input, criticism will not be taken as disloyalty, and change will happen. Obviously, great care should be taken not to make assurances that might not be kept.

Start Lining Up Talent. This is the time to assess who the innovator is, who has or can find ideas, who will measure and analyze, and who could direct a project. In Contino's words, this is the time to " 'pan for gold' in the organization itself, to find people with good potential who are not afraid of change" (Contino & Giuliano, 1991, p. 185). What makes for "good potential"?

> There are such things as innovative personalities: buoyant, optimistic creatures who believe "it can be done" and successfully convey that message to both subordinates and superiors. They are flexible, collaborating easily with others across traditional professional and agency lines in finding new ways to do thing—often by a combination of old ways (Shanahan, 1991, p. 37).

Some years ago, Blau identified those who should not be expected to favor change: "Civil servants who were less competent and received a low rating felt insecure and objected to changes in operations" (1970, p. 257).

Decide Where the Project Will Be Located. Will the project be housed in a staff office or in a line office? There is no orthodoxy on what is best, but locating the project in the line agency takes advantage of knowledge of the operations, establishes a visibility and openness that encourage cooperation, and permits close observation of how the change is proceeding. The chief disadvantage is that measurement specialists, working away from their staff base, are subject to pressure to compromise and there is the risk they may "go native."

Identify Opportunities

Unless it is unambiguously clear that one particular project has no competitors, it is reasonable to start collecting a set of possible projects, each "package" made up of one problem and solution, from which to select the most promising.

Identify Problems. This is a brainstorming phase. Use everyone: the idea people, the analysts, managers, clients, and members of the work force to suggest what they see as obvious problems. Look for unbalanced work loads, lack of equipment or materials, idle time or equipment, backlogs, too much time spent on unproductive activities, delays and slow response, and so on.

Identify Possible Solutions. Using ideas from all sources, especially projects that have worked in similar agencies, try to identify innovations that could ameliorate the problems that have been identified. Work both ways: A new technique may point up an overlooked opportunity for improving the present system.

Make the First Cut. Problems with no visible solution and techniques that fill no perceived need can be ruled out. So can any "package" that is not of relevant scale, that is patently not viable—because of cost, powerful opposition, or any other clearly forbidding difficulty. What remains should be a set of promising possibilities.

Decide on the Project

This phase is devoted to careful culling and comparison of the alternatives. For each package, consider the following points.

Is the Project Attractive? Would it relieve a visible problem? Does it entail undue risk? How long until it begins to pay off?

Estimate the Productivity Gain. Try to estimate possible benefits as compared with costs. If the project will produce savings, the ratio is easy to calculate: same output divided by fewer resources. If the project will improve service quality, there is no established way of assessing the value. One approach is to think in percentages: "If a 10% increase in cost will result in only a 10% increase in quality, then productivity will not be improved."

Be careful in estimating costs. Consider direct costs—such as equipment, consultants, training, and dollars for rewards—and indirect costs—such as any temporary drop in productivity while systems are being changed (Chisholm, 1983, p. 18).

Assess the Feasibility. This is a mental exercise, with some detective work and preliminary fact finding thrown in. It is a vital step taken to avoid future pitfalls and to rule out any project that contains a fatal flaw. Consider what the innovation will require: equipment, training, expertise, or data. Can they be made available? How? Where will they come from? How will they be paid for? Consider whose cooperation will be needed: workers, managers, union, clients, or legislature? Can it be obtained? For what motivators? Can rewards be produced? How?

In short: Is the project operationally, legally, financially, politically, and socially feasible? If not, could it be redesigned to become so? Would it then be worth doing? (See Ruchelman, 1989, p. 51, for a sample public service redesign outline.)

Decide. This is the "go or no-go" decision point. It is also the point for building in desired limitations such as scale, location, or what features would be unacceptable.

Implement the Innovation

The steps in implementing a productivity-enhancing innovation are the same as the steps in implementing most projects. Some basics are reviewed briefly here.

Plan. This is the point to state the objectives of the project in specific form; for example, "reduce absenteeism by 20%" or "have one quality circle in operation within two months." The evaluator should participate in defining the "final product" (Newcomer & Wholey, 1989, p. 202) and in the entire planning phase to ensure that objectives are clear and measurable.

Consider specifically what resources (space, expertise, participators, equipment, and supplies) will be needed. Plan sources and timetables for acquiring them. Identify all the tasks to be done, who will be responsible for each, and what is to be accomplished at each stage.

Organize and Staff. Decide on the structure of the project: how personnel will be grouped and coordinated. Decide the location and the layout of the project. Ascertain that all the important roles are covered: leader, analyst, evaluator, and possible teams, including leaders or facilitators.

Direct and Control. Even in the most participatory ventures, coordination requires that a leader give direction. Start with orientation sessions to explain project goals and reassure remaining misgivings. Provide clear guidance; people will do a more intelligent and creative job of execution if they understand the philosophy, reasons, and purposes that underlie instructions.

Expect problems as the implementation proceeds. An open, participative process facilitates the flow of feedback and makes it more likely that incipient problems will be noticed early on. Control the project by comparing the actual expenditure rate and stage of progress with what had been planned in the budget and timetable. If necessary, intervene to get things back on track and schedule.

Evaluate. As the project proceeds, formatively evaluate how the people, instruments, and techniques are working. Is staff performance good? Are the measurement data yielding the desired information? Are there bugs in the procedure? Use the findings to improve the process. Evaluate summatively: Look back and assess the costs, processes, payoffs, pitfalls, and efficiencies. Find out what went well and what did not. What has been learned?

Disseminate

Every practical experience is a valuable source of information for other practitioners and academics. Share the results through conference presentations, articles for professional newsletters or journals, letters to the editor, reports to governmental associations, or media interviews. Other interested parties can be made aware of techniques and learn what conditions further or undercut success, the benefits to be expected, and the costs and effort that have to be invested. Even failed efforts contain very important lessons. In the absence of any formal central repository of information, this kind of networking creates a corpus of knowledge for everyone to use.

Some Strategic Conclusions

Improvement Is Possible

Productivity improvement is possible in every field and at every level of government. There is no systematic, existential barrier.

Langworthy's systematic analysis suggests that neither agency size, technological approach to policing, population variables, nor type of local government, taken alone or in combination, act as substantial constraints on police organizational structure. . . .

This finding—that the structure of police departments is not mechanistically driven by "immutable" forces—is important, because it means that innovative police leadership . . . can shape police organizations far more effectively than might have been expected on the basis of traditional theory (Huff, 1987, p. 508).

Improvement Need Not Be Difficult If . . .

Productivity improvement techniques are generally a lot simpler and easier than people think. By and large, they are not hard to learn.

> I had an experience once where I had to go out and spend some time with a supervisor of 500 people. He had taken the civil service exam, he had done well, and had been promoted a number of times. All of a sudden, he was in this terrifying situation where his subordinates were upset about a lot of things. They were raising a lot of issues and grievances, and he didn't know what to do. "How do I deal with it?" he asked. I asked if he knew who all those employees were? "Do you know their names?" "No, they are only secretaries and such." So we spent the day going out and talking to employees. As a result, he started creating internal committees to deal with the issues, and in time he was able to answer his own question: employees have good ideas (W. Sullivan in Benton, Contino, Grace, Sullivan, & White, 1989, p. 114).

. . . Practitioners Know What They Are Doing

Practitioners need to understand what they are doing. Granted, good intuition and a little luck can create the occasional success in productivity improvement. But hit or miss is not good enough for circumstances today. Effective, confident, successful improvement can be done reliably and efficiently only if it rests on an understanding of what productivity is, how it is measured, how to diagnose problems, and how to use the set of instrumentalities. Every organization needs to have or have access to someone knowledgeable about the productivity field.

The Future Is Now

Prediction is dangerous, but it seems likely that a great deal of public sector productivity improvement will take place in the near future and in a decentralized, idiosyncratic way, wherever the ground is favorable, but spreading rapidly by contagion and imitation. A new generation of managers is at the threshold, many of them educated in and converts to the productivity field. Public workers and their unions are knowledgeable about their plight and the rising popularity of privatization. They have seen models of successful labor-management collaboration toward improving efficiency, work life quality, and the respect of clients. Measurement systems are essentially in place and, with two decades of research and experimentation behind them, academicians, centers, and professional societies can offer encouragement, models of success, and practical guidance.

Wherever there is a confluence of people who believe in the need and the possibility, productivity improvement will take place. The proliferation of expertise and the current climate of openness to participation and change make that more probable than ever.

References

Ballard, J. A., & Trent, D. M. (1989). Idea generation and productivity: The promise of CSM. *Public Productivity Review, 12,* 373-386.

Benton, F. W., Contino, R., Grace, S., Sullivan, W., & White, B. (1989). Human resources and labor-management cooperation (panel discussion at the Third National Public Sector Productivity Conference, New York). *Public Productivity & Management Review, 13,* 107-116.

Blau, P. (1970). Bureaucracy and social change. In O. Grusky & G. Miller (Eds.), *The sociology of organizations* (pp. 249-260). New York: Free Press.

Brower, M. J. (1983). Massachusetts: Lessons from efforts that failed. In N. Q. Herrick (Ed.), *Improving government: Experiments with quality of working life systems* (pp. 61-69). New York: Praeger.

Chisholm, R. F. (1983). Quality of working life: Critical issues for the 1980s. *Public Productivity Review, 7,* 10-25.

Cohen-Rosenthal, E., & Burton, C. E. (1987). *Mutual gains: A guide to union-management cooperation.* New York: Praeger.

Contino, R. A., & Giuliano, J. (1991). Productivity gains through employee participation at the New York City Department of Sanitation. *Public Productivity & Management Review, 15,* 185-190.

Hayes, F. O'R. (1977). *Productivity in local government.* Lexington, MA: Lexington.

Herrick, N. Q. (1983). *Improving government: Experiments with quality of working life systems.* New York: Praeger.

Huff, C. R. (1987). Organizational structure and innovation in urban police departments. [Review of *The structure of police organizations* and *The new blue line: Police innovations in six American cities*]. *Public Administration Review, 47,* 508-509.

Kee, J., & Black, R. (1985). Is excellence in the public sector possible? *Public Productivity Review, 9,* 25-34.

Mann, S. Z. (1980). The politics of productivity: State and local focus. *Public Productivity Review, 4,* 352-367.

McClure, J. (1986). What to avoid in a productivity improvement effort. In J. Matzer, Jr. (Ed.), *Productivity improvement techniques: Creative approaches for local government* (pp. 24-28). Washington, DC: International City Management Association.

National Commission on Productivity and Work Quality. (1974). *So, Mr. Mayor, you want to improve productivity. . . .* (Stock No. 5203-00049). Washington, DC: Government Printing Office.

Newcomer, K. E., & Wholey, J. S. (1989). Evaluation strategies for building high-perform-ance programs. In J. S. Wholey, K. E. Newcomer, & Associates, *Improving government performance: Evaluation strategies for strengthening public agencies and programs.* Sar Francisco: Jossey-Bass.

Palumbo, D., Musheno, M., & Maynard-Moody, S. (1986). Public sector entrepreneurs: The shakers and doers of program innovation. In J. S. Wholey, M. A. Abramson, & C. Bellavita (Eds.), *Performance and credibility: Developing excellence in public and nonprofit organizations* (pp. 69-82). Lexington, MA: Lexington.

Pennsylvania Department of Community Affairs. (1990). *Intergovernmental cooperation handbook.* Harrisburg: Author.

Podlich, J. (1987, November). (Letter in Project Update). *STEP Update,* p. 2.

Poister, T.H., Hatry, H. P., Fisk, D. M., & Greiner, J. M. (1985). Centralized productivity improvement efforts in state government. *Public Productivity Review, 9,* 5-24.

Poister, T. H., & Streib, G. (1989). Municipal managers' concerns for productivity improve-ment. *Public Productivity & Management Review, 13,* 3-11.

Polansky, L. (1992). Letter to membership, p. 1 of announcement of conference, "Improving Justice Through Innovation," March 11-15, 1992, Dallas, TX.

Ronchi, D., & Morgan, W. R. (1983). Springfield, Ohio: Persisting and prevailing. In N. Q. Herrick (Ed.), *Improving government: Experiments with quality of working life systems* (pp. 42-52). New York: Praeger.

Ruchelman, L. (1989). *A workbook in redesigning public services.* Albany: State University of New York Press.

Shanahan, E. (1991, October). The mysteries of innovative government. *Governing,* pp. 35-47.

Steisel, N. (1984). Productivity in the New York City Department of Sanitation: The role of the public sector manager. *Public Productivity Review, 8,* 103-126.

Swiss, J. E. (1983). Unbalanced incentives in government productivity systems: Misreporting as a case in point. *Public Productivity Review, 7,* 26-37.

Index

269

About the Author

Ellen Doree Rosen, Professor Emerita, recently retired from John Jay College of Criminal Justice, City University of New York, where she has chaired the Department of Public Administration and Economics and coordinated the Master's of Public Administration program. Her area of specialization is organizational performance, and she has taught graduate courses on productivity in the public sector, organization theory, program evaluation, research methods, and human resources management.

Professor Rosen has worked in the public productivity field for almost 20 years. She has been affiliated with the National Center for Public Productivity since 1975, serving for 16 years as associate director; she served 11 years on the editorial board of the *Public Productivity & Management Review*; she organized the Second National Public Productivity Conference. Professor Rosen has directed research projects in productivity measurement, training evaluation, and personnel management for New York

City, New York state, and federal agencies, and conducted numerous workshops, in-service training sessions, and formal courses on public productivity at various campuses.

Professor Rosen's writings include a casebook in public administration and articles on public productivity, employee attrition, and the pathologies of organizations.